English

Grammar for

Communication

G. De Devitiis, L. Mariani and K. O'Malley

General editor: M. Palmer

Longman
London and New York

Longman Group UK Limited,
Longman House, Burnt Mill, Harlow,
Essex CM20 2JE, England
and Associated Companies throughout the world.

First published 1989

Set in Helvetica light
Produced by Longman Group (FE) Ltd
Printed in Hong Kong

ISBN 0 582 00511 6

Acknowledgements

English Grammar for Communication draws
on the notional and functional categories
used by Leech and Svartvik in
A Communicative Grammar of English
(Longman 1975).

Artwork by Printing and Graphic, Bristol.

Contents

This list of contents indicates the main areas dealt with in each chapter and, where appropriate, provides an example of the type of language described. For a more detailed analysis see the General Index at the back of the book.

Section one: Structure

1 The sentence

2 Interrogative and negative sentences

3 Passive sentences

4 Replacing and omitting words

5 Personal, reflexive and reciprocal pronouns

6 Auxiliary verbs and full verbs

24 Permission, obligation and prohibition

25 Influencing the behaviour of other people

26 Feelings and attitudes

27 Language of social situations and discussion

Preface

This grammar is intended to be a reference book to accompany a course of English. It can be used either in class or by the student working alone.

The language dealt with has been selected after analysing the contents of some of the most widely used English language courses, from an elementary to an upper-intermediate level. The grammar itself reaches a level a little above that required for the First Certificate examination of the University of Cambridge.

The book reflects recent developments in language teaching and could be used alongside either courses organised on notional-functional lines (the 'communicative' approach) or to accompany courses following a more traditional structural approach.

The language is mostly organised according to notional and functional categories in order to show how language uses grammatical structures to express concepts and to carry out communicative functions. However considerable space is also given to describing the forms of the grammatical structures themselves.

Important characteristics of this grammar are:
1 *Classification of the language in notional-functional categories*, each of which groups together the most important grammatical structures that the language uses to express a particular concept or to carry out a particular function.
2 An extensive *analytical index* which sets out, in alphabetical order, all the concepts, functions, grammatical categories and all the individual language items which are dealt with.
3 *Layout in two columns*, of which the left is reserved for examples and the right is used for explanatory notes.
4 *Frequent cross-references* (indicated by the symbol ▶) allowing the student to extend the analysis of a particular problem.
5 *Explanations given in simple, clear language*, avoiding technical or confusing terminology wherever possible. A glossary is provided giving simple explanations of essential grammatical terms which may present difficulties.
6 *Attention paid to register*, distinguishing the formal from the informal, in relation to both the written and the spoken forms of the language. Particular consideration is given to informal, or neutral, spoken language. The variety chosen is British English; specific references to American English are made only when it is thought necessary.
7 *Attention paid to pronunciation, stress and intonation* where these features have a particular influence on meaning.

The *Introduction* provides an explanation of the methodological theory underlying this grammar, clarifying fundamental terms like 'concept', 'function', 'situation'. *Both teachers and students are strongly recommended to read the Introduction carefully before using the grammar.*

Introduction

Concepts and communicative functions

All languages are based principally upon two basic human needs:

1 to *identify* everything that is part of our existence:
   - concrete things (e.g. an object, an animal);
   - abstract ideas (e.g. love, intelligence);
   - general concepts (e.g. space, time, quantity);
   - concepts involving logical relationships (e.g. cause and effect);
2 to *communicate* with other people in order to achieve a particular result. For example:
   a) A person who does not have certain information can *ask* another person who will then *give a reply*.
   b) If someone needs to use something which belongs to another person he/she can *ask for permission* to use it. The other person will then *give permission* or *refuse* it.
   c) If someone *makes a suggestion* to another person, the second person may *accept* or *reject* it or, perhaps, *thank* the first person.

Language is therefore used to carry out a variety of communicative functions. It can express our intellectual, moral and emotional attitudes; it can influence the behaviour of other people (by requesting or ordering them to do something); it can establish and maintain social contact (by, for example, simple expressions for greeting people or answering the telephone).

The language of words is not the only means of satisfying these two fundamental human needs of identifying and communicating. There are other forms of language and they are becoming increasingly important (e.g. graphical, mathematical, musical). However there is no doubt that the language of words is still the most important for human communication.

How concepts and functions are expressed

Concepts and communicative functions are not rigidly separate categories. The abstract concept of, for example, *desire* can also be considered as a communicative function when it is seen as a need to *express desire*. The abstract concept of *existence* can be seen as a need to *ask about* or *confirm the existence* of something.

Moreover language expresses both concepts and communicative functions by the same means: through *vocabulary* (individual nouns, adjectives, verbs, etc.) and through *grammatical structures* (the plural of nouns, the position of adjectives, the use of articles, verb tenses, etc.).

Thus, to take an example, the concept of *possibility* can be expressed in English both through *vocabulary* (e.g. **Perhaps he was there**) and through *grammatical structure* (e.g. **He could have been there**).

In the same way communicative functions can be expressed through *grammatical structure* (e.g. to make a suggestion: **What about going to the cinema?**; to ask for permission: **Would you mind if I opened the window?**). But sometimes they can also be expressed simply through vocabulary (e.g. to express approval: **Excellent!**; to greet someone: **Hello!**).

English Grammar for Communication considers primarily the grammatical structures used in English to express concepts and communicative functions. However it also deals with items of vocabulary when they play an important part in such expression. Items of vocabulary are also considered more specifically in a section of the book concerned with the formation of words.

Stress and intonation also play a vital part in expressing communicative functions. The same words, spoken with different stress and intonation, can express a variety of different attitudes on the part of the speaker (e.g. surprise, irritation, sympathy). Variations in stress and intonation may even have the effect of changing the function of the words spoken:

Sit DŎWN. (polite invitation)

Sit DÒWN. (order)

For stress and intonation ▶ Appendix A.

Concepts, functions and grammatical structures

There is no simple, direct relationship between concepts/functions and grammatical structures. A single concept or function can be expressed using a variety of structures. For example the function of *asking someone to do something* can be expressed by any of the following structures:

Can you Could you Would you	lend	me your book?
Would you mind lending		

On the other hand a single structure can be used to carry out a variety of communicative functions. For example, **Can I?** is used, among other things:
– to ask for permission: **Can I come in?**
– to ask someone for something: **Can I have a packet of biscuits, please?**
– to offer to do something: **Can I close the window for you?**

In the Communication section of this book, the structures of English are grouped together not according to formal grammatical categories (pronouns, adverbs, conjunctions, etc.) but according to the meanings or, in other words, the concepts and communicative functions, which they express. The chapter on *Time*, for example, groups together not only the verb forms used to express the concept of present, past and future, but also the prepositions, adverbs and conjunctions which are related to time. Language concerned with the measurement of time (clock time, dates, etc.) is included in the same chapter.

To take another example, modal verbs (**can, may, shall**, etc.) are mentioned in various Communication chapters each time they serve to express a particular function. So the verb **can** appears in the chapters on:
– *Permission, obligation and prohibition* (e.g. **Can I come in?**)
– *Certainty and uncertainty* (e.g. **Driving in the fog can be dangerous.**)
– *Ability* (e.g. **I can speak Spanish.**)

The importance of the context

Since there is no simple direct correspondence between grammatical structures and concepts/functions we must be very careful about interpreting the meaning of a particular structure. The same words can express different concepts and functions and can therefore be understood in different ways in different situations. Let us look at some examples.
a) An affirmative sentence may mean something more than simply an affirmation.

The window's open may be only a statement of fact but, depending on the situation, it may also be understood as a request (= **Can you close it?**).
b) An interrogative sentence is not always simply a question. **Are you using the typewriter?** may be just a question but it may also be a way of asking for permission (= **Can I borrow it?**)
c) The imperative form of the verb is not only used to give orders. In **Joan, meet Margaret** the verb **meet** is a way of introducing someone.
d) The verb tense called *simple present* can refer to a time which is really in the future, as in **Lessons start again next week**. The *present progressive* does not always signify actions which are in the process of happening at this moment. In certain contexts it may refer to a habitual action which the person speaking finds irritating: **Why are you always telling me what to do ?**

In most of these examples what is crucial is the *context*, the particular situation in which the different things are said. The person who is speaking chooses his/her words according to that situation and the person who is listening interprets them in the same way. Understanding the context and, also, using our own knowledge and natural expectations are two fundamental skills in interpreting the real meaning of what people are saying.

If we examine extracts from conversations it often appears at first that information is missing or that there is no obvious connection between what people are saying to each other, as in the following examples:
a) (a dialogue in Paris)

A: Are you leaving for New York tomorrow?
B: There's fog all over northern France.

In this case only our knowledge of the world allows us to interpret correctly the connection between the question and the answer. Based upon our own experience we can deduce that A is aware of B's plan to travel to New York and that B's reply indicates doubt about the prospects for his/her flight and even provides the reason for his/her doubt, namely the presence of fog which may cause a closure of the airports and therefore the possible cancellation of flights.

Notice that B's reply consists of a simple affirmative sentence in which there are neither expressions of doubt nor expressions of cause and effect.

b) MOTHER: Who's taking Martin to school tomorrow?

    FATHER: I'll be going to work at six.

    MOTHER: I'll see to it.

In this case too a number of concepts and communicative functions have not been explicitly presented. Compare the same dialogue where they have been made explicit:

MOTHER: Can you take Martin to school tomorrow? (*request*)

    FATHER: Sorry, I can't because I'll be going to work at six and lessons start at eight. Can you see to it? (*refusal + reason + request*)

    MOTHER: Yes, OK. (*acceptance*)

Again it is only our ability to deduce the logical connections which allows us to interpret the dialogue correctly. Our own experience of the world also helps us. We know, for example, that if the father leaves home at six o'clock he will not be able to accompany his son to school – we presume that lessons start later.

Our natural tendency in speaking is to omit all the information and all the logical connections which can (we presume) be easily deduced by the people we are speaking to.

Formal, informal and neutral language

As we can see, the context is fundamentally important for our choice of the vocabulary, the grammatical structures and also (in the spoken language) the intonation with which we express a particular concept or carry out a particular communicative function. Before making this choice we must consider a number of factors, including:

– our social relationship with the person to whom we are speaking (Is this person a friend, a stranger, a subordinate or someone with authority over us, etc.?)

– our psychological attitude with regard to this person or to the situation in general (Do we feel sympathy, hostility, boredom, tension, etc.?)

– the place in which we find ourselves (Are we at home, in a bank, at an official meeting, etc.?)

– the means of communication (Is it a face to face conversation, on the telephone, a letter, etc.?)

– the subject matter under discussion (Is it about a football match, the rise in inflation, the dismissal of someone from work, etc.?)

All of these factors, and others too, play a part in guiding our choice of language.

The type of language which is acceptable in most situations can be described as 'neutral'. There are, in addition, varieties of language which are more formal and more informal and which can only be used in particular situations. Let us look at some examples.

a) A boy could ask a friend for permission to switch on the television using an informal expression: **Is it OK if I switch on the TV?**

b) A customer in the post office might ask the clerk for a form using a neutral expression: **Could I have one of those forms, please?**

c) A newly-employed typist, who wants to ask a rather severe boss for permission to come into work later the next day, would use a formal expression: **Would it be possible for me to come in later tomorrow?**

The expression used in example (**b**), **Could I . . . ?** would be acceptable in all three situations. However, **Is it OK . . . ?** would probably not be acceptable in situation (**c**) and **Would it be possible . . . ?** would sound absurd in situation (**a**).

The distinctions between formal, informal and neutral are not, however, rigid. Much depends on the attitude of the individual speaker towards these expressions and also on the intonation and manner in which they are spoken.

This grammar indicates where a particular form of language is formal or informal. If no indication is given the language can be considered neutral. A distinction is also made, where necessary, between forms which normally appear only in the spoken language and those which are typical of the written language.

Organisation of the grammar

The book is divided into two principal sections, *Structure* and *Communication*.

The Structure section deals with certain fundamental issues of how the language is put together (e.g. the elements that make up a sentence, the formation of verb tenses, the construction of interrogative sentences). These are essentially general matters of language organisation which do not usually relate to particular concepts/communicative functions (although sometimes there are obvious links, e.g. between the structure of interrogative sentences and the function of asking questions).

The Communication section is basically concerned with how grammatical forms and structures are used to convey particular meanings. The chapters are organised according to concepts/communicative functions. Within the various chapters forms/structures are usually both described and related to these concepts/communicative functions.

How to use this grammar

1 Most pages have two columns. The column on the left contains examples, the column on the right contains explanations about the form and the use of the various structures being dealt with. The numbers and letters of the examples on the left correspond to the numbers and letters of the explanations on the right. This arrangement allows the grammar to be used following either an 'inductive' approach to problems (moving from the examples to the generalisation of the rules) or, alternatively, a 'deductive' approach (moving from the rule to the particular cases presented in the examples).

2 The general index lists, in alphabetical order:
   a) all the concepts and communicative functions dealt with in the grammar (e.g. *desire, regret, giving instructions, reminding* someone to do something)
   b) all the grammatical terms presented in the grammar, listed both as grammatical categories/structures (e.g. adverbs, prepositions, relative clauses) and as individual words (e.g. **rather, towards, whose**).

   Thus, the concept of *limited quantity* (as in **There were very few people**) can be found in the general index under *quantity (limited)*. In addition the index contains references to **few** and to *quantifiers*. Similarly the function of *suggesting* (as in **Shall we go to the cinema?**) can be found in the general index under *suggesting*, but there are also references to **shall** and to *modal verbs*.

3 The cross-references, indicated by the symbol ▶, provide an immediate connection between two paragraphs, whenever this is relevant, without needing to turn to the general index. For example, the cross-references concerning verb tenses provide a link between the meanings of the various tenses (dealt with in the chapter on *Time*) and the corresponding forms of these tenses (dealt with in the chapter on *Auxiliary verbs and full verbs*).

4 The Glossary provides an explanation of all the grammatical terms used in the book which might cause difficulty.

Pronunciation table

Consonants

Symbol	Key word
b	**b**ack
d	**d**ay
ð	**th**en
dʒ	**j**ump
f	**f**ew
g	**g**ap
h	**h**ot
j	**y**et
k	**k**ey
l	**l**ed
m	su**m**
n	su**n**
ŋ	su**ng**
p	**p**en
r	**r**ed
s	**s**oon
ʃ	fi**sh**ing
t	**t**ea
tʃ	**ch**eer
θ	**th**ing
v	**v**iew
w	**w**et
z	**z**ero
ʒ	plea**s**ure

Vowels

Symbol	Key word
æ	b**a**d
ɑː	c**a**lm
ɒ	p**o**t
aɪ	b**i**te
aʊ	n**ow**
aɪə	t**ire**
aʊə	t**ower**
ɔː	c**au**ght
ɔɪ	b**oy**
ɔɪə	empl**oyer**
e	b**e**d
eə	th**ere**
eɪ	m**a**ke
eɪə	pl**ayer**
ə	**a**bout
əʊ	n**o**te
əʊə	l**ower**
ɜː	b**ir**d
i	prett**y**
iː	sh**ee**p
ɪ	sh**i**p
ɪə	h**ere**
uː	b**oo**t
ʊ	p**u**t
ʊə	p**oor**
ʌ	c**u**t

The symbol ' indicates that the following syllable is stressed:
record /'rekɔːd/   cassette /kə'set/

Glossary of grammatical terms

Examples are given in brackets **( )**.

active An active verb form is used when the subject carries out the action of the verb (The cat **drank** the milk) cf *passive*

adjective a word used to describe a noun or pronoun (a **pretty** girl; she's **pretty**) ▶ 8.10–8.15

adverb a word used to describe a verb (He walked **slowly**) or to describe where, when or how an action takes place (I'll meet you **there tomorrow**)

adverb particle a word which forms part of a phrasal verb (I looked **up** the word in a dictionary) ▶ 7.1–7.7

adverb phrase a group of words which functions in the same way as an adverb (He walked **in a slow deliberate way;** I'll meet you **at the station on Friday**)

agent the person or thing that carries out an action, the 'performer', normally introduced using **by** in a passive sentence (The novel was written **by Dickens**) ▶ 3.1

apposition When one noun phrase describes another but is simply placed next to it without being connected by a conjunction or preposition the two phrases are described as being *in apposition* (I visited **Ottowa, the capital city**) ▶ 8.29

article **the** (the definite article) or **a/an** (the indefinite article) ▶ 8.2–8.9

auxiliary verb a verb which can be used together with a full verb in a verb phrase. For example the auxiliary verbs **be, have, do** help to form progressive tenses (She **was** working), perfect tenses (I **have** finished), negative structures (I **don't** like it). Modal auxiliary verbs help to express meanings like possibility, certainty, etc. (He **might** be there; He **must** be there) ▶ 6.1–6.14

base form the simple form of the verb without any suffixes (**go, eat, look**)

clause part of a sentence normally containing both a subject and a finite verb (**The film ended** and **they left the cinema**). For *main clause, subordinate clause, co-ordinate clause* ▶ 1.2

comparative forms and structures involving adjectives or adverbs which are used to make comparisons between two or more things (Shanghai is **bigger** than Hong Kong but Hong Kong is **more densely** populated) cf *superlative;* ▶ 16.2–16.10

complement part of a sentence (after **be, seem, look** and certain other verbs ▶ 8.12) which describes the subject (You look **tired**). Sometimes the complement may describe the object of the sentence (The journey made him **tired**).

compound word two or more words which function together to make up a noun, verb, preposition, etc. (**rush hour; take off; in front of**)

conjunction a word used to join clauses (e.g. **and, but, while, so**) (She did it **while** you were away)

countable noun a noun which is used in both singular and plural form (**chair – chairs; house – houses; city – cities**) cf *uncountable;* ▶ 9.4

demonstratives the determiners/pronouns **this, that, these, those** ▶ 8.16–8.18

determiners words which are normally used at the beginning of noun phrases and have certain grammatical features in common. Determiners include: articles (**a/an, the**); demonstratives (**this, that,** etc.); possessives (**my, your,** etc.); certain quantifiers (**few, some, many,** etc.); certain **wh**-words (**what, which, whose**)

direct speech speech which is written down using exactly the same words as were originally used (He said, 'I don't want the job.') cf *reported speech*

emphasis making one part of a word or sentence appear, or sound, more important than the other parts, for example:

So YOU took the money ▶ 18.1–18.10

emphatic pronouns pronouns used to give emphasis to a noun or another pronoun (She did it all **herself**) ▶ 18.4

finite verb forms which are the basis of a clause or sentence. They can change according to the particular tense and subject (I **am** ready but she **isn't**; I usually **go** by bus but yesterday I **went** by car) cf *non-finite*

formal a style of language used when writing or speaking politely to strangers or superiors; cf *informal*

full verb a verb which is not an auxiliary or modal auxiliary (**eat, take, put**) ► 6.19–6.36

genitive the use of **'s** or **s'** with a noun to indicate *possession* in the widest sense of the term (That's **David's** car) ► 10.7

gerund ► *verbal noun*

imperative a verb form used to give orders and instructions (**Sit** here, please) ► 6.22

infinitive a verb form commonly made up of **to** + *base form* (the **to**-infinitive) (They told me **to wait**) ► 6.27, 6.28.
The infinitive can also be used *without* **to**. (I must **wait**) ► 6.29

informal a style of language used when speaking or writing to people we are familiar with (e.g. family or friends) cf *formal*

intonation the way in which, in speaking, the tone of the voice rises or falls, for example:

A: Are you READY? B: No, I'm NOT
► Appendix A

intransitive verb a verb which is used without an object (**come, go**) cf *transitive*

irregular word a word with forms which are not made according to the normal rules, (**man – men**, *not* **mans; take – took**, *not* **taked**) cf *regular*

linkers/linking words words or phrases which establish a link between two sentences (It's a beautiful house. **On the other hand** it is rather expensive)

main verb the verb that is the basis for the main clause of a sentence. (If you're ready **I'll call** a taxi) For *main clause* ► 1.2

modal auxiliary verbs certain auxiliary verbs with common grammatical features which express meanings like possibility, certainty, etc. (**can, could, will, would, shall, should, may, might, must, ought to, need, dare**) ► 6.15–6.18

non-finite fixed verb forms which do not change according to tense or subject (e.g. infinitive and participle forms) (I hope **to be** back in time; **Feeling** tired, she went to bed) cf *finite*

noun a word used to name a person, a thing, a place, an idea, etc. ► 8.1. A noun can be used as the subject, object or complement in a sentence.

noun phrase a group of words which can function as the subject, object or complement of a sentence (I bought **a black leather jacket**)

object a noun or pronoun referring to something, or somebody, which does not carry out the action of the verb but is affected by it in some way.
The *direct object* is 'directly' affected (Monica burned **the letter**).
The *indirect object* is usually affected by receiving something (The bank lent **me** the money) cf *subject*

passive A passive verb form is used when the subject does not carry out the action of the verb but is affected by it in some way. Passive verb structures consist of **be** + *past participle* (The milk **was drunk** by the cat) cf *active*; ► 3.1–3.6

past participle a verb form made up of *base form* + **-ed** in regular verbs (The building was **destroyed**). For various uses ► 6.23

perfect a verb form made up of a form of the auxiliary verb **have** + *past participle* (The programme **has started**)

person a means of distinguishing between the person/people speaking (first person: **I, we**), the person/people being spoken to (second person: **you**) and the person/people/thing(s) being spoken about (third person: **he, she, it, they**)

phrasal verb a verb that is made up of two elements: *verb + adverb particle* (The plane **took off**) ► 7.1–7.7

phrase two or more words that function together as a noun, verb, adverb, etc. ► 1.1, 1.2

possessive a form used to indicate 'possession' in the widest sense of the term (This is **Neil's** street) ► 10.1–10.14

prefix an element added at the beginning of a word to make a new word (**re**turn, **trans**atlantic, **self**-conscious) ► Appendix D

preposition a word or group of words which usually precedes a noun or pronoun relating it to the rest of the sentence (The car was parked **in front of** a shop)

prepositional verb a verb that is made up of two elements: *verb + preposition* (She **looked at** the advertisements) ► 7.1–7.7

present participle the **-ing** form of a verb when it is used to make a verb tense, and in certain other cases (The children are **sleeping**) cf *verbal noun*; ► 6.25

progressive a verb form made up of a form of the auxiliary verb **be** + *present participle* (The wind **was blowing**)

pronoun a word which is usually related to a noun or noun phrase and may be used for different purposes, e.g. to avoid repeating the noun (Kevin applied for the job but **he** didn't get **it**) or to emphasise it (Kevin **himself** typed the letter).

In addition to personal, possessive and reflexive pronouns certain other words may also function as pronouns. (I've made a cake – would you like **some?**)

quantifier a word or expression used to indicate a degree of quantity. Quantifiers often function as determiners (There were **a lot of** boys but only **a few** girls in the disco)

regular word a word with forms which are made according to the normal rules (**cat – cats; look – looked**) cf *irregular*

relative clause a clause, which may be introduced by a relative pronoun, describing or defining something previously mentioned (Thank you for the present **which you sent me**) ► 8.19–8.29 for *restrictive* and *non-restrictive* relative clauses

relative pronouns the pronouns **who, whom, which, that,** used to introduce a relative clause ► 8.22–8.28

reported speech speech which is reported 'indirectly' without using exactly the same words as were originally used ('I don't want the job.' **He said that he didn't want the job**) cf *direct speech*; ► 22.1–22.10

sentence one or more clauses used to express a statement, a question, an order or an exclamation ► 1.1

short answer/response an answer or response made up of *subject + auxiliary verb* (A: Who said that? B: **I did**) ► 21.4

stress pronouncing one part of a word or sentence so that it is more noticeable than the other parts (in the word **information** /ɪnfəˈmeɪʃən/ the third syllable is stressed; in the sentence **He's ill** the word **ill** would normally be stressed) ► Appendix A

subject a noun or pronoun referring to something or somebody which carries out the action of the verb in an active sentence (**Monica** burned the letter; **The bank** lent me the money). In passive sentences, however, the grammatical subject does not carry out the action of the verb but is affected by it in some way; cf *object, passive*

suffix an element added at the end of a word to make a new word (care**ful**, slow**ly**, open**ed**) ► Appendix D

superlative forms and structures involving adjectives and adverbs which are used to distinguish one member of a group from all the other members (New York is the **biggest** city in America and is also the **most densely** populated) ► 16.2–16.10; cf. *comparative*

syllable a phonetic element, based on a vowel sound, which is used to make up a word. A word may be made up of one or more syllables (**child** – one syllable; **chil dren** – two syllables; **grand chil dren** – three syllables) ► 1.1, 1.2

tense a verb form which gives some indication of when an action takes place (**take** – present; **took** – past)

to-infinitive a common form of the infinitive in which the base form of the verb is preceded by **to** (► 6.27, 6.28)

transitive verb a verb which is used with an object (I **closed** the door; I **saw** a film) cf *intransitive*

uncountable noun a noun which is not normally used with a plural form (**milk, gold, carefulness**) cf *countable noun*; ► 9.4

verb the word in the sentence which usually refers to the action carried out by the subject or the state which the subject is in (Monica **burned** the letter; I **feel** sleepy) *full verb, auxiliary verb, modal auxiliary verb*

verbal noun also called *gerund*: the **-ing** form of a verb when it is used as a noun (**Cooking** can be fun) ► 6.26; cf *present participle*

verb phrase a group of words, usually *auxiliary verb(s) + full verb* which together form the basis of a sentence (Monica **has burnt** the letter; I **was feeling** sleepy)

Section one: Structure

1 The sentence

Language structure

The basic units of the language are as follows:

a) . . . /n/ . . .
b) . . . -man . . .
c) . . . woman . . .
d) **The tall woman . . .**
e) **The tall woman is American,**
f) **The tall woman is American, but her husband is English.**

a) the *phoneme;*
b) the *syllable;*
c) the *word;*
d) the *phrase;*
e) the *clause;*
f) the *sentence.*

Each unit is composed of one or more elements taken from the preceding unit.

1 /m/

   /æ/

   /n/

1 A *phoneme* is a distinctive speech sound. Phonemes do not correspond exactly to the letters of the alphabet. They can be represented by phonetic transcription. For a complete list of phonemes in English ▶ page xiii.

2 /mæn/

   /wʊm/ /ən/

   /ə/ /mer/ /ɪ/ /kən/

2 A *syllable* is made up of one or more phonemes. It contains a vowel sound, which may also have consonant sounds before and after it.

3 man
   woman
   American

3 A *word* is made up of one or more syllables. It can be considered the smallest unit of the language capable of carrying a meaning. For a description of word formation ▶ Appendix D.

4 a) **A big blue car** was parked outside the house.
   She bought **a new dress.**

   b) He **has been driving** for fifteen years.
   The programme **will start** at eight o'clock.

   c) You must put it **in the oven.**
   Please drive **as carefully as possible.**

4 A *phrase* is composed of two or more words which together make up a particular element of a clause (e.g. the subject or the verb). The most important are:
   a) *noun phrases* which can function as *subject* or *object;*
   b) *verb phrases;*
   c) *adverb phrases.*

5 a) While they were waiting at the airport, **the children slept.**
   If you don't know the answer **you can look it up in the dictionary.**

5 A *clause* is a group of words which normally contains both a *subject* and a *finite verb.* It may also contain other elements (e.g. an *object* or an *adverb*). There are three types of clause:
   a) A *main clause* provides a complete expression of meaning and could usually stand independently as a sentence.

b) **While they were waiting at the airport,** the children slept.
If you don't know the answer you can look it up in the dictionary.
Did you notice that woman **who just got off the bus**?
Turning the corner, the driver lost control of the car.

c) **The lift stopped** and **the door opened.**
She called the waiter but **he didn't hear her.**
You can send a telex or **you can telephone the office.**

6 a) **Charles Dickens lived in this house.**
When did he live here?

b) **Close the door, please.**

c) **What an unusual building!**

b) A *subordinate clause* is dependent on a main clause. It cannot, therefore, stand independently as a sentence. It is usually introduced by a *conjunction* (e.g. **if, while**) or a *relative pronoun* (e.g. **who, which**).

NOTE: Sometimes a subordinate clause contains a *participle* or an *infinitive* instead of a subject and finite verb.

c) A *coordinate clause* is one of two clauses which are joined together, neither of which is dependent on the other. They could each stand as independent sentences. They are usually linked by **and, but** or **or.**

6 a) A *sentence* is made up of one or more clauses. It provides a complete expression of meaning. It expresses a *statement*, a *question*, a *command* or an *exclamation*. In the written form it begins with a capital letter and ends with a full stop, a question mark or an exclamation mark.

b) Sometimes a sentence may not have a subject (e.g. in an imperative).

c) Sometimes there may not be a verb (e.g. in an exclamation).

Sentence structure

1.3

1

	Subject	Verb	Object	Adverb
a)	Jack	loves	Sally	passionately.
b)	The minister	will make	a final decision	next week.

The basic grammatical elements of a sentence (*subject, verb, object, adverb*) are made up of either (**a**) single words or (**b**) phrases.

2 a) **What you are saying** is nonsense.

b) She didn't know **that the letter had arrived**.

2 However an entire clause may also function as (**a**) the subject or (**b**) the object of a sentence.

Word order in the sentence

The construction of the *affirmative* sentence in English is based on the following general rules:

1.4

1 **Time flies.**
Nelson died in 1805.
I like a cup of coffee after dinner.

1 The sentence must include a *subject* and a *finite verb*. The subject comes before the verb and is usually placed at the beginning of the sentence.

2 a) **There's** a good film on at the Odeon.
There were some flowers on the table.
There seems to be a mistake here.

   b) **Away** he went.
   £100 it cost me!
   Three hours the film lasts!
   Never have I heard such nonsense.

2 In the following cases the subject is not at the beginning of the sentence:
   a) in sentences introduced by **there**. **There + be** is often used as an 'empty' introductory phrase at the beginning of the sentence. In this case the real subject of the sentence comes after the verb. Sometimes other verbs (e.g. **seem, appear**) can be used with **be**.

   NOTE: In this type of sentence **there** does not function as an adverb of place (▶ 12.18).

   b) in emphatic sentences. In this case we deliberately place an element which is not the subject at the beginning of the sentence to draw attention to it (▶ 18.2). This type of sentence is often followed by an exclamation mark.
   For adverbs at the beginning of the sentence ▶ 1.5.

3 a) Tom likes **Ann** (direct object).
   Speak to **him** (indirect object).
   Ask **me some questions** (indirect and direct object).

   b) Arthur is **rich**.
   She looks **tired**.
   You're **the boss**.

   c) She sings **beautifully**.
   He talked to me **about his problems**.
   I took a taxi **to the station**.

3 A sentence may consist of only a subject and a verb. Other elements which may appear in the sentence and which normally follow the verb, are:
   a) a *direct* and/or an *indirect object*;
   b) a *complement* (i.e. an adjective or noun which follows the verb **be** and certain other verbs ▶ 8.12);
   c) an *adverb* or *adverb phrase*.

For other types of sentence: interrogative sentences ▶ 2.1–2.11; negative sentences ▶ 2.12–2.14; imperative sentences ▶ 6.22, 25.2–25.5; exclamations ▶ 18.8.

Position of adverbs

Adverbs and *adverb phrases* can appear at the beginning or at the end of the sentence. Single word adverbs can also appear in the middle of the sentence.

1.5

1 a) They frequently met. **Consequently** their friendship developed.
I never met him. **However** I knew his reputation.

b) **Obviously** the room hadn't been booked in advance.
Naturally, she speaks German.
She speaks German, **naturally**. (= of course)
Compare:
She speaks German **naturally**. (= in a natural way)

c) **At about midnight** we heard footsteps coming slowly along the corridor.
Yesterday you left the light on in the kitchen all day.

d) **Quickly** he shut the door.

2 a) It **never** stops raining.
She **rarely** went to bed later than ten o'clock.
We **sometimes** go to the seaside in summer.
He is **often** late.
I had **always** wanted to see that film.

b) He is **probably** at home now.
The contract has **definitely** been signed.
Compare:
Perhaps nobody knows him.

c) We have **almost** finished.
The trouble has **really** started.

d) I was **only** trying to help.
The burglars had **even** taken their clothes.
Compare:
You can come **too**.

e) Everybody has **already** left.
He's **still** doing the same job.

f) They **quickly** finished their meal and left the room.

1 Adverbs come at the beginning of the sentence:
a) when the adverb acts as a link with the previous sentence;
b) when the adverb is a *sentence adverb* expressing the point of view of the speaker or making a comment (▶ 13.5). This type of adverb may also come at the end of the sentence. In both cases it may be separated by a comma to avoid confusion of meaning.
c) to avoid placing too many adverbs or adverb phrases together at the end of the sentence (adverbs of time are often placed at the beginning);
d) to give greater emphasis to the adverb.

2 The position in the middle of the sentence is before a one-word verb but after the verb **be**. If there is a compound verb the adverb comes after the first *auxiliary*. Generally only one-word adverbs, not adverb phrases, take this middle position. It is the normal position for:
a) adverbs of frequency;
b) adverbs expressing certainty and uncertainty (▶ 19.1–19.15). Notice that **perhaps** and **maybe** come at the beginning of the sentence.
c) certain adverbs of degree;
d) certain adverbs expressing the concept of inclusion or restriction (▶ 17.1–17.6). Notice that **too** and **as well** normally come at the end of the sentence.
e) certain adverbs expressing a time relationship;
f) Sometimes adverbs of manner can also appear in this position.

3 a) The plane landed **safely**.
I gave him the money **reluctantly**.

  b) She sat **quietly in the corner all evening**.
They were playing records **loudly in their room last night**.

  c) We went **to Vienna by train at Easter**.
The guide took us **to our hotel in his car**.

4 The meal we had was **absolutely** delicious.
She cleaned the house **very** thoroughly.
Compare:
He isn't old **enough** to drive a car.

3 a) Most adverbs, and especially adverb phrases, come at the end of the sentence, after the verb and after the object if there is one.

  b) When there are two or more adverbs together at the end of the sentence they usually appear in the following order: MANNER → PLACE → TIME.

  c) With verbs of movement the normal sequence is: PLACE → MANNER → TIME. Variations are possible for reasons of focus or style.

4 Adverbs are also used to modify adjectives and other adverbs. In this case the adverb normally comes before the word it modifies. But notice that **enough** comes after the word which it modifies.

Position of direct and indirect objects

When a sentence has both a *direct object* and an *indirect object* the word order is as follows:

1.6

1 Jim gave **Jenny a record**.
They sent **me a letter**.
Sheila bought **John a book**.

2 Jim gave **a record to Jenny**.
They sent **a letter to me**.
Sheila bought **a book for John**.

3 Jim gave **it to Jenny**.
They sent **it to me**.
Sheila bought **it for John**.

4 a) Please give **your cheque to the secretary**.
Don't send **the goods to us** yet.

  b) Could you cook **something for my friends**?
I'd like you to get **some fruit for me** from the market.

  c) Thank you for the present you brought **for** me.
I brought my passport **to** the receptionist.

1 If the direct object is a noun, the indirect object normally comes before it, without a preposition.

2 An alternative construction is to place the indirect object, preceded by **to** or **for**, after the direct object. This is less common in informal English.

3 If the direct object is a pronoun, the indirect object normally follows it and is preceded by **to** or **for**.

4 In constructions where prepositions are used:
  a) *To do something* **to** *someone* suggests an action in which the other person is directly involved as some kind of recipient. **To** is used with the following verbs: **give, hand, lend, offer, owe, pass, promise, read, sell, send, show, take, teach, throw, write**.

  b) *To do something* **for** *someone* suggests an action carried out for the benefit of someone without that person necessarily being involved in the action. **For** is used with **book, build, buy, cook, fetch, find, get, keep, leave, make, order, reserve, save**.

  c) Either **to** or **for** may be used with the verb **bring** depending on the meaning.

1.7

1 a) What's the matter? **Tell me**.
So, this is your new flat. Come on, **show us**.
I've got a new job. Haven't I **told you**?

b) Will you **read to the children**?
Write to me as soon as you can.
Compare American English:
Write me as soon as you can.

2 'Come here,' he **said to her**.
He **explained** the rule **to them**.

1 Some verbs can be followed by an indirect object even when there is no direct object. In this case:

a) **Ask, promise, show, teach, tell** are followed by the indirect object without a preposition.

b) **Read, sing, write** are followed by **to** + *indirect object*. (Notice that in American English **to** can be omitted after **write**.)

2 Some verbs are not normally followed by an indirect object unless it is preceded by the preposition **to**: **complain, explain, reply, say, shout, speak, suggest, talk**.

2 Interrogative and negative sentences

Interrogative sentences

2.1

| Shall I open the window?
| Can I come in?
| Why don't you read a book?
| Wasn't it exciting?

An *interrogative sentence* is normally used as a question, a means of asking for information (▶ 21.2). However interrogative structures may also have other functions: for example offering to do something (▶ 26.3); asking for permission (▶ 24.1–24.3); making a suggestion (▶ 25.10); making an exclamation (▶ 2.15, 18.8).

Types of interrogative sentence

Interrogative sentence structures are of three types, as follows:

2.2

1 When did you go to BRİstol?

What TİME is it?

Where's the MİLK?

How far is the STĀtion?

2 Is he a DŌctor?

Do you speak FRĒNCH?

Has she done her HŌMEwork?

3 Is he coming toDĀY or toMŌRrow?

Are you going to paint it RĒD, WHİTE or BLŪE?

Do you like your coffee BLĀCK or WHİTE?

1 **Wh-***questions* ask for information specifically linked to a question word. They are called **wh-***questions* because the question words begin with the letters **wh-** (except for **how**). **Wh-***questions* normally have falling intonation.

2 **Yes/no** questions simply ask for a positive or a negative response. These questions generally have rising intonation.

3 *Alternative questions* ask for a choice between two or more given alternatives. They normally have rising intonation on each of the alternatives except the last, which has falling intonation (▶ Appendix A).

Formation of interrogative sentences

2.3

1 **Are you** working?
Was this poem written by Keats?
Can she do it?

Compare:
You are working.
This poem was written by Keats.
She can do it.

2 **Have they** been working?
Could she have come to the meal?
How many **would you** have liked?

3 **Do** the children go to bed early?
Which books **does** she want?
Did they leave in the morning?

1 The word order of most interrogative sentences is different from that of affirmative sentences (▶ 1.4) because there is inversion of the subject and the auxiliary verb.

2 If there are two auxiliary verbs the subject is placed after the first auxiliary.

3 In the simple present or the simple past, where there is usually no auxiliary verb in an affirmative sentence, the auxiliary verb **do** is introduced (▶ 3.13).

4 a) **Who met** you at the pub?
 How many people saw him?
 Which of them can help me?
 How many students understand this?
 How many students do not understand this?

 Compare:
 b) **Who did you meet** at the pub?
 How many people **did he see**?
 Which of them **can I help**?

5 a) Is **anybody** there?
 Are you going **anywhere** this summer?
 Would you like **anything** to drink?

 b) Compare:
 Is **somebody** there? (I thought I heard somebody)
 Are you going **somewhere** this summer? (you usually go somewhere)
 Would you like **something** to drink?
 Could you get me **some** milk from the fridge?

4 a) In **wh-***questions*, if the **wh-***question* word serves as the subject of the sentence, there is no inversion of subject and auxiliary verb and therefore the addition of the auxiliary verb **do** is not necessary (unless **do** forms part of a negative structure ▶ 2.12).

 b) If the **wh-***question* word serves as the *object* of the sentence there is inversion of the subject and auxiliary verb, as in other interrogative sentences.

5 a) Normally an interrogative sentence contains **any** and compounds of **any,** rather than **some**.

 b) However **some** and compounds of **some** are used when we confidently expect a positive response or wish to encourage such a response. **Some** is also used when we wish to express a more positive or more assertive attitude (e.g. in offering something to somebody, or requesting somebody to do something ▶ 9.9, 9.10).

Interrogative determiners and pronouns

Summary table

2.4

	Pronouns			Determiners
	Subject	*Object*	*Possession*	
People	who which	whom/who which	whose	what which whose (*possession*)
Things	what which	what which		

NOTE: **Who, whom, which, whose** are also used as *relative pronouns*.

1 a) **Who came** yesterday?
 What frightened you?
 Which is your jacket?

 b) **Which team won** the cup?
 Whose car got damaged in the accident?

1 When (**a**) the interrogative pronoun is used as the subject of the sentence or when (**b**) the interrogative determiner refers to the subject there is no inversion of subject and auxiliary verb (▶ 2.3).

2 a) **Who(m) did you** see there?
What do they want?

b) **Which newspaper have you** got?
Whose name did they mention?

2 When (**a**) the interrogative pronoun is used as the object of the sentence or when (**b**) the interrogative determiner refers to the object there is inversion of subject and auxiliary verb (▶ 2.3).

Who, whom

2.5

1 **Who** is your favourite singer?
Who told her to come here?
Who are you going to see?
Whom does the party intend to select as leader?

1 The interrogative pronouns **who, whom** are used to refer to people. The object form **whom** is normally used only in formal English. It is rare in the spoken language. (But see interrogatives with prepositions ▶ 2.9.)

Which

2.6

1 **Which** is your favourite singer, Sting or David Bowie?
I've got tea or coffee: **which** do you prefer?

2 a) There are three books here; **which** is yours?

b) She's got two brothers; **which** of them did you meet?

c) **Which** writer are you more interested in: Joyce or Proust?

3 **Which of the** games did you see?
Which of her friends phoned?
Which of them phoned?
Which of these films is on at the moment?

4 **Which one** would you like, the red one or the black one?
Here are the records: **which ones** are you going to borrow?

1 **Which** is used instead of **who(m)** or **what** (referring to either people or things) when the choice is restricted to a limited number of alternatives.

2 **Which** can function as:
a) subject pronoun;
b) object pronoun;
c) determiner.

3 As a pronoun **which** is followed by **of** before the definite article, a possessive adjective/pronoun, an object pronoun, or a demonstrative.

4 **Which** is often used with the pronoun **one(s)** (▶ 1.5).

What

2.7

1 a) **What**'s the title of her latest book?

b) **What** would you like to eat?

c) **What** newspapers are published on Sunday?
What contemporary writers have been most influential?

1 **What** can function as:
a) subject pronoun referring to things;
b) object pronoun referring to things;
c) determiner referring to either people or things.

2 a) A: **What** is your father?
   B: He's an engineer.

   b) Compare:
   A: **Who** is your father?
   B: He's John Reeves, the film director.

   c) A: **Which** is your father?
   B: He's the one on the left.

2 a) The pronoun **what** may be used with reference to people but generally only to ask about occupations.

   b) **Who** is used when we want to ask for someone's name and precise details.

   c) **Which** is used when we want someone in a group to be pointed out.

Whose

Whose refers to possession (▶ 10.1). It can be used as:

2.8

1 **Whose** is this record?

1 a pronoun (in a more formal style);

2 Compare:
   Whose record is this?

2 a determiner (more common in informal English).

Interrogative pronouns and determiners with prepositions

2.9

1 a) **Who** are you working **for**?
   Which room is he **in**?
   Which of these people did you go **with**?
   What country does he come **from**?
   What did you do that **for**?

1 a) *Interrogative pronouns* and *determiners* may be used as parts of prepositional phrases. When this is done in informal English the question word (**who, which, what,** etc.) comes at the beginning of the sentence and the preposition at the end.

   b) **For whom** are you working?
   From what country did Columbus come?
   In which city could you see the Spanish Steps?

   b) In formal English (e.g. quiz questions) the preposition may be placed at the beginning of the sentence before the question word. In this case the object form **whom** must be used instead of **who**.

2 a) A: **What** does he **look like**?
   B: He's tall and thin.
   A: **What** does the bag **look like**?
   B: It's a black leather bag with a metal handle.

2 The preposition **like** is used with **who** and **what** to make some particular questions.
   a) **what** + **look** + **like** refers specifically to physical appearance.

   b) A: **What is** she **like**?
   B: She's very friendly.
   A: **What's** Seville **like**?
   B: It's a fascinating city.

   b) **What** + **be** + **like** refers, in a more general sense, to personality or characteristics.

   c) A: **Who** does the baby **look like**?
   B: He looks like his father.

   c) **Who** + **look** + **like** refers to physical resemblance to another person.

   d) A: **Who is** she **like**?
   B: She's like her sister – very shy.

   d) **Who** + **be** + **like** refers to resemblance to another person, usually in terms of personality.

Interrogative adverbs

1 a) A: **Where** are you going?
   B: To London.

   b) A: **Where** do you have lunch?
   B: At home.

   c) A: **Where** does she come **from**?
   B: From California.

2 a) A: **When** do you start work?
   B: At eight o'clock.

   b) A: **When** were you born?
   B: In 1969.

3 a) A: **Why** are you late?
   B: Because I missed the bus.

   b) A: **Why** are you taking a taxi?
   B: To get there as quickly as possible.

4 a) A: **How** did you come back?
   B: By train.

   b) A: **How** do you switch the radio on?
   B: Just press this button.

   c) A: **How** are you?
   B: Very well, thanks.

   A: **How** do you do, Mr Grey?
   B: **How** do you do?

5 A: **How old** are you?
   B: Sixteen.
   A: **How long** is it?
   B: Three metres.
   A: **How long** does it take you to get home?
   B: About an hour.
   A: **How far** is the cinema?
   B: Two miles.
   A: **How often** do you come here?
   B: About twice a week.
   A: **How quickly** can you type?
   B: One hundred words a minute.
   A: **How much** is it?
   B: 50 pence.
   A: **How many** oranges would you like?
   B: Ten please.

1 **Where** can mean:
   a) to what place? (movement);
   b) in what place? (position);
   c) from what place? (i.e. Where is her home or place of origin?)

2 **When** can mean:
   a) at what time?
   b) in which month, year, etc.?

3 **Why** can mean:
   a) for what reason?
   b) for what purpose?

4 **How** can mean:
   a) by what means?
   b) in what way?
   c) Notice also the expressions **How are you?** (used as a greeting or to ask about someone's health) and **How do you do?** (used when being introduced to someone).

5 In addition, **how** is used before a number of adjectives, adverbs and quantifiers.

Question tags

2.11

1 a) **Mary's** clever, **isn't she**?
   George has got a new car, **hasn't he**?
   John and Tim can play tennis, **can't they**?
   You'll be eighteen soon, **won't you**?
   I should phone him, **shouldn't I**?
   Jane works in New York now, **doesn't she**?
   Peter arrived yesterday, **didn't he**?
   I'm going too, **aren't I**?

 - b) **She isn't** here yet, **is she**?
   Charles hasn't arrived, **has he**?
   Your friends won't stay long, **will they**?
   You wouldn't do that to me, **would you**?
   I can't leave her now, **can I**?
   The Johnsons don't live here, **do they**?
   Elizabeth didn't talk to you, **did she**?

2 a) It's a nice DAY, ISn't it?
   You don't live in LONdon, DO you?

 b) Sheila's met you beFORE, HASn't she?
   He didn't PAY, DID he?

3 a) So he's late aGAIN, IS he?
   You didn't go to SCHOOL, DIDN'T you?

 b) She's SAFE now, IS she?

 c) Oh, you've found a new JOB, HAVE you?

1 *Question tags* are short interrogative structures which can be added at the end of affirmative or negative sentences. They are constructed in the following way:
   a) If the sentence to which it refers is affirmative, the question tag normally has a negative form (but see **3** below). It is made up of the auxiliary verb in the sentence followed by a personal pronoun corresponding to the subject of the sentence. If the sentence has no auxiliary verb (i.e. if the verb is in the simple present or past tense) the auxiliary **do** is used.
   Notice that the question tag for **I am** is **aren't I?**
   b) If the sentence to which it refers is negative, the question tag is made up of the auxiliary verb without **not** followed by the relevant personal pronoun.

2 Question tags are normally used to ask for confirmation of what has just been said.
   a) If we simply wish to ask for confirmation concerning something we already feel sure of, falling intonation is used. The purpose of this is usually just to elicit a reaction from the other person.
   b) If, on the other hand, we are not sure whether what we are saying is correct, rising intonation is used. In this case the question tag helps to form a more genuine question.

3 There is also another type of question tag in which an affirmative tag follows an affirmative sentence, and a negative tag follows a negative sentence.
   These are not normally 'questions' at all, but are used to express emotional reaction of some kind. They may indicate feelings like:
   a) anger;
   b) worry;
   c) interest.

   In these cases a rising intonation is normally used.

Negative sentences

Formation of negative sentences

2.12

1 She **isn't/is not** from New York.
You **mustn't/must not** smoke.
We **haven't/have not** been talking about you.

Compare:
She**'s** from New York.
You **must** smoke less.
We**'ve** been talking about you.

2 I **don't/do not** live in Glasgow.
She **doesn't/does not** work.
They **didn't/did not** see the film.

Compare:
I **live** in Glasgow.
She **works.**
They **saw** the film.

3 He **hasn't** any friends.
Compare:
He **doesn't have** any friends.

4 Frank can come but **not** Michael.
My pullover is brown, **not** green.

1 An affirmative sentence can be changed into a *negative* sentence by adding the negative particle **not** after the auxiliary verb. If there are two auxiliary verbs **not** comes after the first.
Contracted forms (e.g. **isn't**) are more common in spoken English.
For auxiliary verbs ▶ 6.1–6.14.

2 Affirmative sentences with verbs in the simple present or the simple past, which do not normally have an auxiliary verb, can be changed into the negative by adding the auxiliary **do** followed by **not**.
For simple present ▶ 6.20.
For simple past ▶ 6.21.

3 The full verb **have** (indicating possession ▶ 10.13) is sometimes itself followed by **not** without using the auxiliary **do**.

4 The negative particle **not** can also be used before other parts of the sentence.

Negative pronouns, determiners and adverbs

2.13

Pronouns		Determiners	Adverbs
People	*Things*		
no one nobody	nothing	no neither	never (TIME) nowhere (PLACE) neither, nor (EXCLUSION)
none (of) neither (of)			

1 a) I've got **no** sugar.
There was **nobody** in the street.
Did **no one** tell you?
There's **nothing** we can do.
Personally, I like **none** of his books.
She's been **nowhere** this week.

1 a) A negative sentence normally contains only one negative word. Since the words in the above table automatically make the sentence negative, the negative particle **not** is not included.

b) Compare:
I have**n't** got **any** sugar.
There was**n't anybody** in the street.
Did**n't anyone** tell you?
There is**n't anything** we can do.
I do**n't** like **any** of his books.
She has**n't** been **anywhere** this week.

2 a) **Neither** of the cars was damaged in the crash.

b) There were two paintings on the wall; **neither** painting was very attractive.

c) You don't speak German and **neither/nor** do I.

3 I've **never** been there.
Compare:
I have**n't ever** been there.

b) Notice that sentences with **not** + **any** (or compounds of **any**) have almost the same meaning as sentences with **no** (or compounds of **no**). Sentences with **no** are more emphatic.
For **no** ▶ 9.5–9.7.
For **nobody, no one** ▶ 9.8.
For **nothing** ▶ 9.18.
For **none** ▶ 9.6, 9.7.
For **nowhere** ▶ 9.18.

2 **Neither** is used when referring to two people or things. It can be used as:

a) a pronoun ▶ 9.5–9.7;

b) a determiner ▶ 9.5–9.7;

c) a conjunction ▶ 17.3 – notice that **nor** can also be used in this sense.

3 **Never** (▶ 11.22, 11.43) refers to time. Sentences with **not** + **ever** have the same meaning but are not so commonly used.

For inversion after negative adverbs ▶ 18.2.

Any, some in negative sentences

2.14

1 She didn't say **anything**.
There isn't **any** coffee in the cupboard.
I didn't recognise **anyone** in the office.

2 I don't like **some** of your friends (= some particular individuals).
I didn't know **something** had happened (= a particular incident).

Compare:
I don't like **any** of your friends.
I didn't know **anything** had happened.

3 We **rarely** watch anything on TV.
She can **hardly** say anything in English.
We had **scarcely** any time to relax.
The engine **seldom** gives any trouble.

1 In a negative sentence we normally use **any** and compounds of **any** rather than **some** and its compounds.

2 However **some** is used, even in a negative sentence, when we wish to refer to something or some quantity which is limited or restricted in some way.
Any usually has an unlimited, unrestricted sense (▶ 9.9, 9.10).

3 Some other adverbs have negative implications (e.g. **hardly, scarcely, barely** ▶ 14.4; **rarely, seldom** ▶ 11.43).
We normally use **any** with such adverbs too.

For inversion after negative adverbs ▶ 18.2.

Negative-interrogative sentences

2.15

1 **Aren't you** ready yet?
Why **hasn't she** paid you?
Who didn't come to school today?
Don't you want to come with us?
Couldn't you lend him some money?
Won't you help me?
Isn't it a lovely day! (= What a lovely day it is!)
Doesn't he play well!

1 *Negative-interrogative* sentences are constructed like ordinary interrogative sentences except that the negative particle **not** (contracted to **n't**) is placed after the auxiliary verb.
This type of sentence often expresses surprise, irritation or disappointment, or gives a sense of pleading (▶ 25.6). Negative-interrogative sentences often function as exclamations and so they are sometimes followed by an exclamation mark (▶ 18.8).

2 A: Haven't you finished?
B: Yes. (= I have finished)

A: Can't you drive?
B: No. (= I can't drive)

2 Notice that in English, the answer **yes** to a negative question has an affirmative meaning and the answer **no** has a negative meaning.

3 **Did they not** realise how serious the problem was?
Why **does the government not** do something?

Are you NOT coming?

Does she NOT want a drink?

3 There is an alternative structure for negative-interrogative sentences which is used in a more formal style of English. The negative particle **not** is placed after the subject. This structure is also used when **not** is stressed.

3 Passive sentences

Formation of passive sentences

1 a)
Mr West	marks	the English tests.
(subject)		*(object)*

  b)
The English tests	are marked by	Mr West.
(subject)		*(performer)*

2

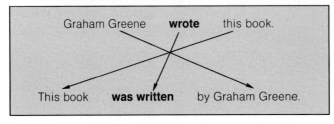

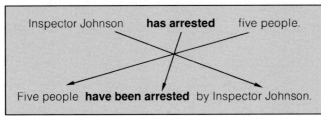

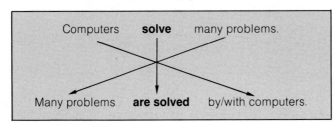

1 a) In a typical *active* sentence the subject carries out the action indicated by the verb. The object is 'passive'; it is affected by this action.

  b) In a *passive sentence* it is the subject which is affected by the action. The 'performer' of the action, if mentioned, is normally introduced using **by**.

2 An active sentence can be transformed into a passive sentence in the following way:
  – The *object* of the active sentence becomes the *subject* of the passive sentence.
  – The passive structure is formed by using the verb **be** in the same tense as the verb in the active sentence, followed by the *past participle* of the original active verb.
  Notice that the verb **be** is plural when the subject of the passive sentence is plural.
  – The subject of the active sentence is introduced using the preposition **by** (or **with** for 'instruments').

3.2

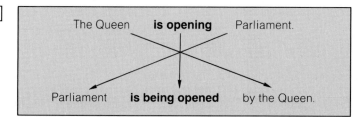

The passive of *progressive* forms is obtained by using the progressive form of **be** (e.g. **am being**) followed by the *past participle* of the original active verb.

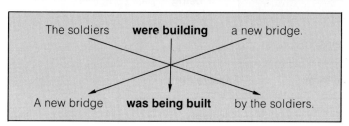

3.3

1

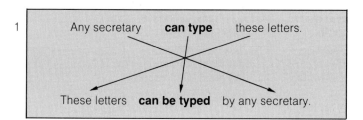

1 When the active sentence contains a modal verb, the passive structure is formed by using *modal verb + passive infinitive without* **to**. (▶ 3.4, 3.6)

2

Anybody **could have said** that.

That **could have been said** by anybody.

2 If the modal verb is followed by a past infinitive without **to,** the passive construction is *modal verb + past passive infinitive without* **to** (▶ 3.4, 3.6).

3.4

1 a) I want **to be left** alone.

   b) He must **have been killed** in an accident.

2 She doesn't like **being taken** to her grandmother's.

1 a) The passive of the infinitive is formed by **(to) be** + *past participle.*

   b) The *past passive infinitive* is formed by **(to) have been** + *past participle.*

2 The passive of the **-ing** form is **being** + *past participle.*

3.5

1 **Is this seat** taken?
Has the house been sold?

1 Passive *interrogative* sentences are formed by inverting the subject and first auxiliary verb.

2 This seat **isn't** taken.
The house **hasn't** been sold.

2 Passive *negative* sentences are formed by using **not** after the first auxiliary verb.

3 This exit is **not to be used** by the general public.
Not being informed of the delay, I got more and more worried.

3 The negative form of the passive infinitive is **not (to) be** + *past participle*, and the negative of the passive **-ing** form is **not being** + *past participle.*

Summary table: active and passive forms

3.6

Verb tense	Active form	Passive form
simple present	writes	is written
present progressive	is writing	is being written
simple past	wrote	was written
past progressive	was writing	was being written
present perfect	has written	has been written
past perfect	had written	had been written
present infinitive	(to) write	(to) be written
past infinitive	(to) have written	(to) have been written
-ing form	writing	being written
past of the **-ing** form	having written	having been written

Passive structures: possibilities

3.7

1 Everybody speaks English here.
English is spoken by everybody here.

1 Verbs can be transformed from active into passive if they are followed by a direct object, i.e. if they are *transitive*.

2 They have turned off the radio.
The radio has been turned off.
They looked at me with suspicion.
I was looked at with suspicion.

2 With *phrasal* or *prepositional verbs* (▶ 7.1) the preposition or adverb particle remains immediately after the verb.

3.8

He gave me a book.
1 **I was given a book.**
2 **A book was given to me.**

She promised him £200.
1 **He was promised £200.**
2 **£200 was promised to him.**

They told me a story.
1 **I was told a story.**
2 **A story was told to me.**

If a verb is followed by both a direct object and an indirect object, two passive constructions are possible: either (**1**) the indirect object or (**2**) the direct object can be transformed into the subject of the passive sentence. Notice that in (**2**) the indirect object is normally preceded by **to**.
Transforming the indirect object into the subject (**1**) is more common, but this depends on the focus intended or required.

Verbs of knowing and thinking in the passive

3.9

1 They think that he is in Spain.
It is thought that he is in Spain.
People said that she had properties abroad.
It was said that she had properties abroad.
Everybody supposed that he was English.
It was supposed that he was English.
We agreed that we should leave in the morning.
It was agreed that we should leave in the morning.
They have arranged that the house should be sold.
It has been arranged that the house should be sold.

2 a) They **consider him to be** a suitable candidate.
He **is considered to be** a suitable candidate.
They **felt the examination to be** too easy.
The examination **was felt to be** too easy.

b) She **was said to have** properties abroad.

1 With certain verbs linked to the idea of 'knowing', 'thinking', etc. an impersonal passive structure using **it** as an empty subject is possible: **it** + *passive verb* + **that**. Such a structure is possible with the verbs **believe, consider, expect, feel, find, know, report, say, suppose, think, understand**. It is also common with the verbs **agree, arrange** and **decide**.

2 a) Many of the verbs mentioned in the previous paragraph can also be followed by *object* + **to-***infinitive*. Another passive structure can be formed with these verbs by transforming the object into the subject, followed by *passive verb* + **to-***infinitive*.

b) With **say** the active structure mentioned in **2a** above is not possible. However, the passive structure is possible.

For **expected** and **supposed** to express obligation ▶ 24.4, 24.6, 24.9, 24.10.

Alternative passive structures

3.10

1 My leg **got broken** in the accident.
Many houses **got damaged** in the storm.
My car **got smashed up** in an accident last week.

2 She **got married** to a Chinese.
I'll **get dressed** in a minute.
We **got lost** in the fog.

1 In informal English the verb **get** may be used in a similar way to **be** as an auxiliary in the formation of a passive sentence. This is particularly common when referring to damage, injury or accident.

2 There are also a number of common expressions constructed in the same way, e.g. **get confused, get divorced, get dressed, get engaged, get lost, get married, get washed**. They have a *reflexive* rather than a truly *passive* meaning.

Active structures with passive meaning

3.11

> My car **needs washing** (= needs to be washed).
> That shirt **wants ironing** (= needs to be ironed).
> This proposal **requires examining** (= needs to be examined).

In informal English the verb **need** and, more rarely, **want** may be followed by the active **-ing** form (verbal noun) to express a passive meaning. In formal English, **require** + **-ing** form has a similar meaning.

For **need, require** and **want** see also ▶ 6.35.

4 Replacing and omitting words

4.1
English uses a variety of means to avoid repeating words which have already been mentioned. In certain cases, the words can simply be omitted and the context will make the meaning clear. In other cases, instead of repeating the same words, other words can be inserted in their place. These replacement words are principally *pronouns*, certain *adverbs* and *auxiliary verbs*.

Substitution

Pronouns and possessive adjectives

4.2

1   John   and   Sue   came to the party.
    He   arrived at nine, but   she   was late.

2   I borrowed   this book   from   Philip .
    Can you give   it   back to   him ?

3   She was ill , but I didn't know   it .
    I didn't know   it   but   she was ill .

Personal pronouns, both (**1**) subject and (**2**) object (▶ 5.1), are used to take the place of nouns which have been previously mentioned. **It** (**3**) can also refer back, or forward, to a whole clause or sentence (▶ 5.3).

4.3

1   Paul   likes   his   new   secretary ;
    he says   her   typing is excellent.

2   Sheila   and   her   parents   live in
    separate   flats   now;   theirs   is bigger.

To avoid the repetition of a noun referring to the possessor we use (**1**) *possessive adjectives* and (**2**) *possessive pronouns* (▶ 10.2, 10.4). Possessive pronouns can refer both to the possessor and to the thing possessed.

4.4

Can you see   the house on the corner ?
 That's   where I live.
A: The weak point of the novel is its plot.
B: Well, I don't agree with   that .

Demonstrative pronouns (▶ 8.18) can be used to replace elements of a sentence, or a whole sentence, previously mentioned.

4.5

1 A: I'd like to buy   a tie .
   B: What kind?
   A: I want   one   with red stripes.

1 The pronouns **one** and **ones** can be used to avoid the repetition of countable nouns. **One** replaces a singular noun, **ones** replaces a plural noun.

A: Can I have some apples please?

B: Which ones would you like?

A: The big ones over there.

2 A: Which tie do you like best?

B: I like **the blue** one .

A: What kind of tie would you like?

B: I'd like **a red** one .

C: I'd like one with red stripes.

(*not* **a one**)

2 *Articles* can be used before **one(s)** but **a/an** can only be used when **one** is preceded by an adjective.

3 A: I'm looking for some glasses .

B: What about these (ones) on the

shelf? Which (ones) do you prefer?

3 **One(s)** can be used or can be left out after **this, that, these, those** and **which**.

4.6

 Bananas were cheap at the market today,

so I bought some .

I'm looking for some cigarettes but I

cannot find any .

Several students took the test, but

 none (of them) passed it.

Certain *quantifiers* (▶ 9.5) can be used to replace previously mentioned nouns.

Adverbs

4.7

1 Why don't we stop here ? Harrods

is a fantastic place for shopping.

2 I used to live in Spain years ago ;

I was happy then .

I'm very depressed these days . In fact,

I've never been so depressed as now .

The adverbs **here/there** (▶ 12.18) and **now/then** (▶ 11.21, 11.24) can replace expressions of place and time. They may be used to refer forward to (**1**) an element not yet mentioned, or (**2**) back to something which has already been mentioned.

4.8

A: I wonder if Paul is coming to the party .

B: He told me so . (= He told me that he

would come)

So and **not** avoid the repetition of entire clauses which have previously been mentioned. This happens particularly after verbs like **believe, guess, hope, imagine,**

A: I think ⬚ Martha will be late ⬚, as usual.

B: I hope ⬚ not ⬚. (= I hope that she won't be late)

A: Don't you think ⬚ we should buy a new record player ⬚?

B: No, I don't think ⬚ so ⬚. (= I don't think we should buy a new record player)

suppose, tell, think, and the expression **I'm afraid. So** replaces an affirmative clause and **not** a negative clause.

For **if so, if not** ▶ 20.13.

Auxiliary verbs

4.9

1 George ⬚ smokes ⬚ a lot. I never ⬚ do ⬚. (= I never smoke)

2 A: Who ⬚ came to school yesterday ⬚?

   B: I ⬚ did ⬚. (= I came to school yesterday)

3 She'll gladly help you if she **can**. (= . . . if she can help you)

1 The auxiliary verb **do** (▶ 6.12, 6.13) can be substituted for another verb previously mentioned.

2 **Do** can also be used to avoid repeating an entire clause. (The subject, however, must be included.)

3 Other auxiliary and modal auxiliary verbs can also be used to carry out this second function of **do** (▶ 6.2, 6.15).

4.10

My wife ⬚ reads the paper ⬚ after breakfast, but I prefer to ⬚ do it ⬚ in the evening.
Somebody ⬚ took ⬚ the money. Did you ⬚ do it ⬚?

The full verb **do,** followed by **it, this, that** or **so,** can be substituted for another ordinary verb which has already been mentioned (▶ 6.14).

Omission

Nouns which have previously been mentioned are commonly omitted after:

4.11

1 I only have one egg, but I need **three** (eggs) to make this cake.
Rick was **the first** guest to arrive. Kathy was **the second** (guest to arrive).

2 The doctor's already seen three people. Who's **the next** (person he's going to see)?

1 cardinal and ordinal numbers (▶ 9.19);

2 **the next** and **the last** (▶ 11.23);

> 3 Rome and Paris are beautiful cities. In fact, among **the most beautiful** (cities) I've ever seen.

3 superlatives (▶ 16.2, 16.3).

In the examples the omitted words are in brackets.

4.12

> 1 A: Have you seen her before?
>   B: No, I haven't. (= I haven't seen her before)
>
> 2 I like science-fiction films. Do you? (= Do you like science-fiction films?)

A full verb which has previously been mentioned is commonly omitted after an auxiliary verb in (**1**) *short answers* and (**2**) *short questions* (▶ 21.4).

4.13

> A: What are you doing?
> B: Watching TV. (= I'm watching TV)
>
> A: What should I do?
> B: Just leave her alone. (= You should just leave her alone)
>
> A: Got a cigarette to give me, Anne? (= Have you got a cigarette?)
> B: Yes, here you are.

In the context of questions and answers, it is also possible to omit the subject and auxiliary verb which come before the main verb.

4.14

> She closed the door but (she) didn't lock it.
> I want some bread and (I want) a bottle of wine.
> Robert has sold his house and (he has) left for America.
> You can listen to a record or (you can) watch TV.
>
> Compare:
> I'll phone you when I get home.
> She's happy wherever she goes.
> If you don't like this film you can watch another one.

In clauses which are joined by the conjunctions **and, but** and **or** it is often possible to omit various elements in the second clause.

NOTE: This is usually not possible with other conjunctions.

4.15

> I told her to come, but she doesn't want **to** (= to come).
> I hate getting up early, but I have **to** (= to get up early).
>
> Compare:
> We must make that telephone call. Shall we stop here **to make it**?

After many verbs the **to**-*infinitive* can be reduced to the particle **to** to avoid repeating a previously mentioned verb.
This, however, does not apply to the infinitive of purpose (▶ 15.8).

4.16

> A: Does it take more than an hour to get there?
> B: **Yes** (it does).
> A: What time did you get back home last night?
> B: **At eleven**.

In answering questions it is unusual to repeat all the words that appear in the question. Depending on the situation it may be possible to answer **yes** or **no,** or **yes/no** followed by a short response, or simply to provide the information requested (▶ 4.9, 6.4, 21.4).

5 Personal, reflexive and reciprocal pronouns

Personal pronouns

Form

5.1

		Personal pronouns	
		Subject	*Object*
Singular	1st person 2nd person 3rd person	I you he she it	me you him her it
Plural	1st person 2nd person 3rd person	we you they	us you them

Use

5.2

1 **I** live in London.
   We work for Rolls Royce.
   Follow **me**, please.
   Meet **us** at the station.

2 Where do **you** study, Mary?
   Alan and John, are **you** American?
   Now, children, I'll tell **you** what to do.

3 a) Martin is tired. **He**'s in bed.
       Peter lives here now, and Jane lives with **him**.

   b) I can't find Anne. Is **she** at home?
       Where's Mrs Richards? I want to speak to **her**.

   c) Look at that monkey! Isn't **it** funny?
       This box is empty. There is nothing in **it**.

   d) When she told Mary to stay, I didn't like **it**.
       (= I didn't like her telling Mary to stay)

   e) Peter and Jane come from Dublin; **they** are Irish.
       Can you see those shops? My house is behind **them**.

1 *First person pronouns* are used to refer to the person who is speaking **(I/me)** or a group of people including the person who is speaking **(we/us)**.

2 *Second person pronouns* refer to the person or the group of people to whom we are speaking **(you)**.

3 *Third person pronouns* are used to refer to specific persons or things previously mentioned:
   a) a male person **(he/him)**;
   b) a female person **(she/her)**;
   c) an animal or inanimate object **(it)**;
   d) an entire clause **(it)**;
   e) people, animals or things in the plural **(they/them)**.

Compare:
My cat is so lazy! **He**'s always sleeping.
I like my old car. **She**'s never given me any trouble.

Notice that **he/him** and **she/her** can be used to refer to animals, especially pets, when the sex of the animals is known. **She/her** is also sometimes used to refer to ships, boats and cars.

5.3

1 **I**'m hungry.
  She loves you.

2 a) A: Who's there?
      B: It's **me**.
      It was **him** who started the argument.

  b) Give **him** some money.
     Tell **me** a story.

  c) I went with **her**.
     You can sit beside **me**.
     Harold is taller than **me**.
     Liz is as old as **him**.

  Compare:
  Harold is taller than **I am**. (more formal)
  Liz is as old as **he is**. (more formal)

  d) A: Who's got a cigarette?
     B: **Me**.

     Compare:
     B: **I have**. (more formal)

     A: Who did that?
     B: **Him**.

3 It was **he** who started the argument. (formal)

4 Compare:
  Do you mind **me** opening the window?
  Do you mind **my** opening the window? (more formal)

1 *Subject personal pronouns* are used as the subject of the verb.

2 *Object personal pronouns* are used in all other cases:
  a) as object or complement of the verb, including the verb **be**. But see **3** below.
  b) as indirect object (▶ 1.4);
  c) after a preposition, including **than** and **as** in comparisons (▶ 16.4, 16.7);
  d) in one word answers (▶ 21.4).

3 Notice that in sentences introduced by the 'focussing' expression **it** + **be** (▶ 18.6) formal English uses a subject pronoun.

4 Notice that in the construction *verb* + *pronoun* + **-ing** form (▶ 6.33) formal English uses a possessive adjective.

Other uses of **it**

5.4

1 a) What's the time? – **It**'s four.
     What date is it? – **It**'s May 1st.
     What's the weather like? – **It**'s cloudy.
     It's hot in here.
     It's four miles from the station to the school.

1 The pronoun **it** is also used, with non-specific reference, in the following cases:
  a) in expressions of time, weather, temperature, price, distance and measurement in general (▶ 9.24);

b) **It**'s nice and quiet here.
It's very dangerous here in Beirut.

c) **It seems** that you're not interested in the job.
It would appear that she has been here before.

d) **It was John** who came first. (= John came first)
It's the firm that is going to pay.
(= The firm is going to pay)
It was in Rome that I first met her.
(= I first met her in Rome)

e) Who is **it**? – **It**'s Paul.
Hello! **It**'s Jane here.

2 a) **It** makes me happy **to see you again**.
It is clear **that she doesn't like me**.
It is important for him **to leave**.

Compare:
To see you again makes me happy.
(unnatural)
That she doesn't like me is clear.
(unnatural)

b) I find **it** interesting **to meet new people**.
She considers **it** essential **that we should all come to the meeting**.

b) to refer to a situation in general.
c) as the subject of impersonal verbs (e.g. **appear, happen, seem**);
d) in 'focussing' structures, to emphasise particular words or expressions. (▶ 18.6);
e) in referring to the identity of people.

2 a) English tends to avoid having an infinitive or a clause beginning with **that** as the subject of a sentence.
It is used as the grammatical subject instead, so that the real subject can appear at the end of the sentence.

b) **It** is also used as an object pronoun when an infinitive or a clause beginning with **that** is referred to by an adjective. **It** is placed immediately before the adjective.

For use of **it** in passive sentences ▶ 18.41.

Use of **you, they, one** as indefinite pronouns

5.5

1 a) **You** want to be happy.
One wants to be happy. (more formal)
You've got to take life as it comes.
One never knows what tomorrow will bring. (more formal)
One must not waste **one's** money. (more formal)

b) **You** go straight on and then **you** take the second on the left.
First **you** press the start button and then **you** choose a programme.

2 a) **They** have opened a new supermarket.

b) **They** say this shop is expensive.
(= **People** say this shop is expensive)

You and **they** can be used, in informal English, as *indefinite* pronouns, referring to people in general. When used in an indefinite sense, **you** has a more general meaning than **they**.

1 a) **You** in this sense includes both the speaker and the person he/she is speaking to as well as other people in general. More formally, **one** is used as an alternative to **you**. Note the possessive form **one's**.

b) **You** is also used in a general sense when giving instructions or explanations.

2 Indefinite **they** excludes the speaker and the person he/she is speaking to. It may indicate (**a**) an indefinite group of people (e.g. the authorities or the government), or (**b**) people in a more general sense. In this case it can be replaced by **people**.

Reflexive pronouns

Form

5.6

Singular	1st person	myself
	2nd person	yourself
	3rd person	himself
		herself
		itself
Plural	1st person	ourselves
	2nd person	yourselves
	3rd person	themselves

NOTES
Reflexive pronouns follow the same rules of agreement (for person, number and gender) as personal pronouns (but notice the distinction between **yourself** (singular) and **yourselves** (plural); ▶ 5.2. **Oneself** is the reflexive equivalent of the indefinite pronoun **one** (▶ 5.5).

Use

5.7

1 a) They washed **themselves**.

   b) I have bought **myself** a new car.

   c) Tom does everything for **himself**.
      One should not keep everything for **oneself**.

   d) (You) Behave **yourself**!

   e) She told me **herself**.
      The headmaster **himself** contacted my family.

2 a) He **prides himself** upon speaking so many languages.

   b) I **enjoyed myself** at the party.
      Compare:
      I **enjoyed** the film.

      She **found herself** in an unknown place.
      Compare:
      She **found** a ring in the park.

      He's **hurt himself**.
      Compare:
      He **hurts** me when he talks like that.

1 Reflexive pronouns can be used when they refer to the same person or thing as the subject of the sentence. Grammatically they can function:
   a) as object;
   b) as indirect object (▶ 1.4);
   c) after a preposition.

   In imperatives (**d**) the subject of the sentence is implied.
   Reflexive pronouns are also used as in (**e**) for emphasis (▶ 18.4).

2 a) In English very few verbs are used only as reflexive verbs. One example is **to pride oneself**.

   b) Many common verbs (e.g. **dress, enjoy, find, hurt, lose,** etc.) can be followed either by a normal object or by a reflexive pronoun.

3 a) I get up at seven, **wash** and **dress**.
Do you **shave** every day?

b) What time do you **get up**?
Please **stop** in front of the gate.
She **fell asleep** after a couple of minutes.

4 Put on **your jacket**.
Take off **your hats**.
She washed **her hair** before getting dressed.
I've hurt **my hand**.

5 I work **by myself** (= on my own).
They came **by themselves** (= on their own).

3 a) When referring to actions which are normally carried out on oneself, the reflexive pronouns are often omitted (e.g. after **change, dress, dry, wash,** etc.).

b) In many cases verbs which are used reflexively in other languages have a corresponding verb in English which is not reflexive. For example: **fall asleep, get up, hurry, put on, sit down, stop, take off** are not used with a reflexive pronoun.

4 Notice that, unlike some European languages, English uses a *possessive adjective* and not a reflexive pronoun when talking about actions connected with articles of clothing and parts of the body (► 10.3).

5 Expressions like **by myself, by yourself,** etc. have the same meaning as **on my own, on your own,** etc.
For **own** ► 10.3.

Reciprocal pronouns: each other, one another

5.8

1 The soldiers killed **each other**. (= Each soldier killed the other)
All the students in the class helped **one another**. (= Each student helped others in the class)

2 They looked at **each other**. (= Each of them looked at the other)
They looked at **themselves** in the mirror. (= Each of them looked at himself or herself)

1 The *reciprocal pronoun* **each other** is used to refer to an action carried out by two or more subjects not on themselves but each on the other subject. The pronoun **one another** is used in the same way, especially if there are more than two subjects.

2 Notice the difference of meaning between **one another/each other** and **themselves**.

6 Auxiliary verbs and full verbs

Auxiliary verbs

Why we use auxiliary verbs

6.1 In English a verb can sometimes be used on its own, in its basic form: for example **study** in **They study history** conveys both the lexical meaning of **study** and the reference to *habitual action* in the *present* signalled by the *simple present* tense form.

On other occasions, however, the verb in its basic form is not sufficient in itself to convey both the lexical meaning of the word and other supplementary information (e.g. about person, tense, aspect, interrogation, negation). For example, in **She studies history** we need the suffix **-s** in order to refer the action to a third person singular subject; in **He is studying now** we need both another verb form **(is)** and a suffix **(-ing)** to convey the meaning of the *progressive aspect*. In **I have written a letter** a verb form **(have)** and a suffix **(-en)** are necessary to express the *perfect* aspect. And in **Do they speak English?**, **do** is used to make an *interrogative* structure.

Thus, side by side with *full* verbs, such as **study, write** and **speak,** which carry the basic lexical meaning, English uses the verbs **be, have** and **do,** as *auxiliary verbs.* These auxiliary verbs 'help' full verbs to convey the extra information about tense, aspect, interrogation, negation, etc.

Auxiliary verbs and modal auxiliary verbs

6.2 Some other verbs are used in English to add information to the basic lexical meaning of a full verb. For example, in **It may rain tomorrow, may** is used by the speaker in order to show that he/she considers the event (*raining*) as *possible;* **must** in **I must get back immediately** shows that the speaker thinks the action (*get back*) is *necessary;* **can't** in **She can't be sixty yet – she looks so young!** is used to show that the speaker is *certain* of something because he/she has come to some *logical conclusion* (*she looks too young to be sixty*).

Such verbs (**may, must, can't** in the examples above) and others (fully listed in 6.15) are called *modal auxiliaries* because they help to convey the *logical modality.* This means the way in which the speaker considers the action expressed by the full verb to be possible, probable or certain; necessary or permissible; hypothetical or desirable; etc.

The *auxiliary* and *modal auxiliary* verbs share some common features, which are described in 6.3. The auxiliary verbs **be, have** and **do** are then dealt with in 6.5–6.14. The *modal* auxiliary verbs are dealt with in 6.15–6.18, while the forms of *full* verbs are treated starting from 6.19.

In general, this chapter is concerned with *verb forms:* it deals with the categories of words which are used in English as verbs and with the rules by which different verb tenses and moods are constructed. The *meanings* which these verb forms may express are dealt with in other chapters (especially Chapter 11 – *Time*), and references are given to the relevant paragraphs.

A list of auxiliary and modal auxiliary verbs

6.3

The auxiliary verbs in English are:

be ▶ 6.5–6.7;   **have ▶** 6.8–6.11;   **do ▶** 6.12–6.14.

Notice that in some cases these verbs are *not* used as *auxiliaries,* but as *full* verbs (▶ 6.7, 6.10, 6.11, 6.14).

The *modal auxiliary verbs* are: **can/could; may/might; shall/should; will/would; must; ought to.** (▶ 6.15, 6.16).

The verbs **need, dare** and **used to** can also function as *modal auxiliaries* in some cases (▶ 6.17, 6.18).

Features shared by auxiliary and modal auxiliary verbs

1 a) We **aren't/are not** coming tonight.
They **haven't/have not** finished yet.
You **mustn't/must not** cross the road here.

b) They **haven't/have not been** arrested yet.
He **couldn't/could not have** told the truth.

1 a) A *negative* structure with auxiliary and modal auxiliary verbs is obtained by placing **not** after the auxiliary.
In the spoken language and in informal written English **not** is usually contracted to **n't** and joined to the end of the auxiliary verb like a suffix.

b) Two auxiliaries or a modal and an auxiliary can be used in conjunction. **Not** is then placed after the *first* auxiliary.

2 **Are you** coming tonight?
May I cross the road here?
Have they been arrested yet?
Could he have told the truth?

2 *Interrogative* structures are formed by placing the *first* auxiliary verb before the subject.

3 **Weren't you** invited to the party?
Hadn't she been there before?
Don't you know what to do?

Compare:
Were you not invited to the party?
Had she not been there before?
Do you not know what to do?

3 A *negative-interrogative* structure is formed by placing the *first* auxiliary verb with **n't** before the subject.
Notice that in formal English an alternative structure is possible. **Not** can be placed after the subject. This structure may be used when **not** is stressed. Otherwise it is very rare (▶ 2.15)

4 a) **We're/We are** just leaving.
She'll/She will phone you tomorrow.
They'd/They would love to see you.

b) **Tom's/Tom is** sleeping.
Tom's/Tom has gone home.
She'd/She had already left.
She'd/She would do it.

c) A: Is he American?
B: Yes, **he is**. (*not* **he's**)
Robert hasn't been to Berlin but **I have**. (*not* **I've**)

4 a) Auxiliaries and modal auxiliaries have contracted forms which are used in the spoken language and in informal written English (▶ 6.5, 6.8, 6.12, 6.15).

b) Notice that **'s** may mean both **is** and **has**; **'d** may mean both **had** and **would**.

c) The contracted affirmative forms cannot be used in short forms, e.g. in short responses (▶ 21.4).

6.4

1 Tom **was sleeping** when I arrived.
They **have gone** out.
We **should talk** to him some time.

1 Auxiliary verbs are normally followed by a full verb in the form of a *participle* or *infinitive without* **to** form (▶ 6.1, 6.2).

2 a) You don't smoke, **do you**?

b) A: Who's lent you the money?
B: Mary **has**.
A: Will you write to me?
B: Yes, **I will**, don't worry.
A: I went to New York last week.
B: **Did you** really?

2 In certain cases an auxiliary verb may appear *without* a full verb. This can happen when the full verb has already been mentioned and can therefore be clearly recognised in the context. This happens in the following cases:
a) in question tags (▶ 2.11);
b) in short responses (▶ 21.4);

c) A: Mary will pass her exams.
   B: **Yes, she** certainly **will**.
   A: Tim hasn't found a job yet.
   B: Oh yes, **he has**!
   A: You drink too much!
   B: But **I don't**!

d) I'm living here at the moment, **and so is she**.
Martha can't swim, **but I can**.
He doesn't like thrillers and **neither do I**.
We have already paid our bill, **but you haven't**.

c) when a speaker expresses agreement or disagreement with (or contradicts/denies) something that has just been said (▶ 21.4);

d) in clauses that use shortened structures to avoid repeating all the content of a previous clause or sentence (▶ 4.9, 5.3, 16.4, 16.7, 17.3).

Be

Be: forms

6.5

	Present	Past
I you he/she/it	am ('m) are ('re) is ('s)	was were was
we you they	are ('re)	were
Past Participle: been		

NOTES
Contracted forms are given in brackets.
For features shared by auxiliary verbs ▶ 6.3, 6.4.

1 **He isn't** coming.
They aren't listening to her.
Compare:
He's not coming.
They're not listening to her.
I'm not driving.

2 The book **is being** translated.
The message **has been** sent.

1 Instead of using the contracted negative particle **n't** (▶ 6.3) we may use the contracted form of **be** followed by **not**. Notice that **amn't** is not used in standard British English.

2 In other tenses **be** follows the normal rules for the formation of the tense.

Be as auxiliary verb

Be is used as an auxiliary verb in the following cases:

6.6

1 He **was carried** to hospital.
   Will Parliament **be opened** next week?

2 a) Mary**'s playing** the piano in the lounge.

   b) He **was watching** TV when I came in.

   c) I**'ve been waiting** for hours.

   d) John **had been living** with her for a year
      when they separated.

   e) This time next Monday I **will be flying**
      home.

   f) By the end of this term I **will have been
      studying** English for three years.

3 a) You **are to go** up to your room immediately.

   b) The President **is to make** a speech
      tomorrow to Congress.

1 When it is followed by the *past participle* to
   form the *passive* (▶ 3.1–3.6);

2 When it is followed by the **-ing** form (*present
   participle*) to form progressive tenses:
   a) *present progressive* (*present of* **be** + **-ing**
      form) (▶ 11.3);
   b) *past progressive* (*past of* **be** + **-ing** *form*)
      (▶ 11.7);
   c) *present perfect progressive* (**have been** +
      -ing *form*) (▶ 11.5);
   d) *past perfect progressive* (**had been** +
      -ing *form*) (▶ 11.9);
   e) *future progressive* (**will be** + **-ing** *form*)
      (▶ 11.16);
   f) *future perfect progressive* (**will have been**
      + **-ing** *form*) (▶ 11.18);

3 The form **be** + **to-**infinitive may (**a**) indicate
   obligation (▶ 24.6), or (**b**) refer to future
   plans (▶ 11.13).

Be as full verb

6.7

1 a) The Isle of Man **is** in the Irish Sea.
      They**'re** students here.
      Benjamin Franklin **was** American.
      If you**'re** hot, take off your jumper.
      I **was** so cold that I couldn't sleep.
      She**'ll be** five next week.
      The picture **is** 6 feet by 3.

   b) **There is** a nurse with her now.
      Were there many people at the concert?

   c) **It's** very cold in winter here.
      Hello! **It's** me, Bob.
      It's obvious that he's not coming.

2 **Be** quiet.
   Don't be angry with me.

1 **Be** is not always used as an *auxiliary* verb. It
   can also be used, as a *full* verb, acting as a
   verbal link between subject and noun or
   adjective complement. In such cases (**a**) it
   refers to the existence of, or gives information
   about, someone or something. Sometimes (**b**)
   there (▶ 1.3) or (**c**) **it** (▶ 4.2, 4.10) can be
   used as 'empty' subjects.

2 **Be** can be used as a full verb to refer to
   temporary states. It can then be used in
   imperative structures, including a negative
   imperative with the auxiliary **Don't**.

Have

Have: forms

6.8

	Present	**Past**
I you he/she/it	have ('ve) have ('ve) has ('s)	had ('d)
we you they	have ('ve)	
Past Participle: had		

NOTES
Contracted forms are given in brackets.
For features shared by auxiliary verbs ▶ 6.3, 6.4.

1 I **haven't** finished.
   They **hadn't** done the work.

   Compare:
   I**'ve not** finished.
   They**'d not** done the work.

2 The train **will have** left by now.

1 Instead of using the contracted negative
   particle **n't** (▶ 6.3) we may use the
   contracted form of **have** followed by **not**.

2 In other tenses, where **have** is used as an
   auxiliary verb, it follows the normal rules for
   the formation of the tense.

Have as auxiliary verb

6.9

a) I **have seen** him before.
b) I **had seen** him before.
c) I **will have finished** by tomorrow.
d) She seems **to have lived** here.
e) **Having said** that, he went out.

Have is used as an *auxiliary* verb in the
formation of perfect tenses, as follows:
a) *present perfect* (**have** + *past participle*)
   (▶ 11.4, 11.5);
b) *past perfect* (**had** + *past participle*)
   (▶ 11.8, 11.9);
c) *future perfect* (**will have** + *past participle*)
   (▶ 11.18);
d) *past infinitive* (**(to) have** + *past
   participle*) (▶ 6.27, 6.30);
e) *past of the* **-ing** *form* (**having** + *past
   participle*) (▶ 6.24).

Have as full verb

6.10

1 a) He **has**/He**'s got** a cottage on the lake.
       She **had**/She**'d got** some money.

   b) They **have**/They**'ve got** to go.
       They **had**/They**'d got** to call the doctor.

   c) It **has**/It**'s got** to be him.
       It **had** to be him.

2 a) He **hasn't got**/He **doesn't have** a cottage
       on the lake.
       Has he **got**/**Does** he **have** a cottage on
       the lake?
       She **hadn't got**/She **didn't have** any
       money.
       Had she **got**/**Did** she **have** any money?

   b) They **haven't got**/They **don't have** to go
       back.
       Have they **got**/**Do** they **have** to go back?

1 **Have** is used as a *full* verb to express (**a**)
   possession (▶ 10.13). When followed by the
   to-*infinitive* it can express (**b**) *obligation*
   (▶ 24.7) and, in the affirmative form, (**c**) *logica*
   deduction (▶ 19.4). In all these cases it is
   very common, especially in informal English,
   to use contracted forms followed by **got** in
   the simple present (and, less commonly, in
   the simple past).

2 When **have** expresses (**a**) possession and (**b**)
   obligation, the *negative* and *interrogative*
   structures of the simple present and the
   simple past can be made in two alternative
   ways:
   – by treating **have** as an auxiliary verb
     followed by **got** (more common in British
     English), *or*
   – by treating **have** as a full verb (without **got**)
     and using the auxiliary verb **do/does/did**
     (especially in American English).

6.11

1 a) I usually **have some milk** before going to
       bed.
       Have a cigarette.
       What time did you **have lunch** today?

   b) I **had Tony with me** for a week.

   c) Sheila **had her driving test** yesterday.
       We**'ve had no problems** at all with the
       baby.

   d) **Did you have a nice time**?
       I had a lovely weekend at the seaside.

2 She**'s having a big party** for her birthday.
   He **was having breakfast** when I came in.

3 a) She **had better** hurry up.

   b) The publishers **had** the book **translated**
       into Spanish.

1 **Have** is used as a *full* verb in a number of
   particular expressions with the meaning of:
   a) taking food or drink;
   b) receiving guests;
   c) undergoing experiences;
   d) passing the time, etc.

   In these cases the structure **have** + **got**
   cannot be used, and the negative and
   interrogative structures of the simple present
   and the simple past are constructed using
   the auxiliary verb **do/does/did**.

2 In these cases **have** can be used in the
   progressive tenses.

3 **Have** is also used in the following
   constructions:
   a) **had better** to express obligation (▶ 24.5);
   b) **have something done** and **have**
       somebody do something in the
       causative sense (▶ 15.11).

Do

Do: forms

6.12

	Present	**Past**
I you he/she/it	do do does	did
we you they	do	
Past Participle: done		

NOTES
For features shared by auxiliary verbs ▶ 6.3, 6.4.

Do as auxiliary verb

Do is used as an *auxiliary* verb followed by the *infinitive without* **to** of a full verb:

6.13

1 **Does** he **smoke**?
He **didn't understand** the problem.
Didn't they **tell** you?

2 She **did** leave on the Thursday.

3 I can read faster than you **do**.

1 to form the *negative*, *interrogative* and
negative-interrogative structures of the
simple present and the simple past of full
verbs (▶ 6.20, 6.21);

2 in emphatic forms (▶ 18.5);

3 to avoid repeating a verb which has already
been mentioned (▶ 4.9, 4.10).

Do as a full verb

Do is used as a *full* verb in the following cases:

6.14

1 A: What do you **do**?
B: I'm a teacher.
A: What are you **doing**?
B: I'm studying.
A: Why did you **do** that?
B: Because I needed the money.

Compare:
What are you **making**?
They **make** cars in that factory.
When she has **made** a decision she keeps to
it.

1 to express the idea of carrying out an activity
or a particular action. In this case the
negative and interrogative structures of the
simple present and the simple past are
constructed using the auxiliary verb **do**.
In some languages, the same word is used
for **do** and **make** but in English these words
have different meanings: **make** is used more
in the sense of building or creating
something so that there is a *product* of some
kind at the end of the activity.

2 A: Mrs Parker, I'd like you to meet Mr Reeves.
B: **How do you do,** Mr Reeves?
C: **How do you do,** Mrs Parker?

3 I had no time to pay the bill, so I asked Jimmy to **do it**.
She had left early in the morning and nobody knew why she **had done that**.

2 in the expression **How do you do?** used in formal *introductions* (▶ 27.1), i.e. when introducing oneself and in responding to an introduction.

3 followed by **it, so, this, that** to avoid the repetition of another full verb already mentioned (▶ 4.10).

Modal auxiliary verbs

Forms

6.15

The modal auxiliary verbs given in the following table have only a present form (**can, may, shall, will**) and a corresponding past form (respectively, **could, might, should, would**). The verbs **must** and **ought to** have only one form.

For the various communicative functions that these verbs can perform, check the individual entries in the index.

Forms			
Affirmative		Negative	
Not contracted	*Contracted*	*Not contracted*	*Contracted*
can	—	cannot	can't
could	—	could not	couldn't
may	—	may not	—
might	—	might not	mightn't
shall	'll	shall not	shan't/'ll not
should	—	should not	shouldn't
will	'll	will not	won't/'ll not
would	'd	would not	wouldn't/'d not
must	—	must not	mustn't
ought to	—	ought not	oughtn't

NOTE: For features shared by auxiliary verbs ▶ 6.3, 6.4.

Features of modal auxiliary verbs

6.16

1 a) I **can** swim.
He **can** swim.

1 Notice the following features of modal auxiliary verbs:
a) They have only the limited number of forms previously mentioned (▶ 6.15).

b) I **have been able to** swim for three years.
I'm proud of **being able to** swim.
He **has had to** go to hospital.
I don't like **having to** take a taxi.

b) When there is no equivalent form using a modal verb (e.g. if a past participle or **-ing** form is required), alternative structures or expressions have to be used. These are mentioned in the chapters on the communicative functions of modal auxiliaries (see Index).

2 We **should leave** now.
Compare:
We **ought to leave** now.

2 Modal auxiliary verbs are followed by an *infinitive without* **to** (however, **ought to** and **used to** keep the particle **to**).

3 They **might have telephoned** yesterday evening.
You **must have known** about it last year.

3 They can be followed by a *past infinitive without* **to** to refer to *past* time, e.g. **may have come, could have gone,** etc.
Used to is an exception.

Need, dare

6.17

1 a) **Need** you go out so often?
He **needn't** pay now.
Dare you go?
He **daren't** tell me.

b) **Do** you **need to** go out so often?
He **doesn't need to** pay now.
Do you **dare to** go?
He **doesn't dare to** tell me.

2 a) I **need to** see a doctor.
He doesn't **dare to** show his face.

b) The car **needs** to be serviced.
If she **dares** to come here she'll be sorry.

c) We **needed** more time.
I never **dared** to criticise them.

d) **Do** they **need** any help?
I **didn't dare** to tell him.

1 The verbs **need** (▶ 24.6, 24.9, 24.10) and **dare** can be used (**a**) as modal auxiliary verbs followed by an *infinitive without* **to,** or (**b**) as full verbs. As *modal auxiliary* verbs they are used in interrogative and negative structures but rarely in affirmative structures.

2 **Need** and **dare** are more commonly used as full verbs. In this case they:
a) are followed by the **to-***infinitive*;
b) have **-s** in the third person singular of the simple present;
c) have the past forms **needed** and **dared**;
d) have negative and interrogative structures with **do** in the simple present and simple past.

Used to

6.18

He **used to** live here.
He **didn't use to** play tennis.
Did he use to work for Ford?

The modal auxiliary verb **used to** (▶ 11.10) is used only in the past. It is used in two negative structures (**used not to** and **did not/didn't use to**) and two interrogative structures (**used he to ...?** and **did he use to ...?**). The forms with **did** are more common. The others are very formal.

Full verbs

Regular and irregular verbs

6.19 English has both *regular* and *irregular* full verbs. The *past* and *past participle* forms of a *regular* verb can be constructed from the *base form* (which corresponds to the *infinitive* without the particle **to**). The *past* and *past participle* forms of *irregular* verbs must be learnt individually (see Appendix E).

	Base form	**Past form**	**Past participle**
Examples of *regular* verbs	work listen watch	worked listened watched	worked listened watched
Examples of *irregular* verbs	eat go come	ate went came	eaten gone come

Simple present

6.20

1

I you	work	eat
he/she/it	work**s**	eat**s**
we you they	work	eat

1 The simple present (▶ 11.3) *affirmative* forms (except for the third person singular) correspond to the base form for all verbs, both regular and irregular. The third person singular takes a final **-s**.

For modifications in the spelling of the third person singular form ▶ Appendix C. For the pronunciation of final **-s** ▶ Appendix B1.

2

a)	I/you/we/they	do not/don't	work.
	He/she/it	does not/doesn't	eat.

b)	Do	I/you/we/they	work?
	Does	he/she/it	eat?

c)	Don't	I/you/we/they	work?
	Doesn't	he/she/it	eat?

2 The *negative, interrogative* and *negative-interrogative* structures are formed with the auxiliary verb **do** (third person singular **does**) in the following way:
a) *negative: subject +* **do not/don't** *or* **does not/doesn't** *+ base form of the full verb;*
b) *interrogative:* **do/does** *+ subject + base form;*
c) *negative-interrogative:* **don't/doesn't** *+ subject + base form.*

Simple past

6.21

1

Base form	Simple past
Regular verbs	
work	work**ed**
watch	watch**ed**
Irregular verbs	
eat	ate
go	went
come	came

1 The simple past (▶ 11.6) of *regular* verbs is obtained by adding the suffix **-ed** to the base form. *Irregular* verbs have various past forms (▶ Appendix E).

For modifications in the spelling of the simple past form ▶ Appendix C.
For the pronunciation of final **-ed** ▶ Appendix B2.

2

I/you	worked.
He/she/it	ate.
We/you/they	went.

2 The simple past is invariable for all verbs, regular and irregular.

3 a)

I/you		work.
He/she/it	did not	
We/you/they		eat.

b)

	I/you	work?
Did	he/she/it	
	we/you/they	eat?

c)

	I/you	work?
Didn't	he/she/it	
	we/you/they	eat?

3 The *negative, interrogative* and *negative-interrogative* structures are formed using the auxiliary **did** in the following way:
a) *negative: subject +* **did not/didn't** *+ base form* of the full verb;
b) *interrogative:* **did** *+ subject + base form*;
c) *negative-interrogative:* **didn't** *+ subject + base form*.

Imperative

6.22

1 **Come** here, please.
  Open the window!
  Take off your coat!
  Be good now.

2 **Don't open** the window!
  Don't take off your coat!
  Don't be silly!

3 D̀O **come** in.

  D̀O **be** quiet, please.

1 Imperatives can be expressed using the *base form* of the verb. This form can refer to both the second person singular and plural.

2 *Negative* imperatives can be expressed by placing **do not/don't** in front of the affirmative form.

3 **Do** can be placed in front of the simple imperative form to express different attitudes, such as politeness or irritation (▶ 25.2). In this case **do** is stressed.

For **let** in imperative expressions ▶ 25.4.

Past participle

6.23

1

Base form	Simple past	Past participle
Regular verbs		
work watch	worked watched	worked watched
Irregular verbs		
eat go come	ate went came	eaten gone come

1 The past participle of *regular* verbs is identical to the simple past form. With *irregular* verbs the past participle has various forms (▶ Appendix E).

2 a) We**'ve** just **arrived**.
   She **had left** the week before.
   By this time tomorrow I **shall have finished**.
   I must **have met** him before.

   b) She **was seen** with a man last night.

   c) **Woken** by the storm, I got up and closed the windows.

   Compare:
   Because I **had been woken** by the storm, I got up and closed the windows.

   d) The **written** translation will be ready tomorrow (= the translation which has been written).
   I am very **interested** in basketball.

2 The past participle is used:
   a) with the auxiliary verb **have** to construct perfect tenses and past infinitives (▶ 6.9);
   b) with the auxiliary verb **be** to construct passive forms (▶ 3.1–3.6);
   c) in participle phrases that refer to a following noun or pronoun, indicating, for example, *cause* (▶ 15.6). Compare the complete clause (*subject* + *passive verb*).
   d) as an adjective, with passive meaning (compare present participle ▶ 6.25)

-ing form

6.24

1 work/work**ing**
   watch/watch**ing**
   eat/eat**ing**
   go/go**ing**

1 The **-ing** form of all verbs, regular and irregular, is obtained by adding the suffix **-ing** to the *base form*. The **-ing** form can function as either a *present participle* (▶ 6.25) or *a verbal noun* (gerund) (▶ 6.26).

   For modifications in the spelling of the **-ing** form ▶ Appendix C.

2 **Not seeing** him, I phoned home.

2 Negative structures with the **-ing** form are formed by placing **not** in front of it.

3 a) **Having spent** all he had, he went back home.

   b) I don't remember **having spent** all that money.

3 To refer to past time, we can use **having** + *past participle* in both (**a**) participle and (**b**) verbal noun structures.

-ing form as present participle

	6.25

The **-ing** form is used as a *present participle* in the following cases:

1 She**'s working** in Ottawa now.
What **was** he **doing** when you went in?

1 with the auxiliary verb **be** to construct progressive forms (▶ 6.6);

2 **Watering the garden,** I found a snake.
Having no money, he desperately needed a job.

2 in participle phrases indicating, for example, *time* or *cause* (compare ▶ 6.23);

3 The **crying** mother was taken away.
(= the mother who was crying)
This book is really **interesting**.

Compare:
I am **interested** in this.

3 as an adjective, with active meaning (compare ▶ 6.23).

-ing form as verbal noun

	6.26

The **-ing** form is used as a *verbal noun* (gerund) in the following cases:

1 **Reading** is his favourite pastime.
Do you like **swimming**?

1 as the subject or object of a sentence (▶ 6.32, 6.33);

2 He went out **without saying** a word.
Call me **before going** to bed.
This machine is used **for processing** information.

2 after prepositions;

3 I don't do **much reading**.
A little learning is a dangerous thing.
No smoking.
No parking here.

3 after determiners;

4 This is an **adding machine** (= a machine for adding).
There's a **writing desk** in the corner (= a desk for writing).

4 in compound nouns (▶ Appendix D6).

Infinitive

	6.27

1 a)

(to)	work	live	watch
	eat	go	come

1 a) The *present infinitive* corresponds to the base form of the verb. It is commonly preceded by the particle **to** (forming the **to-***infinitive*). For the *infinitive without* **to** ▶ 6.29.

b)

(to)	have worked	have lived
	have eaten	have gone

b) The *past infinitive* is constructed using **(to) have** + *past participle*.

2	not (to) work	not (to) have worked
	not (to) eat	not (to) have eaten

2 The *negative* structures with the infinitive are formed by placing **not** in front of them.

Present infinitive with **to**

6.28

The *present infinitive with* **to** (the **to**-*infinitive*) is used in the following cases:

1 a) I decided **to buy** that house.
   I hope **to see** you soon.

 b) I want you **to stay** here.
   She told her sister **to do** the shopping.

2 I've never **found out how to save** money.
  I don't **know what to do**.
  She was **wondering who to ask** for help.

3 He's going to the USA **to learn** English.

4 There's a lot of homework **to do** (= that must be done).
  He needs someone **to play** with (= with whom he can play).

5 She seemed **surprised to see** me.
  She's very **difficult to teach**.
  This cake is very **easy to make**.
  You're **impossible to talk** to!

6 a) **It was hard to understand**.
   It's silly to cry about it.

 b) **It was nice of him to take** me home.
   It's hard for Anne to bring up a family without a husband.

7 **To learn** a foreign language is useful.
  Compare:
  It is useful **to learn** a foreign language.

1 (**a**) after many verbs, including (**b**) verbs normally followed by an *object (noun or pronoun)* + **to**-*infinitive* (▶ 6.34);

2 after certain verbs when they are followed by **how, what, when, where, whether, who**. These verbs include **ask, consider, discover, explain, find out, know, show, tell, understand, wonder**.

3 to express *purpose* (▶ 15.8);

4 referring to a preceding noun or pronoun (with a meaning similar to that of a relative pronoun ▶ 8.29);

5 after many adjectives;

6 a) after **it** + **be** + *adjective*;

 b) There is also a variation of this construction adding **of/for** + *noun/object pronoun*.

7 as the subject of a sentence. In this case, however, the construction with **it** is much more common (▶ 5.4).

For infinitive reduced to the particle **to** ▶ 4.15.

Present infinitive without **to**

6.29

The *present infinitive without* **to** is used in the following cases:

1 We **must get** back as soon as possible.
  Should we **tell** him the truth?
  I'll be home by five.

1 after modal auxiliary verbs (but note **ought to** and **used to** ▶ 6.15, 6.16). For **need** and **dare** (▶ 6.17.)

2 a) **Let** me **see** what you've bought.
   She won't **let** me **do** anything in the home.

   b) He **had** his secretary **type** all the reports.
   I'll **make** him **change** his mind.

3 I **saw** him **leave** before midnight.
   She **heard** me **make** that phone call.

4 I'd **rather/would rather** stay here with you
   tonight.
   It's late, you**'d better/had better go** now.

5 I want **to go and see** what's happening.
   There's nothing **to do but wait**.

6 **Why spend** more if you can pay less?
   Why not go out for a walk?

2 a) after **let** (▶ 24.1–24.3, 25.4, 25.10);
   b) after **have** and **make** with causative
   meaning (▶ 15.11);

3 after verbs of perception like **feel, hear, see,**
   etc. (for more information on possible
   constructions with such verbs ▶ 6.36);

4 after the expressions **would rather** (▶ 26.12)
   and **had better** (▶ 24.5);

5 after **and, but, except, or, than** used to link
   two infinitives;

6 after **why** and **why not** (▶ 25.10).

Past infinitive

6.30

1 I **was to have met** her at the station, but she
   cancelled the journey.

2 a) I **should have bought** more bread.
   You were lucky, you **might have had** a
   serious accident by driving so fast.
   I **must have read** this book before.
   You **could have offered** to help me.
   I arrived in the late afternoon – it **would
   have been** six or half past.

   Compare:
   She **ought to have checked** the accounts
   more carefully.

   b) By the year 2000 the population **will have
   reached** 30 million.

1 The past infinitive form **to have** + *past
   participle* is used after **be** in 'future in the
   past' constructions (▶ 11.17) to refer to
   events which did not take place.

2 a) The *past infinitive without* **to** can be used
   after modal verbs to refer to *past* time
   (▶ 6.16), usually to talk about events
   which did not take place or could have
   happened.
   NOTE: **Ought** is followed by infinitives
   with **to.**

   b) After **shall** and **will** the past infinitive
   usually refers to a past seen from the
   perspective of a future moment (▶ 11.18).

For more information, check the individual
modal verbs in the index.

Verbs followed by the infinitive and/or by the **-ing** form

6.31

Many verbs are commonly used in conjunction with other verb forms: infinitives (with or without **to**) and
-ing forms (verbal nouns or present participles). The phrase with the infinitive or the **-ing** form then
usually functions as the object of the main verb.

Verbs followed by the **-ing** form

6.32

1 Try to **avoid using** the car.
I used to **enjoy reading** detective stories.
Fancy meeting John at the party!
When she **finished speaking,** she sat down.
This course **involves doing** a lot of homework.
Do you **mind getting** up early?
I won't **risk missing** the train; I'll take a taxi.
He **suggested going** to the cinema.

2 Do you **feel like having** a walk?
She's **given up teaching.**
Please **leave off hoovering** the carpet; the baby's sleeping.
We are **looking forward to receiving** your reply.

3 I **can't help smoking** when I'm nervous.
It's no use crying over spilt milk.
It's worth having a look at this church.
Don't **waste your time** just **watching** TV.
I **am used to waiting** for the bus for a long time.
Compare:
I **used to wait** for my girlfriend outside the station.

4 a) Why don't you **come skating** with me?
   I usually **go shopping** on Friday afternoons.
   We **went swimming** last Sunday.

   b) Don't **keep looking** at me!
   She **kept asking** me for money.

1 Verbs commonly followed by the **-ing** form (verbal noun) (▶ 6.24, 6.26) include:

admit	endure	mind
advise	enjoy	miss
allow	escape	pardon
anticipate	excuse	permit
appreciate	face	postpone
avoid	fancy	practise
consider	finish	recollect
contemplate	forbid	resent
defer	forgive	resist
delay	imagine	risk
deny	involve	suggest
detest	mention	understand
dread		

2 Most verbs followed by prepositions or adverb particles (▶ 7.1) are used with the **-ing** form.

3 Some compound expressions are also followed by the **-ing** form:
be accustomed to
be used to (compare **used to** ▶ 6.18, 11.10)
burst out (laughing, crying)
can't help
can't bear/stand
it's no fun/good/use
it's worth
keep (somebody waiting)
spend/waste time/money (doing something)

4 a) **Go** and **come** can be followed by the **-ing** form when used in expressions connected with sports and other (mainly physical) activities.

   b) **Keep** is also followed by the **-ing** form, with the meaning of 'continue'.

Notice that in both (**a**) and (**b**) above the **-ing** form functions as a *participle* phrase (▶ 6.25) rather than as the object of the main verb.

6.33

1 I'm **considering taking up** engineering.
I **can't bear being** late.

2 I **can't bear him being** late.
Can you **imagine Peter doing** the housework?

3 I **can't bear his being** late.
Please **forgive my interrupting** like this.

4 Do you **mind my smoking**?
Compare:
Do you **mind if I smoke**?

1 When the verbs and expressions listed in the previous paragraph are followed immediately by the **-ing** form, the subject of both verb forms is presumed to be the same person.

2 Some of these verbs and expressions can also be followed by a *noun* or *object pronoun* before the **-ing** form. In this case the **-ing** form refers to the noun or object pronoun.

3 In more formal English, possessive adjectives can be used instead of object pronouns.

4 Notice that **mind** can also be followed by a clause beginning with **if.**
For uses of **mind** ▶ 24.1, 25.6–25.8.

Verbs followed by the **to-**infinitive

6.34

1 She **agreed to leave** in the morning.
Did you **decide to sell** the car?
He **happened to meet** Susan at the station.
Where did you **learn to speak** English?
Would you **undertake to pay** me back?
I'll **pretend not to see** you.

1 Verbs commonly followed by the **to-***infinitive* (▶ 6.27, 6.28) include:

afford	determine	offer
agree	endeavour	plan
appear	fail	prepare
arrange	happen	pretend
attempt	hesitate	promise
care	hope	refuse
choose	learn	seem
consent	manage	swear
decide	neglect	undertake

Notice the negative form with **not to**.

2 a) The police **advised us to see** a lawyer.
The doctor **allowed her to go** home.
He **persuaded me to sign** the contract.
Will you **remind me to switch** off the video?

2 a) Verbs commonly followed by a *noun* or *object pronoun* + **to-***infinitive* include:

advise	instruct	persuade
allow	intend	prefer
ask	invite	recommend
command	leave	remind
encourage	like	request
expect	mean	teach
forbid	need	tell
force	oblige	want
get	order	warn
hate	permit	wish
help		

b) I **recommended their leaving** at once.

b) Notice that many of these verbs can also be used in other structures, e.g. followed by a possessive adjective and an **-ing** form (verbal noun) (▶ 6.33).
For verbs followed by the *infinitive without* **to** ▶ 6.29

Verbs followed by either the infinitive or the **-ing** form

6.35

1 He **began to shout/shouting**.
   I **propose to put off/putting off** the meeting.
   When did you **start to suspect/suspecting** her?

1 Some verbs can be followed by either the **-ing** form (verbal noun) or the **to**-*infinitive* with almost no difference in meaning. Such verbs include **begin, continue, intend, propose, start**.

2 Your hair **needs cutting/to be cut**.

2 The verbs **need, require** and **want** may be followed by an active **-ing** form or by a passive infinitive (▶ 3.11).

Some other verbs can be followed either by the infinitive or by the **-ing** form (verbal noun), but often with a *difference in meaning*.

6.36

1 I **hate watching/(to watch)** television.
   Do you **like going/(to go)** to the cinema?

1 When talking about feelings in general, **hate, like, love** and **prefer** are usually followed by the **-ing** form, more rarely by the **to**-*infinitive*.

2 a) I **prefer to start** work as early as possible.
      I **hate to see** good food wasted.
      I **like to see** my doctor at least once a year.

   b) I **love to see/(seeing)** children enjoying themselves.

2 These verbs are usually followed by the **to**-*infinitive* when they refer to more *specific* actions, as in (**a**). But often the choice depends more on *style*, e.g. to avoid using two **-ing** forms in quick succession, as in (**b**).

3 **Would you like to go** out for a meal?
   I'd love to have a holiday at Easter.

3 **Would hate/like/love/prefer** are followed by the **to**-*infinitive*.

4 a) I'll never **forget sitting** next to the King.
      He **regretted lending** her so much money.
      I **remember meeting** her just after the war.

4 a) **Forget, regret** and **remember** are followed by the **-ing** form when they refer to memories, thinking about the past. The forgetting, regretting or remembering is *later* than the action referred to by the other verb.

   b) I **forgot to post** your letter.
      We **regret to inform** you that the shipment will be delayed.
      Remember to shut the window!

   b) The **to**-*infinitive* is used if **forget, regret** and **remember** refer to an action that does *not* come before the forgetting, regretting or remembering.

5 a) **Stop talking** like that!
      I **stopped wearing** short trousers when I was eleven.

5 a) **Stop** followed by the **-ing** form refers to the ending of an action.

   b) He **stopped to light** a cigarette.
      They **stopped to look** at a shop window.

   b) **Stop** followed by the **to**-*infinitive* refers to the interruption of one action with the purpose of carrying out another. In this case **to** means **in order to** (i.e. infinitive of purpose ▶ 15.8).

6 a) She **tried cleaning** the carpet with a special liquid.
   Why don't you **try taking** an aspirin?

   b) I **tried** hard **to convince** him, but it was no use.
   Hold your arms up high and **try to touch** the ceiling.

7 a) Do you **mean to work** all night long?

   b) Accepting this job **means working** long hours.

8 She won't **allow smoking** here.
   Did she **allow you to smoke**?

9 Can you **help (to) wash** the dishes?
   I **helped John (to) mend** his car.
   I **can't help feeling** embarrassed about the situation.

10 a) I **saw** her **do** the washing up. (= I saw her do it from beginning to end)
    I **heard** him **play** a beautiful sonata.
   b) I **saw** her **doing** the washing up. (= I saw her do it but only for a moment)
    I **heard** him **playing** the piano.

6 a) **Try** followed by the **-ing** form refers to an *experimental* action.

   b) **Try** followed by the **to-***infinitive* refers to the *effort* involved in carrying out the action. There is an implication that the action is difficult to perform.

7 a) **Mean** followed by the **to-***infinitive* refers to an intention (▶ 26.8).

   b) **Mean** followed by the **-ing** form has the same meaning as **involve.**

8 **Advise, allow, forbid** and **permit** may be followed by the **-ing** form (▶ 6.32) or by an *object* + **to-***infinitive* (▶ 6.34).

9 **Help** (+ *object*) can be followed by an infinitive *with or without* **to**. But notice that the expression **can't help** (meaning 'can't avoid') is followed by the **-ing** form (▶ 6.32).

10 Some verbs of perception (**hear, notice, see,** etc.) can be followed either by the infinitive without **to** or by the **-ing** form. In the first case (**a**) the action is perceived *in its entirety*, from the beginning to the end. In the second case (**b**) *only part* of the action is perceived.

7 Phrasal and prepositional verbs

Composition of phrasal verbs and prepositional verbs

7.1 Particularly in informal English, certain verbs are made up of more than one word (e.g. **look up, put up**). A verb is combined with an adverb particle (a *phrasal verb*) or a preposition (a *prepositional verb*) and, as a result, can take on a new meaning.

1 *Phrasal verbs:*
The flowers we planted last winter are beginning to **come up**.
Can you **put away** all these things, please?

Prepositional verbs:
The policeman **ran after** the thief but couldn't catch him.
She **laughed at** me when I told her the story.

2 *Phrasal verbs:*
He couldn't stand his job any more, so he **gave** it **up**.
(**give up** = renounce)
Have you finished? Time has **run out**!
(**run out** = come to an end)

Prepositional verbs:
I can't find my purse. Can you help me **look for** it?
(**look for** = try to find)
We'll **call on** you tomorrow.
(**call on** = visit)

1 The new meaning may have a logical link with the original meaning of the verb and the adverb or preposition.

2 Very often, however, the new meaning has no obvious connection either with the original meaning of the verb or with the adverb or preposition. In this case it is necessary to consult a dictionary to find out the meaning.

For a list of common phrasal and prepositional verbs ▶ Appendix G.

7.2

1 *Phrasal verb:*
We can **carry on** our talk tonight. (**carry on** = continue)

Prepositional verb:
The success of the enterprise **depends** very much **on** the weather.

2 a) She will **consent to** this agreement.
She will **consent to** it.
We **live on** our salary.
We **live on** it.

b) Could you **turn** the TV **off**?
Could you **turn off** the TV?
Fill in this form, please.
Fill this form **in**, please.
Could you **turn** it **off**?
Fill it **in** please.

1 The same word may be classed as an *adverb particle* or as a *preposition*, and be combined with different verbs to form *phrasal verbs* or *prepositional verbs* respectively. A dictionary will clarify whether a verb should be considered *phrasal* or *prepositional*.

2 An important difference between phrasal and prepositional verbs is that:
a) with prepositional verbs the preposition always comes *before* the object;
b) with phrasal verbs the adverb particle can come *either before or after the object,* if it is a noun. However, if the object is a *pronoun,* the adverb particle comes *after it.*

3 a) He made **up** a STÒRY /ʌp/

He made a story **UP** /ʌp/

b) They shouted **for** HELP /fə/.

3 Another difference is that:
a) the adverb particle is normally stressed and has main stress (▶ Appendix A4) when it comes after the object;
b) the preposition is normally unstressed.

7.3

They have **switched off the machine**.
The machine has been **switched off**.
She **looked after the children** very well.
The children were very well **looked after**.

In a passive sentence with a phrasal or prepositional verb, the adverb particle or preposition comes immediately after the verb (▶ 3.7).

7.4

Let's **get down to** business now.
If somebody accuses you, I'll **stand up for** you.

There are also verbs that are followed by both an adverb particle and a preposition (*phrasal-prepositional verbs*). These verbs follow the same rules as prepositional verbs.

7.5

1 I will never **approve of** his **wasting** so much money.
Don't stop now; **carry on working** for a little while.

2 He **set out to do** his homework but his thoughts were somewhere else.

1 A verb following a phrasal or prepositional verb is normally in the **-ing** form (verbal noun) (▶ 6.32).

2 However, in some cases (e.g. to express purpose), the following verb may be in the **to-**infinitive.

Individual verbs can be checked in a dictionary.

Section two: Communication
8 Identification and description

8.1

One of the main jobs of any language is to provide names to refer to the universe around us. This means providing names which allow us to identify:

1 types of people, animals or objects (e.g. **girl, horse, book**). These words are called *common nouns*;
2 abstract ideas (e.g. **poverty, success, fear**). These are called *abstract nouns*;
3 groups of people, animals or objects (e.g. **crowd, herd, set**). These are called *collective nouns*;
4 individual people, animals, places or objects (e.g. **Helen, Lassie, Chicago, the Titanic**). These are called *proper nouns* and are usually written with a capital letter at the beginning.

This chapter will examine the words which frequently accompany nouns (articles, adjectives. demonstratives, relative clauses) to specify or describe who or what is being referred to.

For the formation of the plural form of nouns and problems related to countable and uncountable nouns ▶ 9.2–9.4.

The articles

Form and pronunciation

8.2

```
1            Consonant sounds
             bus /bʌs/
             film /fɪlm/
   the /ðə/ unit /ˈjuːnɪt/
   a /ə/     European /jʊərəˈpɪən/
             one-way street /wʌn weɪ striːt/
             house /haʊs/

             Vowel sounds
             apple /æpl/
   the /ðɪ/ egg /eg/
   an /ən/ uncle /ʌŋkl/
             MP /em piː/
             FBI man /ef biː aɪ mæn/
             hour /aʊə/


2 Are they really THE Crown Jewels? /ðiː/

  I asked you to get me A bottle of beer, not
  six bottles. /eɪ/
```

1 The *definite article* has only one form **(the)** which never changes. However the pronunciation depends on the first sound of the following word. It is pronounced: /ðə/ before a consonant sound including /j/ and /w/; /ðɪ/ before a vowel sound, including words beginning with an unpronounced 'h' (e.g. **hour, honest, heir, honour**).
The *indefinite article* has two forms:
a /ə/ before a consonant sound;
an /ən/ before a vowel sound.

NOTE: English spelling is not a safe guide to pronunciation. The form and pronunciation of the articles depend on the *pronunciation* of the following word, not on the *spelling*.

2 When the definite article is stressed it is pronounced /ðiː/. The indefinite article **a**, when stressed, has the pronunciation /eɪ/. Stressed **an** is pronounced /æn/.

The definite article

8.3

The *definite article* usually refers to something specific, something 'definite' (but ▶ 8.5). It is normally used in front of a noun when the speaker assumes that the listener knows who or what is being referred to. The listener may know this because:

1 I watched a concert and a film on TV. **The concert** was good but I didn't like **the film**.

1 the noun has already been mentioned;

2 **The development of electronics** has been surprising.
The car that I saw was a Ford.

2 the noun is immediately defined by additional information;

3 Let's call **the doctor** (= the family doctor).
Give me **the paper** (= the paper that you are holding).

3 the context makes it obvious what is being referred to;

4 **The sky, the earth, the sun,**
the Pope, the weather, the South Pole,
the Reformation

4 the noun refers to something of which we assume there is only one.

The indefinite article

8.4

The *indefinite article* refers to something unspecified, something 'indefinite'. It is used before a singular noun when the speaker has no reason to assume that the listener can identify it more precisely.

1 There's **a bus stop** round the corner.
Can I have **a cake**?
I spent my holidays with **a friend**.
She's **a nice person**.

1 The indefinite article would, therefore, normally be used the first time a noun is mentioned or if it does not refer to a specific person or thing.

2 a) **Cars** are very expensive nowadays.
Supermarkets don't open on Sundays.

   b) I use **cream** to make the sauce.
She doesn't like **milk**.

2 The indefinite article is not used before:
   a) plural nouns;
   b) uncountable nouns (nouns which are not normally used in the plural).

Generic reference and specific reference

8.5

We may wish to refer not to one particular person or thing (e.g. a specific book) but to an entire category (e.g. 'books' in general). This is called *generic reference*.

1 a) **Computers** are often used for scientific research.
Matches can be dangerous.

   b) **The computer** is often used for scientific research.
The Giant Panda has become a rare species.

   c) **A computer** is often used for scientific research.
A gentleman always pays his debts.

   d) Very little has been done for **the handicapped**.
The rich get richer and **the poor** poorer.

1 Generic reference can be made using:
   a) the plural form of the noun, without the definite article;
   b) the singular form of a countable noun, with the definite article. This is common in the field of science and technology.
   c) the singular form of a countable noun, with the indefinite article;
   d) an adjective (functioning as a noun) representing a whole class, preceded by the definite article (▶ 8.13).

2 I like **tea; coffee** makes me nervy.
He was hungry for **success**.

2 Uncountable nouns (including abstract nouns) used in a generic sense appear without an article.

Summary table

8.6

Nouns	Structures for types of meaning	
	Generic	*Specific*
1 Singular countable	a dog/the dog	the dog
2 Plural countable	dogs	the dogs
3 Uncountable	wine	the wine

Generic reference	Specific reference
1 **A dog** can be useful to protect your home. **The dog** was one of the first animals to be domesticated.	**The dog** from next door is in our garden.
2 **Dogs** can be a nuisance in cities. **International flights** are delayed because of a strike.	Do you remember **the dogs** we had when we were children? **The international flights** listed below are cancelled.
3 Do you like **wine**? I'm fond of **classical music**.	**The wine** we had in that restaurant was awful. **The music** in the show was excellent.

NOTE: In English, nouns may still be considered generic even when they are accompanied by adjectives or other nouns which limit their reference to some extent (e.g. **international flights, classical music, twentieth century art**).

Special uses of **the**

8.7   The definite article is used in the following cases:

1 I can play **the piano,** not **the guitar.**

1 to refer to musical instruments that people can play;

2 (I'm going to) **the mountains, the seaside, the country, the cinema, the theatre, the office, the shops.**

2 to refer to certain places in a generalised way;

3 **the Mississippi, the Pacific Ocean, the Panama Canal, the Alps, the Shetlands, the Sahara, the USA, the USSR, the German Federal Republic**

3 before names of rivers, seas, canals, mountain chains, groups of islands, deserts and names of countries which refer to a union or a federation (also in certain other particular cases (e.g. **the Sudan**) ▶ 8.9).

Special uses of **a/an**

8.8 The indefinite article is used in the following cases:

1 He is **an architect**. She wants to be **a nurse**.	1 before the names of professions;
2 A: There's **a Miss Frost** waiting for you. B: Is she **the Miss Frost**, the writer? A: No, she's **a Miss Frost** but not the famous writer.	2 before a proper name to indicate a person whose exact identity has not been established;
3 What **a lovely poster**! What **an interesting book**! Compare: What **lovely posters**! What **interesting books**!	3 after **What** in exclamations in front of a singular countable noun, but not in front of plural nouns;

4 a) **a couple, a dozen, a half, a hundred, a lot of**
   b) **fifty pence a kilo**
   a hundred miles an hour
   three times a week
   Compare:
   fifty miles per hour
   four times per day
	4 a) in certain quantifying expressions;
	   b) to indicate rates of price, frequency, speed, etc.
	   Per is sometimes used in more formal English.

Cases in which articles are not used

8.9 Articles are *not* used in the following cases:

1 **Mr Brown, Dr Humphrey, Lady Diana, President Bush, Uncle John** Compare: **the Johnsons** (= Mr and Mrs Johnson and family) Is he THE **Stephen Spielberg**, the film director?	1 before proper names of people (with or without titles). However notice the use of **the** to refer to a family and the use of the stressed form /ðiː/ to refer to one particular individual (▶ 8.8).
2 **Africa, Liverpool, France, Lake Ontario, Mount Everest**	2 before names of continents, cities, countries, lakes or mountains (with some exceptions: e.g. **the Congo, the Sudan, the Hague**);
3 **NATO** /neɪtəʊ/ (= the North Atlantic Treaty Organisation) **UNESCO** /juːneskəʊ/ (= the United Nations Educational, Scientific and Cultural Organisation)	3 before the names of organisations represented by initial letters but pronounced as words (acronyms);

4 **Dinner** is ready.

Compare:
We had **a very good dinner** last night.
Mr Green gave **a dinner** to celebrate his promotion.

4 before names of meals, except when they are described or specified in some way;

5 Can you play **cards**?
Swimming is my favourite sport.

5 before names of games or sports;

6 She has certainly had **smallpox** and **measles**.

Compare:
I've got **a cold/a headache/a temperature**.
I've got (a) toothache/(a) stomachache.

6 before names of illnesses, although there are some common exceptions;

NOTE: **A toothache** and **a stomachache** are more common in American English.

7 Put **your hat** on **your head**.
Take off **your coat**.

7 when talking about parts of people's bodies, or clothes. These are usually specified by using a *possessive adjective* (▶ 10.3).

8 She goes to **university** (= as a student).
He's in **hospital** (= as a patient).
If you have a temperature you should stay in **bed**.
Home is where I hang my hat.

Compare:
He walked past **the university** (= the building).
He's in **the hospital** (= the building, not necessarily as a patient).
She was sitting on **the bed** (= a specific bed).
The headteacher telephoned **the homes** of all the pupils who were absent.

8 before certain nouns referring to places (**church, college, court, hospital, prison, school, town, university**) when we are not thinking of a specific building but are referring to the institution in a more abstract sense.
The nouns **bed, work** can be used without an article in a similar way.
When the noun **home** is not defined in any way it is also used without an article.

9 **by bus, by train, by bicycle, by plane, by phone, by telex**

9 before names of means of transport and communication preceded by the preposition **by** (▶ 13.7);

10 a) **on Sunday, in February, at Easter, in 1942**

b) **in** (the) **spring, in** (the) **winter**

c) **at dawn, at noon, at sunset, at night**

Compare:
in the morning, in the evening

10 a) before names of days, months, festivals and also before years;
b) before names of seasons **the** is optional;
c) before moments during the day (and also before **night**) preceded by the preposition **at**;
Notice that *periods* of the day are usually preceded by **in the**.

11 Do you speak **English**?
German is a difficult language.

11 before names of languages;

12 I usually watch **TV** in the evening.
Would you like to listen to **the radio**?

12 before **television**; but notice the use of **the** before **radio**;

13 a) GIRL DIES IN FIRE
MINERS LOSE PAY RISE

b) crystal = substance solidified in geometrical form

c) Read instructions first. Check plug. Select correct record speed.

d) Sign contract immediately. Letter follows.

13 in particular types of abbreviated language:
a) newspaper headlines;
b) dictionary definitions;
c) instructions;
d) telegrams.

Adjectives

Use and form

8.10

1 Can I have the **big** apple?
He was **fat.**

1 Adjectives help to specify, or at least give more information about, the nouns or pronouns to which they refer.

2 Jane is a **tall** girl.
A group of **tall** men were standing at the door.
I live in a **small** flat.
All my friends live in **small** flats.

2 Adjectives in English are invariable. They have only one form which does not alter for masculine or feminine, singular or plural.

For a list of adjectives used with particular prepositions ▶ Appendix H.

Adjectives in front of the noun

8.11

1 He's a **good** singer.
They own a **large** house.
True love never dies.

1 Normally adjectives go in front of the noun to which they refer.

2 I met a **beautiful, blonde German** girl.
My wife wants a **big, round, wooden** table.
They live in a **little, old, stone** cottage in the country.
She was wearing a **long, yellow, silk** dress.

2 When there are two or more adjectives together describing people or things they tend to appear in the following order:

SIZE	→ AGE	→ COLOUR →
(small)	**(old)**	**(black)**
SHAPE	→ ORIGIN	→ MATERIAL
(round)	**(English)**	**(metal)**

3 Volkswagens are **good, reliable** cars.
We stayed in a **dirty, uncomfortable** hotel.

Compare:
She wore a **black and white** skirt.
The architect designed a **concrete and glass** building.

3 Adjectives in front of the noun usually have commas between them. **And** is not normally used except when two adjectives describe the same characteristic (e.g. colour or material).

Adjectives in other positions

8.12

1 a) He's **young**.
The music was **nice**.

b) Christine got **annoyed**.
They felt very **tired**.
You look **wonderful** tonight.
The frying bacon smelt **delicious**.
That sounds **interesting**.

1 a) An adjective may follow the verb **be** (i.e. it may be used as the complement of a sentence). It is then separated from the noun or pronoun to which it refers.
b) In certain cases other verbs may link an adjective with the noun or pronoun to which it refers (e.g. **become, fall, feel, get, grow, keep, look, prove, seem, smell, sound, taste**).

2 The children felt **afraid** and ran away.
Experiments were performed on animals which were **alive**.

Compare:
The **frightened** children ran away.
Experiments were performed on **live** animals.

2 Certain adjectives can only be used after the verbs mentioned in **1** above and not in front of the noun to which they refer (e.g. **afraid, alike, alive, alone, asleep, unable**).

3 a) **Something important** was going on.
Everyone available came to help.

b) You've made a comment **worthy** of consideration.
The man **walking** beside her is her fiancé.
The car **used** in the bank robbery was found.

c) Make my coffee **strong,** please.
He painted the door **green**.
Everybody considers Henry **honest**.

3 In the following cases the adjective comes after the word to which it refers:
a) with compounds of **some, any, no, every** (▶ 9.18);
b) when the adjective is part of a longer phrase. Present and past participles are often used in this way, although they commonly behave like ordinary adjectives and go in front of the noun (▶ 6.23, 6.25).
c) when an adjective refers to the object of the sentence but is also linked to the verb, completing or extending the meaning of the verb.

Adjectives used as nouns

8.13

The Japanese have a distinctive style of cooking.
We're collecting money for **the blind**.
Nobody knows how to help **the unemployed**.
The rich have no real sympathy for **the poor**.

An adjective preceded by the definite article can be used to refer to an entire category of people or things (▶ 8.5). This often happens with certain nationality adjectives (▶ 8.15), adjectives referring to physical or social problems (e.g. **blind, sick, unemployed, homeless**) and certain others (e.g. **rich, poor, old, young, good, bad**).

Nouns used as adjectives

8.14

> Our friends live in a beautiful **country house**.
> Isn't this **record sleeve** nice?
> The **Lonely Hearts Club Band** will play here next week.

Words which are normally considered nouns may also function as adjectives by being placed in front of other nouns so that they define or qualify them in some way (▶ compound nouns: Appendix D6).

Nationality adjectives and nouns

8.15

Nationality adjectives and nouns are always written with a capital letter. They can be divided into four groups:

1 **Chinese** restaurants are often not expensive.
The Chinese invented paper.

1 The adjective and the noun are the same in both singular and plural. This group includes adjectives ending in **-ese** (e.g. **Japanese, Portuguese,**) and also the adjective **Swiss**.

2 **Italian** tailors are famous all over the world.
The Italians are well-known for their sense of style.

2 The adjective and the singular noun are the same but the plural noun is formed with **-s**. This group includes adjectives ending in **-an**, e.g. **German(s), American(s), Russian(s),** and also **Israeli, Pakistani, Greek**.

.3 My **Danish** friends come to see me every year.
The Danes are renowned for being very tolerant.

3 The adjective and the noun have distinct forms, e.g. **Polish/Pole(s), Swedish/ Swede(s), Spanish/Spaniard(s)**.

4 **English** shoes are in fashion now.
On the trip I met two **Englishmen** and an **Irishman**.
The English are considered a rather reserved people.

4 The noun is formed by adding **-man/woman** (singular) or **-men/women** (plural) to the adjective. To indicate the entire people the definite article is placed before the adjective. This group includes **English, Irish, Welsh, French, Dutch**.

Demonstratives

Forms and uses

8.16

	Indicating nearness	Indicating distance
Singular	this (table)	that (table)
Plural	these (tables)	those (tables)

Demonstrative adjectives and pronouns are used to identify, and distinguish between different things by relating them to ideas of nearness and distance. Demonstratives are therefore linked to the concept of space and, in particular, to the distinction between the adverbs **here/there** (▶ 12.18) and the prepositions **near/far from** (▶ 12.11). Demonstrative adjectives belong to the class of words that can come at the beginning of a noun phrase, called *determiners*.
Notice that **that** as a demonstrative is always pronounced /ðæt/ (Compare **that** as a relative pronoun ▶ 8.24).

Demonstrative adjectives

8.17

1 Will you sit in **this** chair here, please?
Is your father leaving **this** week?
I want to pay **this** time.
These things should never be revealed.

2 Look at **that** girl over there.
I'm not interested in **those** people.
Do you remember **that** time when we missed the plane?
We were young and happy in **those** days.

3 Which shirt would you like? **This** one or **that** one?
I don't want these cigarettes. I want **those ones** over there.

1 The demonstrative adjective (or determiner) **this** (plural **these**) indicates nearness to the speaker (not necessarily only in terms of space but also in time, or even psychologically). This is similar to the concept of **here** (▶ 12.18).

2 The demonstrative adjective **that** (plural **those**) indicates distance (in space, in time or psychologically). This is similar to the concept of **there** (▶ 12.18).

3 Demonstrative adjectives are often followed by **one(s)** (▶ 4.5) to refer to a countable noun which has already been mentioned.

Demonstrative pronouns

8.18

1 What are you going to do with **that**?
This is my new car.
These are your records, aren't they?

2 **This** is what she told me . . .
. . . and **that**'s the end of the news.

3 **This** is Frank, my boyfriend.
(*on the telephone*)
Hello. Is **that** Annie? **This** is Roger here.

1 **This/these** and **that/those** may also function as *pronouns*.

2 **This** and **that** may refer, more vaguely, to whole sentences or ideas.

3 Demonstrative pronouns do not normally refer to people except when introducing or establishing the identity of someone (especially on the telephone).

Relative clauses

Use of relative clauses

8.19

1 The man, **who was seventy years old,** retired.
The car, **which was dark red,** stopped.

Compare:
The **old** man retired.
The **red** car stopped.

1 Instead of using an adjective to describe a noun we can give a description by adding a clause to the sentence.
This type of clause, describing or providing more information, is called a *relative clause*.

2 It's raining, **which is a pity**.
There were many people in the theatre, **which frightened him**.

2 The function of a relative clause is not always so clearly linked to that of an adjective. A relative clause may refer to one particular noun (as in **1** above) but it may also refer to an entire clause. In the first example **which is a pity** refers to the fact that *it's raining*. In the second example **what frightened him** was the idea that *there were many people in the theatre*.

Restrictive and non-restrictive relative clauses

8.20

1 Bicycles, **which are very popular,** are a cheap form of transport.
The President, **who was visiting Rome,** met the Pope.
The diet recommends oranges, **which contain Vitamin C**.

1 There are two types of relative clause. One kind simply gives a little more information about someone or something. This extra information is incidental and is not the main point of the sentence. The clause could be omitted without distorting the meaning. This type of relative clause is called *non-restrictive* (or *non-defining*).

2 Bicycles **which don't have lights** are dangerous.
The pupils **who hadn't done the homework** were punished.
The assistant brought the books **which the customer had ordered**.

2 *Restrictive* (or *defining*) relative clauses define and limit what is being referred to. They are therefore an essential part of the sentence and cannot be omitted without altering the overall meaning. In the first example only bicycles **which don't have lights** are dangerous. The relative clause *restricts* the reference to one particular defined person, thing or group.

Punctuation in relative clauses

8.21

1 The girl, **who was reading a newspaper,** looked up.
(= There was only one girl present and she was reading a newspaper)

1 The incidental, non-essential nature of the non-restrictive clause is indicated by the *commas* which separate it from the rest of the sentence.

2 The girl **who was reading a newspaper** looked up.
(= There were a number of girls present but only one looked up: the one who was reading a newspaper)

2 The restrictive relative clause, which is an essential part of the sentence, is not isolated by commas.

Relative pronouns

8.22

At the beginning of the relative clause there is normally a word (**who, which, that,** etc.) which refers back to the person or thing we are talking about. These words are called *relative pronouns*.
The choice of the relative pronoun depends on:
a) whether it is referring to a *person* or a *thing*;
b) the *role* of the pronoun in the relative clause (*subject, object*);
c) whether the relative clause is *restrictive* or *not*.

Who, which, whom

8.23

1 Take the report **which** is on the desk.
The woman **who** was sitting here has gone.
Will you give me the newspaper **which** you've read?

2 a) That's the assistant **who** sold me the shoes.
That's the girl **who** I met at the concert.

b) He's the man **who** we were talking **about**.
I can't find the record **which** I wanted to listen **to.**

3 a) This is a fresco by the artist **whom** we mentioned.
Compare:
The artist **who** painted this fresco was a genius.

b) He was not qualified for the job **for which** he applied.
We discovered the person **from whom** he received the money.

4 The two workers, **both of whom** were exhausted, sat down.
We didn't like the food, **most of which** was tasteless.

1 For things the relative pronoun is **which** and for people it is usually **who** in informal English.

2 In informal English:
a) **who** is used as both subject and object of the clause;
b) when the relative pronoun is dependent on a preposition the preposition comes at the end of the clause.

3 In formal English:
a) if the relative pronoun is not the subject of the relative clause, **whom** is used instead of **who**;
b) if the relative pronoun is dependent on a preposition, the preposition comes in front of the pronoun and not at the end of the clause.

4 The forms **of whom** and **of which** are used after certain quantifiers (**both, all,** etc.
▶ 9.5, 9.6).

That

8.24

1 The actor **that** I like best is Paul Newman.
The man **that** was driving was clearly drunk.
The car **that** crashed was completely destroyed.

2 She's the teacher **that** I spoke **to**.
The train **that** we travelled **in** was old.

3 Is there **anything that** I can do?
That's **all that** she said.
It was **the most delicious** meal **that** I've ever eaten.
It was the **only** film **that** she ever made.

1 **That** may also serve as a relative pronoun but only in restrictive relative clauses. Especially in informal English it is used instead of **who(m)** or **which,** acting as either subject or object.

2 If a preposition accompanies the relative pronoun **that,** the preposition must be placed at the end of the clause and never immediately in front of **that.**

3 **That** is normally used as the relative pronoun after certain quantifiers **(some, any, no, every, all, few, little, much)**, after superlatives and after **only**.
Notice that **that** as a relative pronoun is pronounced /ðət/. (Compare **that** as a demonstrative ▶ 8.16).

Whose

8.25

A man **whose** wife had telephoned left the meeting.
There are housing problems in the capital city, **whose** population has grown rapidly.
Compare:
There are housing problems in the city, the population **of which** has grown rapidly.

Whose functions as a *relative adjective* (i.e. it is used before a noun at the beginning of a relative clause). It indicates *possession* in the widest sense of the word (▶ 10.1). It can be used to refer to both people and things. With reference to things the alternative construction using **of which** is possible (▶ 8.23).

Omission of relative pronouns

8.26 It is very common to omit the relative pronoun **(who(m), which, that)** whenever this is possible, especially in informal English. The relative pronoun may be omitted:

1 Have you seen **the house (**that**) they've bought**?
Compare:
The house, which they have bought, is on the corner.

1 in restrictive relative clauses (but *not* in non-restrictive clauses);

2 **The assistant (**who**) I spoke to** was very helpful.
Compare:
The assistant who served me was very helpful.

2 when it is *not* the subject of the relative clause;

3 **The road (**which**) he was driving on** was dangerous.
Compare:
The road on which he was driving was dangerous.

3 when it does not follow immediately after a preposition.

NOTE: **Whose** can never be omitted.

Summary table

8.27

	Subject	**Object**	**Possessive**
People	who, (that)	who(m), (that), ø	whose, of whom
Things	which, (that)	which, (that), ø	whose, of which

NOTES: **That** can be used only in *restrictive* relative clauses.
ø = the relative pronoun can be omitted.

Replacing relative pronouns

8.28

When, where, why, what, how can be used to replace the relative pronouns **which** or **that**.

1 The day **when** he left was Monday.
Compare:
The day **on which** he left . . .

2 The city **where** I live is by the sea.
Compare:
The city **in which** I live . . .

3 The reason **why** they came is obvious.
Compare:
The reason **for which** they came . . .

4 a) I didn't like **what** I saw.
Compare:
I didn't like **the things which** I saw.

b) I didn't like **everything that** I saw.
(*not* **everything what**)
That's **all that** he said.
(*not* **all what**)

5 This is **how** you do it.
Compare:
This is **the way in which** you do it.

1 **When** can replace **in/on which** in expressions of *time*.

2 **Where** can replace **in/at/on/to which** in expressions of *place*.

3 **Why** can replace **for which** with reference to *reason*.

4 a) **What** can be used as an alternative for the idea of **the thing(s) which/that**.

b) Notice that **what** replaces both a noun and a relative pronoun. It cannot therefore be used immediately after a noun or pronoun in the same way as **that** or **which**.

5 **How** can replace **the way in which** with reference to *method*.

Alternatives to relative clauses

8.29

Sometimes, instead of a complete relative clause, we find shorter phrases describing or providing more information. These are like simplified forms of relative clauses.

1 Students **wishing** to take the exam must give their names.
The girl **writing** a letter saw nothing.

Compare:
Students **who wish** to take the exam must give their names.
The girl **who was writing a** letter saw nothing.

2 The operation **carried out** yesterday was a success.
Compare:
The operation **which was carried out** yesterday was a success.

1 The *present participle* of the verb may appear without a relative pronoun or an auxiliary verb.

2 The *past participle* alone may replace a relative pronoun and a verb in the passive.

3 The **first guest to arrive was** Mike.
   The **best thing to do** is to call the police.
   The **only student to pass** the exam was Claire.

   Compare:
   The **first guest who arrived** was Mike.
   The **best thing which you can do** is to call the police.
   The **only student who passed** the exam was Claire.

3 The **to-***infinitive* form of the verb may replace a complete relative clause. This happens especially after ordinal numbers (**first, second,** etc.), superlatives, and after **next, last, only**.

4 The jacket **in the car** is mine.
   Compare:
   The jacket **which is in the car** is mine.

4 The reduction of the relative clause may be taken even further leaving no verb at all, only a phrase with a *preposition*.

5 The driver **with long hair** couldn't see properly.
   Compare:
   The driver **whose hair was long** couldn't see properly.

5 In informal English, clauses with the relative pronoun **whose** are often replaced by *prepositional phrases* using **with**.

6 **Mrs Thatcher, the Prime Minister,** made a speech.
   Lagos, the capital of Nigeria, is a port.

   Compare:
   Mrs Thatcher, **who is the Prime Minister,** made a speech.
   Lagos, **which is the capital of Nigeria,** is a port.

6 Two noun phrases which refer to the same person or thing may simply be placed side by side without using a relative pronoun or a verb to connect them. The two noun phrases are then described as *in apposition*.

9 Quantity

9.1

This chapter is concerned with the different ways in which the concept of *quantity* can be expressed in English. It considers the distinction between *singular* and *plural* and between *countable* and *uncountable*, ways of referring to various *degrees of quantity*, and the use of *numbers*.

Singular and plural

Plural form of nouns

9.2

An essential distinction in quantity is between *singular* and *plural*. Nouns in English normally have a different form for singular and plural.

---

1 There was a taxi waiting.
There were taxi**s** waiting.

1 To form the plural we usually add **-s** to the singular form.
For the pronunciation of the ending **-s** ▶ Appendix B1.
For changes in spelling ▶ Appendix C.
There are, however, several exceptions, as follows:

2 a)

man	**men**
woman	**women**
foot	**feet**
tooth	**teeth**
child	**children**
mouse	**mice**

2 a) A few nouns have very different forms for singular and plural.

b)

sheep	**sheep**
deer	**deer**
fish	**fish**
aircraft	**aircraft**
spacecraft	**spacecraft**
Chinese	**Chinese**
Swiss	**Swiss**

b) Some other nouns have exactly the same form for both singular and plural. Certain nationality words are of this type (▶ 8.15).

NOTE: The plural form **fishes** is sometimes used for a limited number of fish viewed as individual creatures rather than a collective mass.

Compare:
Polar bears eat **fish**.
There were three little **fishes** swimming in the pool.

c)

crisis	**crises**
oasis	**oases**
appendix	**appendices/appendixes**
formula	**formulae/formulas**
referendum	**referenda/referendums**
(datum)	**data**

c) Some nouns of Greek or Latin origin can have Greek or Latin plural forms. Sometimes there exist two possible plural forms.
The singular form **datum** is rarely used.

d) Have you got three **pennies?**
(= three coins of 1p each)
The ticket costs 50 **pence**.

d) The plural of **penny** is **pennies,** referring to the individual coins, or **pence,** referring to a sum of money.

Possible confusion between singular and plural

9.3

1 The **police were** called immediately.
Some **people haven't** paid.
The **cattle were** taken to the market.

1 Some nouns which appear to have a singular form are in fact *plural*.

2 No **news is** good news.
Darts is a popular pub game.
Measles is a common illness among children.
Physics was my favourite subject.

2 Some nouns which appear to have a plural form are in fact *singular*. Names of some games, diseases and academic subjects are in this category.

3 The British **government is** led by the Prime Minister.
The **government are** developing a new policy.
The **crowd is** getting very excited.
Now the **crowd are** leaving the stadium.

3 Some nouns referring to *groups* may be followed by either a *singular* or a *plural* verb form, depending on whether the group is being considered as a single unit or a collection of individual members. Common examples are: **army, audience, class, club, company, crowd, family, government, group, public, team**.

4 There **are** some **scissors** in the drawer.
Compare:
Is there **a pair of scissors** in the drawer?

4 Names of some objects consisting of two parts are plural (e.g. **glasses/spectacles, pants, scissors, tights, trousers**).

5 **£30 was** a lot to pay for a hat.
Fifty square metres isn't enough.

5 Expressions of *measurement* (e.g. amounts of money) are followed by a singular verb.

6 **A number of** speakers **objected** to the proposal.
A lot of noise is coming from that room.
A lot of newspapers are in financial difficulties.

6 The expressions **a number of, a group of** are followed by a *plural* verb. **A lot of** may be followed by either a *singular* or a *plural* verb, depending on the noun to which it refers.

Countable and uncountable nouns

9.4

Most nouns have both a singular and a plural form. They are names of objects or people or concepts which can be counted (e.g. **potatoes, policemen, superstitions)** and are therefore called *countable nouns*.

Other nouns (generally referring to substances) are not considered as countable in this way. For example, **water, sugar, tea** cannot be counted (although they can be measured in other ways – **a glass of water, a kilo of sugar, a cup of tea**). These nouns can be called *uncountable*.

1 **Charity** is the greatest virtue.
The main element in their diet is **cheese**.

1 Nouns used in an uncountable way are not normally preceded by the indefinite article **a/an** and do *not* appear in a plural form.

2 Oxfam is a major **charity** (= a charitable organisation).
French **cheeses** have great prestige (= particular types of cheese).

2 However in particular circumstances the same nouns can be considered countable.

3 Can I have two **teas** and two **beers,** please?
How many **coffees** have you drunk today?

3 Some uncountable nouns, like **tea, coffee, beer,** etc. can be used in the plural form in the sense of **a cup of** or **a glass of**, etc. in informal language.

4 The **spaghetti was** overcooked and soft.
Your **advice has** been useful.
This **furniture is** very expensive.
Her **hair is** fair.
The **news was** broadcast from London.

4 Not all languages have the same idea about what is countable or uncountable. The following nouns are used in an *uncountable* way in English: **advice, furniture, hair, information, money, luggage, news, spaghetti, travel, work**.

5 Let me give you **a piece of advice**.
There were just three **pieces of furniture** in the room.

5 Some uncountable nouns can be made countable by using the expression **a piece of/pieces of**.

6 **Work** was hard to find – nobody gave me **a job**.
Travel is her passion – she's planning **a journey** to Africa.

6 Some nouns which are considered uncountable have countable equivalents with a very similar, but more specific, meaning (e.g. **work/job; travel/journey; money/coin**).

Degrees of quantity

9.5 Varying degrees of quantity can be expressed using the *quantifiers* in the following table. Other expressions of quantity are discussed in the relevant section.

	With countable and uncountable nouns	Only with countable nouns	Only with uncountable nouns	With reference to two
Absence of quantity	no			neither (of)
Limited quantity		few (of)	little (of)	
Indefinite quantity	some (of) any (of)	several (of)		
Sufficient quantity	enough (of)			
Considerable quantity	most (of)	many (of)	much (of)	
Total quantity	all (of)	every each (of)		both (of) either (of) each (of)

Structures with quantifiers

9.6 The quantifiers in the table are grammatically similar in many ways:

1 There was **no noise** from the engine.
Most children like sweets.
Neither team was very impressive.

1 They can all be used immediately in front of a noun (like adjectives; but see **3** below).

2 I've got some tickets. Do you want **any**?
I'll take **both.**
We couldn't eat the apples. **Every one** was bad.
There were several candidates but **none** were/was suitable.

2 They can also be used as *pronouns*, except for **no** and **every** which must take the forms **none** and **every one** to carry out this function (for the form of the verb after **none** ▶ 9.7).

3 a) **Some of the** money was stolen.
Most of my memories are happy ones.
None of these people deserve to succeed.

b) **Every one of us** is responsible for this disaster.
Some of them couldn't read.
I'm going to punish **all of you.**

A: **Most of my** students come from middle-class families.
B: Really? I don't think **any of mine** do.

If you haven't got any sandwiches you can eat **some of mine**.

3 They are followed by **of**:
a) if there is an article **(a, an, the)**, a possessive adjective **(my, your, his,** etc.) or a demonstrative adjective **(this, that, these, those)** before the noun;
b) if they are used before a personal or possessive pronoun.
In these cases **none of** and **every one of** are used instead of **no** and **every**.

NOTE: **All** and **both** can also be used without **of** ▶ 9.13, 9.14.

Absence of quantity

9.7

1 We'd got **no** money. (= We had**n't** got **any** money)
There were **no** seats on the bus. (= There were**n't any** seats) (= There were **none**)

1 **No, none, not . . . any** all express the idea of complete absence of quantity. **No** and **none** are more emphatic than **not . . . any**.

2 a) We **never** have **any** time just to talk.
Nobody noticed **any** sign of the burglary.

2 a) **Any** cannot be used alone to convey a negative sense. It must be accompanied by a negative word (**not, never, nobody,** etc.).

b) **No** newspapers are published on Christmas Day. (*not* **not any**)

b) **Any** in this sense can never be used as the subject of a sentence (▶ 9.10).

3 None of the books **has/have** that kind of information.
The jackets looked nice but none of them **was/were** the right colour.

3 When **none** is used with a plural noun the following verb may have either a singular or a plural form.

4 **Neither** food **nor** drink **was/were** available after ten p.m.
Neither the buses **nor** the trains **were** working.
Because we had little time we saw **neither** the Vatican **nor** the Colosseum.
Neither the President **nor** the Congress **has** the power to ignore the Constitution.

4 Particular expressions are used to refer to two people or two things. If we wish to give a negative meaning **neither . . . nor** can be placed in front of the relevant nouns. If the two nouns are both singular the verb that follows is usually singular but may also be plural. When the nouns are plural the verb is also plural.

For **neither . . . nor** with reference to inclusion ▶ 17.3.
For **either . . . or** with reference to alternatives ▶ 17.8.
For structures with **no, none, neither** ▶ 9.6.

Limited quantity

9.8

1 (Very) **few** people really understood the book.
He eats (very) **little** meat.
Few (= **not many**) accidents result from mechanical faults.
He has **little** (= he doesn't have **much**) experience in the work.

1 **Few** (before plural countable nouns) and **little** (before uncountable nouns) express the idea of a limited, small quantity and suggest a *negative* attitude on the part of the speaker who implies that the quantity mentioned is not enough, or not as much as wanted or expected. **Few** is equivalent to **not many**, **little** to **not much**. **Few** and **little** are often accompanied by **very**.

2 You take **too little** rest. That's why you're always so tired.
Pupils became **so few** that the school closed.
He took **so little** interest in the work that eventually he was dismissed.

2 **Few** and **little** can both be preceded by **so** or **too**. (▶ 14.8).

3 a) **A few** visitors came to see me in hospital and the time passed quite quickly.
We managed to save **a little** money, just enough to buy an old car.

Compare:
Few people came to see me and I felt quite lonely.
We had very **little** money, not enough to buy a car.

3 a) When **few** and **little** are preceded by the indefinite article **a** they have a more *positive* sense. In this case they no longer have the negative implication of **not much** or **not many** and take on a meaning more like the neutral term **some**.

b) **Few** people showed **any** interest.
A few people showed **some** interest.
Little is known about **any** of the participants.
A little is known about **some** of the participants.

b) This positive/negative difference is shown by the following usage:
any (or compounds of **any**) is used in sentences with **few, little**;
some (or compounds of **some**) is used in sentences with **a few, a little** (▶ 2.14).

> 4 With **a bit** of luck they should manage.

4 In informal English **a bit** can be used instead of **a little**.

For structures with **few, little** ▶ 9.6.

Indefinite quantity

Some

9.9

> 1 There's **some** money for you in the drawer.
> We ate **some** cheese.
> I'll need **some** tools to do the job properly.
> Take **some** aspirins.

1 **Some** is used in *affirmative* sentences. It expresses the idea of *indefinite* or *neutral quantity* without having either positive or negative implications. It can be used with uncountable nouns or with plural countable nouns and, in this case, it can be considered the plural form of the indefinite article **a/an**.

> 2 We spent **some** time in HAMburg. /səm/
>
> I'll give you **some** MONey. /səm/
>
> Compare:
> We stayed for **SOME** days in Berlin. /sʌm/
>
> I can give you **SOME** money. /sʌm/

2 **Some** is usually unstressed and is pronounced /səm/ when it is used immediately before a noun.
If **some** is stressed it emphasises the idea of *a number of, a quantity of*. In this case it is pronounced /sʌm/.

> 3 There are **(some)** people who don't like classical music.
> I think I'll have **(some)** tea.
> Please buy me a melon, **some** apples and oranges, **some** bread and cheese.

3 **Some** can be omitted when we do not want to emphasise the idea of **a number of, a quantity of**.
In a list **some** is not normally repeated before every noun.

> 4 I love ice-cream. Please give me **some**. /sʌm/
> **Some** of the rooms are empty. /sʌm/

4 **Some** can also be used as a pronoun (▶ 9.6). In this case it is usually stressed and is pronounced /sʌm/.

> 5 a) Can you give me **some** information?
> Would you like **some** tea?
> Could I take **some** of these brochures?
> Do you think you could give me **some** help?
>
> b) Did you see **some** letters on the table?
> Are you going to buy me **some** sweets?

5 In certain cases **some** is used in *interrogative* sentences to convey positive implications. **Some** is used:
a) when the interrogative sentence is not really a question, in the normal sense of the word, but is a means of carrying out another function (e.g. making a *request* or an *offer* ▶ 25.6, 26.3);
b) when the speaker is expecting, or hoping for, or wanting to encourage, an affirmative response.

> 6 He visited **several** countries on the trip.

6 **Several** (before plural countable nouns) means **more than a few**.

For structures with **some, several** ▶ 9.6.

Any

9.10

1 Is there **any** money in the drawer?
Did you eat **any** cheese?
Will I need **any** tools to do the job properly?
Did you notice **any** magazines?
He asked me if I had noticed **any** magazines.

2 Are there **(any)** people who don't like music?
Have we got **(any)** milk?

3 Are there ˊANy people who don't like music?
(= Do people like this really exist?)

Have we got ˊANy milk?
(= even a very small amount)

4 a) Come and see me ˋANy time you want.
(= no matter when)

ˋANy person who believes that must be crazy.
(= no matter who he/she is)

b) **Any** bus will take you to the station.
Have you got **any** money at all?
Compare:
Some buses go to the station but not all of them.
I've got **some** money but probably not enough.

5 If you have **any** problems, give me a ring.

1 **Any** expresses the idea of *indefinite quantity* in *interrogative* sentences, both direct and reported (▶ 22.7). In this case it can be used with uncountable nouns or with plural countable nouns.

2 **Any,** in interrogative sentences, is normally unstressed and can be omitted.

3 **Any** may be stressed to give a sense of emphasis.

4 a) Stressed **any** may appear in affirmative sentences with the particular sense of *no matter who/what/where*, etc. It may be used with the subject of the sentence (▶ 9.7).

b) Generally, in both affirmative and interrogative sentences, **any** has an unlimited, unrestricted sense whereas **some** is used to refer to a quantity which is limited or restricted in some way (▶ 2.14).

5 **Any** also appears in conditional sentences (▶ 20.6).

For structures with **any** ▶ 9.6.

Sufficient quantity

Enough

9.11

1 You won't have to stand. There are **enough** chairs.
I haven't got **enough** money to go on holiday.
Eat some more food if you haven't had **enough**.

The most commonly used quantifier to refer to *sufficient quantity* is **enough**. It can be used to refer to both countable and uncountable nouns and is placed in front of the noun. It can also function as a pronoun.

For structures with **enough** ▶ 9.6.
For **enough** as an adverb of degree ▶ 14.7.

Considerable quantity

9.12

1 **A lot of** people were attracted by the market and **lots of** money changed hands.
We had **a lot of** difficulty in finding the street.

1 The most common way of expressing the idea of *considerable quantity* is by using **a lot (of)**, or, in informal English, **lots (of)**. Both these expressions can be used with all nouns, countable and uncountable.

2 Have you got **much** free time?
  Do you know **many** people here?
  You don't need **much** water to make the soup.
  There aren't **many** students in this class.
  Do you eat **much** fruit? – Yes, I eat **a lot of** oranges.
  Many imported goods are on sale in the shops.
  Pollution has damaged **much** of the coastline.

3 The fire caused **a great deal of** destruction – **a large number of** houses were burned.
  There was **plenty of** food for everyone.
  He soon made **plenty of** friends.

4 **Most** candidates were promising reforms.
  Most Scotch whisky is made for export.

2 **Many** (with plural countable nouns) and **much** (with uncountable nouns) normally appear only in interrogative and negative sentences. In affirmative sentences they are usually replaced by **a lot of**. However, in formal English, **much** and **many** are sometimes used in affirmative sentences. **Much** and **many** may be preceded by **so** and **too** (▶ 14.8).

3 Other expressions often used to refer to considerable quantity are **a large number (of)** (before plural countable nouns) and **a great deal (of)** (before uncountable nouns). In informal English **plenty (of)** can be used with all nouns.

4 **Most,** meaning **the majority of,** can be used with both countable and uncountable nouns.

For structures with **many, much, most** ▶ 9.6.

Total quantity

All

9.13

1 **All** cows eat grass.
  All hope has been lost of finding survivors.

2 **All (of) the** cows were in the next field.
  All (of) my friends are away on holiday.
  All (of) these problems can easily be solved.

3 I've told you **all that** I know.
  He lost **all that** he possessed in the war.

4 The audience **all** left the theatre.
  The money is **all** in the safe.
  They have **all** finished.

5 I've lost them **all**.
  She's seen it **all** before.

1 **All** can be used with both countable and uncountable nouns.

2 When the following noun is preceded by an article, a possessive adjective or a demonstrative, either **all** or **all of** may be used.

3 In modern English it is not very common to use **all** as a pronoun on its own except when it is followed by a relative clause.

4 **All** can be placed next to the verb, after the noun or pronoun to which it refers. The position is immediately before the verb, but after the verb **be** or the first auxiliary verb.

5 **All** can be placed immediately after a personal pronoun.

For structures with **all** ▶ 9.6.

Both

9.14

1 We went to Germany, France and Spain. We had a good time in **all** these countries.
We stayed in Barcelona and Valencia. **Both** cities were very interesting.

2 **Both** vehicles were damaged.
Both a car **and** a bus were damaged.

3 **Both (of) (the)** teams were tired after the game.
Both (of) my parents are retired.
I'm interested in **both (of) these** jobs.

4 The twins **both** love music.
The salt and pepper are **both** on the table.
My wife and I can **both** drive.

5 I like them **both**.

6 **Both** flats **are** attractive.
Each has its own particular advantage.
Both of the robbers **were** armed.
Each was carrying a gun.

---

1 The equivalent of **all** when referring to two people or two things is **both**.

2 **Both** can refer to a plural noun or to two nouns linked by **and**.
For **both** used to express inclusion ▶ 17.2.

3 When the following noun is preceded by an article, a possessive adjective or a demonstrative, either **both** or **both of** may be used.
Notice that **the** can also be omitted.

4 **Both** can be placed *after* the noun or pronoun to which it refers, in a position immediately before the verb, but after the verb **be** or the first auxiliary verb.

5 **Both** can be placed immediately after a personal pronoun.

6 Notice that **each** (▶ 9.15) can also be used to refer to two people or two things. However **both** considers the pair together as a whole and is followed by a plural verb. **Each** considers the individual members of the pair separately and is therefore followed by a singular verb.

For structures with **both** ▶ 9.6.

Each, every

9.15

1 **All** the workers have signed the contract.
Every worker has signed the contract.
Each worker has signed the contract.

2 **Every** city in Spain is interesting.
Every citizen has the right to be protected.

3 **Each** city has its own distinctive character.
There were ten people in the office and **each** one was concentrating on his own particular job.

---

1 **Every** and **each** can only be used with singular countable nouns and therefore the following verb has a *singular* form. But they express the idea of totality, like **all** + *plural noun*, and in many cases the meaning is similar.

2 However, **every** is a generalising word, referring to individuals but really grouping them together into a mass.

3 **Each,** on the other hand, breaks down the mass into separate individuals.

4 The children **each** took an apple.
You are **each** responsible for cleaning your own room.
We were **each** given a job to do.

5 He sent us **each** a Christmas card.

4 **Each** can be placed *after* the noun or pronoun to which it refers, in a position immediately before the verb, but after the verb **be** or the first auxiliary verb.

5 **Each** can also be placed immediately after an indirect object.

NOTE: **Each** (but not **every**) can be used to refer to two people or two things (▶ 9.14). For structures with **every, each** ▶ 9.6.

Whole

9.16

Whole, meaning **entire,** does not function in the same way as the other quantifiers mentioned in paragraphs 9.5, 9.6.

1 Did you read the **whole** book?
My **whole** career was destroyed.
This **whole** situation is your responsibility.

1 It can be used as an *adjective* with singular countable nouns when they are accompanied by an article, a possessive adjective or a demonstrative. **Whole** comes after such words.

2 She just sat and watched **the whole of the** time.
You've ruined **the whole of our** holiday.
I didn't like **the whole of that** film.

2 The expression **the whole of** can be used before singular nouns (both countable and uncountable) when they are accompanied by an article, a possessive adjective or a demonstrative.

Adverbs of quantity

9.17

He talks **very little,** but he thinks **a lot**.
Now that I'm not working **very much,** I have time to read **a great deal**.
You work **too much**.
I liked the film **so much** that I decided to see it twice.
I feel **a bit** tired.

Little, a bit, much, a lot, a great deal can also be used as adverbs of quantity, indicating the same degree of quantity as when they are used as adjectives or pronouns.
Little and **much** may be preceded by **so** and **too** (▶ 14.8).

Compounds of **some, any, no, every**

9.18

	somebody	anybody	nobody	everybody
Referring to **people**	someone	anyone	no one	everyone
Referring to **things**	something	anything	nothing	everything
Referring to **places**	somewhere	anywhere	nowhere	everywhere

1 Did you hear **anything**?
Yes, I heard **something** on the stairs.
Everyone came to the lecture but **nobody** understood it.
I left the paper **somewhere** in this room.

2 Did you meet **anyone interesting**?
I haven't done **anything special** this week.

3 **Everything** we did **was** a mistake.
Has everybody got **their** copy of the book?

4 **No one** noticed him leaving the room.
None of the telephones was/were working.
None of my friends like classical music.
Everyone was satisfied with the meal.
When I opened the box I saw that **every one** of the eggs was broken.

5 **Somebody** has stolen my car.
Compare:
Some people think smoking should be banned. (*not* **Somebody thinks . . .**)

6 **One of us** will help you. (*not* **Somebody of us . . .**)
Every one of them wanted to go. (*not* **Everyone of them . . .**)

1 The compounds which appear in the table follow the same rules as **some, any, no, every**.

2 An adjective referring to these compound words is placed after them (▶ 8.12).

3 All these compounds, including the compounds of **every,** are followed by a *singular* verb but **everybody/everyone** may be accompanied by a plural pronoun or possessive adjective. (This is often done when referring to a mixed group of males and females.)

4 **No one** and **everyone** (which always refer to people) must not be confused with **none** and **every one** (which can be used with **of** and may refer to people and things) (▶ 9.6).

5 **Somebody** and **someone** refer to a single person; they cannot be used to refer to 'people in general'.

6 These compound words are not normally used with **of** + *personal pronoun*.

Numbers

9.19

Numbers			
Cardinal	*Ordinal*	*Cardinal*	*Ordinal*
1 one	first	10 ten	tenth
2 two	second	11 eleven	eleventh
3 three	third	12 twelve	twelfth
4 four	fourth	13 thirteen	thirteenth
5 five	fifth	14 fourteen	fourteenth
6 six	sixth	15 fifteen	fifteenth
7 seven	seventh	16 sixteen	sixteenth
8 eight	eighth	17 seventeen	seventeenth
9 nine	ninth	18 eighteen	eighteenth

Numbers			
Cardinal	*Ordinal*	*Cardinal*	*Ordinal*
19 nineteen	nineteenth	30 thirty	thirtieth
20 twenty	twentieth	31 thirty-one	thirty-first
21 twenty-one	twenty-first	40 forty	fortieth
22 twenty-two	twenty-second	50 fifty	fiftieth
23 twenty-three	twenty-third	60 sixty	sixtieth
24 twenty-four	twenty-fourth	70 seventy	seventieth
25 twenty-five	twenty-fifth	80 eighty	eightieth
26 twenty-six	twenty-sixth	90 ninety	ninetieth
27 twenty-seven	twenty-seventh	100 a hundred	hundredth
28 twenty-eight	twenty-eighth	1,000 a thousand	thousandth
29 twenty-nine	twenty-ninth	1,000,000 a million	millionth

Cardinal numbers

9.20

1 a) 0.67 = **nought** (or (b) **zero** in American English) point six seven

 c) Tel. 63302 = six double three **oh** two

 d) Liverpool 2 (two) – Everton 0 **(nil)**

 e) −2°C = two degrees below **zero**

2 13 thir'teen /ˌθɜːˈtiːn/   14 four'teen /ˌfɔːˈtiːn/
 30 'thirty /ˈθɜːti/   40 'forty /ˈfɔːti/

3 269   two hundred **and** sixty-nine
 76,842   seventy-six thousand eight hundred **and** forty-two
 89,561   eighty-nine thousand five hundred **and** sixty-one

Compare:
269   two hundred sixty-nine
(in American English)

4 a) A dozen, two **dozen**
 100   a/one **hundred**
 300   three **hundred**
 4,000   four **thousand**
 2,000,000   two **million**

 b) **Hundreds** of people came.
 We lost **thousands** of pounds.

1 The number **0** has different names.
 a) In Britain it is called **nought** (nɔːt).
 b) In American English it is called **zero** (and increasingly in British English too).
 c) As part of a telephone number or postal code, it is pronounced like the letter **O** /əʊ/.
 d) As a sports result it is called **nil** (in tennis **love**).
 e) As a degree of temperature it is called **zero**.

2 In speech, word stress is important to help distinguish between the numbers **13** and **30**, **14** and **40,** etc.

3 The numbers from **21** to **99** are written with a hyphen. Between the hundreds and the rest of the number the word **and** is inserted in British English (but not in American English). Notice the use of a *comma* (not a full stop) to divide the thousands from the rest of the number when it is written in figures (▶ 9.22).

4 **Dozen, hundred, thousand, million** do not take **-s** in the plural (**a**), except when they are used as indefinite expressions (**b**).

5 Four **plus** three equals seven.
Ten **minus** four equals six.
Three **times** four equals twelve.
Eight **divided by** four equals two.

5 In arithmetic calculations the terms **plus, minus, times** and **divided by** are used to refer to, respectively, *addition, subtraction, multiplication* and *division*. The verb is usually in the singular form.

Ordinal numbers

9.21

1		
1st	first
2nd	second
3rd	third
4th	fourth

1 After **third, th** is added to the cardinal number to form the corresponding ordinal. In written English an ordinal number can be indicated by adding the last two letters of the word to the numerical figure.

2 a) fi**ve** – fi**f**th
twel**ve** – twel**f**th

b) ni**ne** – nin**th**
eig**ht** – eig**hth**

c) twent**y** – twent**ie**th
thirt**y** – thirt**ie**th

2 There are some modifications of spelling and pronunciation:
a) **ve** /v/ at the end of the cardinal number changes to **f** /f/;
b) **e** and **t** at the end of the cardinal number are dropped;
c) **y** at the end of the cardinal number changes to **ie**.
In these last two cases there are no changes in pronunciation.

3 January 21st (January **the** twenty-first)
Henry VIII (Henry **the** Eighth)

3 Ordinal numbers are used, among other things, to refer to the date (▶ 11.46) and the names of kings, queens, popes etc. In these two cases the article **the** is always pronounced, although not always written, before the ordinal number.

Fractions, decimals and percentages

9.22

1 a) $\frac{1}{2}$ a/one half
$\frac{2}{3}$ two third**s**
$\frac{3}{4}$ three quarter**s**
$\frac{4}{5}$ four fifth**s**
$\frac{11}{16}$ eleven **over** sixteen
(eleven sixteenth**s**)
$\frac{101}{586}$ a hundred and one **over** five hundred and eighty-six

1 a) Fractions are made up of a cardinal number and an ordinal number (which may take on a plural form with **-s**). More complex fractions can be expressed using **over**.

b) We waited for three quarters ($\frac{3}{4}$) **of** an hour.

b) When a fraction refers to a following noun the preposition **of** is used.

c) **Half (of)** the city was destroyed.
Only **half of them** replied to my letter.
The journey took **half an hour**.

c) **Half** can be used without the preposition **of**, except before personal pronouns; **of** is not normally used before **hour**.

d) The project lasted **one and a half years/a year and a half**.
The film was over after **one and a half hours/an hour and a half**.

e) **One third** of the **soldiers were** killed.
Two thirds of the **work was** done.

2	0.2	nought point two
	1.34	one point three four
	2.75	two point seven five

3	25**%**	twenty-five **per cent**
	8.4**%**	eight point four **per cent**

d) $1\frac{1}{2}$ can be expressed in two different ways.

e) The verb following a fraction is singular or plural, in agreement with the noun and not the fraction.

2 Numbers after the decimal point are read one by one (like telephone numbers). English uses a *full stop*, not a comma, to indicate the decimal point (▶ 9.20).

3 **%** is read (and may also be written) **per cent**.

Use of **a** and **one**

9.23

He bought **a/one** pound of apples.
There were **a/one** hundred thousand people in the square.
He was very kind to me and lent me **a** book.
He only got **one** free ticket but there were many more available.
One car will be enough – there are only three of us.

In English, unlike many languages, the indefinite article **a/an** is different from the number **one**.
A/an is used in an indefinite way when we do not want to imply a contrast with other possible quantities; we use **one** when we wish to express the idea of 'just one, no more than one' in contrast with other possible quantities.

Measurement

9.24

1 a) A: **How long** is the runway at this airport?
 B: It's 2 kilometres **long**.
 A: **How high** is that hill?
 B: It's 1,000 feet **high**.
 A: **How deep** is this lake?
 B: It's 500 metres **deep**.

 b) A: **What** is the **length** of this runway?
 B: It has a **length** of 2 kilometres.
 A: **What** is the **width** of that road?
 B: It has a **width** of 20 metres.
 A: **What** is the **thickness** of this wall?
 B: It has a **thickness** of 2 feet.

1 a) The most common way of asking for and giving information about *dimensions* is:
 A: **How** + *adjective*, is it?
 B: It's 2 metres + *adjective*.

 b) In very formal English an alternative structure is also used:
 A: **What is the** + *noun* of this object?
 B: It has **a** + *noun* **of** (2 metres).
These two structures can be used to refer to:
length (adjective: **long**);
height (adjective: **high/tall**);
width (adjective: **wide**);
depth (adjective: **deep**);
thickness (adjective: **thick**).

NOTE: For people the concept of *height* is expressed using the adjective **tall**. **Tall** or **high** may be used to refer to buildings and trees.

2 a) A: **How far** is (it to) the station? (*or* **What** is the **distance** to the station?)
   B: It's **about** 10 miles.
   A: **How warm/cold** is it today? (*or* **What** is the **temperature** today?)
   B: It's 20 degrees.
   A: **How big** is this room? (*or* **What** is the **size/area** of this room?)
   B: It's **exactly** 25 square metres.
   A: **How old** is your aunt? (*or* **What**'s your aunt's **age**?)
   B: She's **at least** 40.

b) A: **How much** does the case **weigh**? (*or* **What** is the **weight** of the case? *or* **How heavy** is the case?)
   B: It is/weighs 15 kilos.
   A: **How much** does the car **cost**? (*or* **What** is the **price** of the car? *or* **How expensive** is the car?)
   B: It is/costs £6,000.

c) A: **How long** does it **take** to get there?
   B: It takes 20 minutes.

3 Prices have gone up **by exactly** 5% compared with last year.
The temperature has risen **by at least** 3 degrees since yesterday.

2 a) Similar structures are used to refer to other types of measurement: *distance, temperature, area, age.*

b) To refer to *weight* and *cost* an additional structure is also possible:

How much + *subject* + *verb*

c) To refer to *time required* only one structure is possible:

How long + *subject* + *verb*

3 The preposition **by** is used to indicate the amount by which one measurement is greater or less than another.

NOTE: In the examples above (**2a** and **3**) notice the use of expressions like **about, exactly, at least** to qualify the figures given.

10 Possession

10.1 This chapter is concerned with the concept of *possession* and the language used to answer the question **Whose?**

The idea of *possession* can be expressed by means of *possessive adjectives, possessive pronouns,* the **s**-*genitive,* the construction **of** + *possessor,* the verb **have** and certain other verbs.

These constructions are not always used to indicate that something 'belongs' to someone in a literal sense. They may indicate different types of relationship:

my home town = the town where I was born
a friend **of his** = a person he is friendly with
Angela**'s** decision = the decision that Angela took

Possessive adjectives

10.2 The possessive adjectives are one way of indicating to whom something 'belongs'.

Personal pronouns	Corresponding possessive adjectives
I you he she it we you they	my your his her its our your their

NOTE: Do not confuse **its** (possessive adjective) with **it's** (short form of **it is** and **it has**).

Characteristics of possessive adjectives

10.3

1 I'm afraid I've lost **my** pen.
They couldn't find **their** passports.

1 They always come before the noun to which they refer and they are not immediately preceded by most *determiners,* e.g. articles (**the** or **a/an**), demonstratives (**this, that,** etc.), quantifiers (**some, many,** etc.), or a number.

2 a) Can I borrow **some of your** records?
Two of their children died in the war.

2 a) A quantifier or a number can precede a possessive adjective if accompanied by **of** (▶ 10.6, 10.9).

b) He's wasted **all (of) his** money.
Both (of) her parents live abroad.
I've already typed **half (of) your** letters.

b) **All, both** and **half** can be used without **of** before a possessive adjective.

3 **My friend** is in hospital.
Most of **my friends** were there.

3 The same form of a possessive adjective is used to refer to both singular and plural nouns.

4 **Jim** came to the party with **his** sister.
   Jane didn't come with **her boyfriend**.
   This **plant** has lost all **its** leaves.

5 a) I'll tell you a story **my father** used to tell
       me.

   b) Isn't it time you got **your hair** cut?
       She broke **her hip** falling down the stairs.

       Compare:
       The diplomat was shot **in the head** by the
       terrorist.
       He felt a terrible pain **in the stomach**.

   c) The singer appeared on the stage
       wearing **his** famous pink jacket.
       Don't forget to take **your** umbrella when
       you go out.
       We often spend **our** holidays abroad.

   d) She was in **her** mid-twenties when I met
       her.
       You'll have a good pension in **your** old
       age.

6 Walter and I no longer share a flat; he's got
   his own flat now.
   Why don't you use **your own** lighter instead
   of taking mine?
   Why are you looking at my book? Haven't you
   got **your own**?
   Now that she's ten she wants to have **a
   bedroom of her own**.

4 The form of the third person singular
   depends on the *gender of the possessor* and
   not of the person or thing possessed.

5 English differs from many other languages in
   using possessive adjectives to refer to:
   a) members of one's own family (speaking to
       outsiders);
   b) parts of the body;
       NOTE: In certain expressions, usually
       referring to injury or pain, **the** can be
       used instead of a possessive adjective.
   c) clothes, personal possessions and even
       abstract concepts which are closely
       linked to the possessor;
   d) periods/stages of life (in certain idiomatic
       expressions).

6 Possessive adjectives can be given greater
   emphasis by using the word **own**.
   Own can be used as a pronoun and also in
   the special structure **a** + *noun* + **of** +
   possessive + **own**.

Possessive pronouns

10.4 Possessive pronouns are also used to indicate to whom something or someone 'belongs'. But
possessive *adjectives* accompany a noun whereas possessive *pronouns* take the place of the noun.

Possessive adjectives	Corresponding possessive pronouns
my	mine
your	yours
his	his
her	hers
our	ours
your	yours
their	theirs

NOTE: There is no possessive
pronoun corresponding to the
possessive adjective **its**.

NOTE: Possessive pronouns, unlike
possessive adjectives, are always
given a degree of stress in the
sentence:
  A: Give me my book.
  B: It's not YOURS, it's MINE.

10.5 Possessive pronouns have the same structural characteristics as possessive adjectives:

1 Shall we use your car instead of **mine**?	1 They are never preceded by the definite or indefinite article.
2 The jacket is **hers** and the shoes are **hers** too.	2 The same form is used to refer to both singular and plural nouns.
3 David drank his coffee but Mary left **hers**. They paid the bills separately: he paid **his** and she paid **hers**.	3 The form of the third person singular depends on the *gender of the possessor* and not of the person or thing possessed.

Of + possessive pronoun

10.6 The construction **of** + *possessive pronoun* can be used instead of the corresponding possessive adjective when the phrase contains any of the following items:

1 This is Mr Hayes, **a** friend **of mine** (= one of my friends).	1 the indefinite article;
2 **This** book **of yours** is very boring.	2 a demonstrative adjective;
3 We've been listening to **some** cassettes **of ours** (= some of our cassettes).	3 a quantifier;
4 Jane came to see us with **two** cousins **of hers** (= two of her cousins).	4 a number. See also ▶ 10.9.

The s-genitive and possessive noun forms

10.7

1 **Philip's car** is a Fiat, isn't it? Have you ever met **that girl's mother**? **Sophie's Choice** is a beautiful film. **Beethoven's symphonies** are simply wonderful.	1 The **s**-*genitive* is another means of indicating possession, in the widest sense of the term. The name of the *possessor* (usually a person) comes before the name of the thing or the person which is *possessed*. The possessor is followed by an *apostrophe* and **s**; the thing possessed is not accompanied by the definite article. For the pronunciation of **s** ▶ Appendix B1.
2 **The soldiers' barracks** were very uncomfortable. **The Johnsons' flat** is not larger than mine.	2 Notice that with this construction regular plural nouns which already finish in **-s** are followed only by an apostrophe.
3 **The children's shouts** were heard all over the place. There has been a lot of controversy over **women's rights**.	3 Irregular plural nouns (i.e. those that do not end in **-s**) are followed by an apostrophe and **s**.

4 Of course I know **Charles's sister**: she's a friend of mine. Do you think that **Socrates' works** are difficult to read? That happened at the same time as **Jesus' birth**.	4 Singular nouns which finish in **-s** are usually followed by an apostrophe and **s**. Certain famous classical and biblical names are often followed only by an apostrophe.
5 Don't you like **Tim and Sue's flat**? I think it's very nice. Yesterday I borrowed **my brother-in-law's car**.	5 When the possessors have two or more names, or when the name is made up of more than one word, only the last word is followed by an apostrophe and **s**.

Omission of nouns after **s**-genitive

10.8 In the following cases the noun referring to the thing or the person possessed can be omitted:

1 I always have lunch at **my mother's** on Sundays. Can you please buy some potatoes at **the greengrocer's** down the road? They got married in **St Paul's**.	1 when the context makes it obvious what is being referred to. This is particularly the case with place names (e.g. **house, church, shop, restaurant**);
2 Whose shirt is that? Can it be **William's**? I read **Shelley's poems** but not **Byron's**.	2 when we wish to avoid unnecessary repetition.

Of + **s**-genitive and possessive noun forms

10.9 The construction **of** + **s**-*genitive* can be used when the phrase contains:

1 This is Henry, **a** schoolmate **of my brother's** (= one of my brother's schoolmates).	1 the indefinite article;
2 Our teacher thinks that **this** play **of Shaw's** is one of his best.	2 a demonstrative adjective;
3 We've been listening to **some** records **of Michael Jackson's** (= some of Michael Jackson's records).	3 a quantifier;
4 **Two** colleagues **of my husband's** came to dinner.	4 a number. See also ▶ 10.6.

The construction **of** + possessor

0.10

1 It's **Mike's** birthday next week.
Do you agree with the **Government's** policy?
Look at **that bird's** colours!

2 Are these the cigarettes **of the boy who was here last night**?
Is she the daughter **of that man with the glasses**?

3 The temperature **of the water** in the swimming pool is about 18°C.
The progress **of technology** has been enormous this century.
I wonder why the windows **of that house** are always shut.

1 The **s**-*genitive* is normally used when the possessor is a person, a group of people or an animal.

2 However, the construction **of** + *possessor* is normally used when the possessor is a person who is subsequently identified or qualified in some way.

3 The construction with **of** is also normally used when the possessor is not a person or an animal.

Other uses of the **s**-genitive

0.11

In some cases the **s**-*genitive* is used to refer to a possessor which is not a person or an animal, for example:

1 Has **today's mail** come yet?
A good night's rest will make you feel better.
We have **two months' holiday** every summer.

2 I filled the car with **ten pounds' worth** of petrol.

3 Some people say that J.S. Bach is **the world's greatest composer**.
The present government's policy seems to be disliked by everybody.

4 He lives only **a stone's throw** from here (a very small distance).

1 in some expressions connected with time;

2 in expressions containing the word **worth**;

3 with 'things' which really refer to groups of people;

4 in a number of idiomatic expressions.

Nouns used as adjectives

0.12

After the accident the **car doors** (= the doors of the car) wouldn't open any more.
Let's give her a bunch of **spring flowers**!
The **school headmistress** is not in at the moment. Can you ring later?

In many cases it is possible to avoid using both the **s**-*genitive* and the construction **of** + *possessor* by simply placing one word in front of another so that it functions like an adjective (▶ 8.14 and Appendix D6).

Verbs of possession

The verb **have**

10.13

1 Mrs Redford**'s got/has** a really nice house.
She **hasn't got/doesn't have** many friends,
I'm afraid.
How much money **have you got/do you
have** with you?

2 I often **have** colds in winter.
Compare:
Have you **got** a cold?

3 **Do** you ever **have** colds in winter?
Do you **have** a cold?

1 The most commonly used verb to refer to
possession in its widest sense is **have (got)**.
For the forms of **have** ▶ 6.8.

2 In British English, **have** tends to refer to
permanent possession, **have got** to
possession at one particular time.

3 In American English, **have** is used for both
meanings.

For the various other uses of **have**
▶ 6.9–6.11.

Other verbs of possession

10.14

1 a) The house you visited **belongs** to me.

A: Do you **own** a flat?
B: No, I'm just renting my flat.
Compare:
A: **Have** you **got** a flat?
B: Yes, I'm renting one in the city centre.

b) He **belongs** to the Labour party.

2 He doesn't **possess** any property.

1 a) The verbs **belong** and **own** are also used
to refer to possession but in a more
legalistic sense.

b) **Belong** also means 'be a member' (of a
club, a party, an organisation, etc.).

2 The verb **possess** has the same meaning as
own but is used only in formal English.

11 Time

11.1
This chapter is concerned with the ways in which English deals with the concept of *time*. The first part of the chapter examines the relationship between time and verb form. The chapter then goes on to look at how prepositions and adverbs are used to locate events in time and to interrelate events occurring at the same time or at different times. The expression of the measurement of time through clocks and calendars is also considered.

Information about the *formation* of verbs can be found in Chapter 6.

Time, tense and aspect

11.2
The verb in English is related to time by means of *tense forms* and various auxiliary or modal auxiliary verbs used to indicate *aspect*.

1 *Regular forms:*
   a) He **lives** in Italy.
   b) He **lived** in England.

   Irregular forms:
   a) I **speak** English.
   b) I **spoke** to him yesterday.

2 a) He **is staying** with us at the moment.

   b) We **were watching** TV when the lights went out.
   At ten o'clock they **were** still **sleeping**.

   c) At this time next year they **will be studying** at university.

3 a) We **have bought** the tickets so we can go in now.

   b) He **had** already **gone** when I arrived.

   c) By nine o'clock the workers **will have finished.**

4 Richard **has been living** in that flat for the past three years.
   In two months' time we **will have been working** in this factory for ten years.
   The manager **must have been** preparing this plan for months.

1 Verbs in English have only two simple tense forms:
   a) the *present;*
   b) the *past.*
   There is no special form to express the *future:* for this purpose English uses various structures (e.g. with **will,** or **going to** ▶ 11.11 – 11.16).

2 Verbs in English have two aspects: the *progressive* aspect and the *perfect* aspect. The *progressive* aspect (which is expressed by the *auxiliary verb* **be** + **-ing** form/*present participle*) implies that the activity is *incomplete* at the moment referred to. The activity may be in (**a**) the present, (**b**) the past, (**c**) the future.

3 The *perfect* aspect (which is expressed by the *auxiliary verb* **have** + *past participle*) relates a happening at one moment of time with a *later* moment of time in either (**a**) the present, (**b**) the past or (**c**) the future.

4 Both aspects may be in operation *at the same time* and either, or both, may combine with other auxiliary or modal auxiliary verbs (e.g. **will, going to, must**) to create even more complex verbal structures.

NOTE: The *aspect* forms are often referred to as *tenses* (e.g. the *present progressive* tense, the *present perfect* tense), although strictly speaking verbs in English have only two tense forms (see **1** above).

Present time

The simple present and the present progressive

11.3

1 You can't see the doctor now; she**'s examining a patient**.
Wait for me! I**'m coming**.
Look, there's Mike! He**'s going** into that shop.

2 We **live** in London.
I **go** to work by bus.
She always **drinks** coffee for breakfast.
Water **boils** at 100°C.
Compare:
Water **will** boil at 100°C.
She's very kind. She**'ll** always help other people.

3 a) I**'m staying** in a hotel for a couple of weeks.
She**'s not eating bread** while she's on the diet.
John**'s playing** football this season for a change.

b) Maradona **passes** to Valdano who **shoots**.
Now the Queen **enters** the House of Commons and all the MPs **stand up**.
I **take** the bowl and **put** it in the oven.

c) Why **are** you **always borrowing** my books?
Laura annoys me – she**'s always complaining**.

1 If we are speaking about an activity that is happening *precisely at this moment* the *present progressive* is normally used (▶ 6.6).
NOTE: Some verbs are not often used in the progressive form (▶ 11.19).

2 To refer to a *permanent* state of affairs or to an activity that happens from time to time or repeatedly, but not necessarily at this very moment, the *simple present* is used (▶ 6.20).

NOTE: The auxiliary verb **will** (▶ 6.15, 6.16) is sometimes used to refer to characteristic behaviour.

3 There are some variations to this basic division between the *simple present* and the *present progressive*, for example:
a) The *present progressive* is used instead of the *simple present* when the speaker wishes to suggest that an activity is taking place *temporarily*, even if not at this very moment.

b) When an activity happens at the moment of speaking and is concluded at that same moment, the *simple present* is often used. This may be the case in TV or radio commentaries, for example, where the speaker wants the listeners to feel close to the action, or when someone is demonstrating how to do something.

c) The *present progressive* can also be used for repeated activities with **always**. This usually suggests an attitude of irritation about things that happen too often.

Past linked to present

The present perfect

11.4

1 a) I**'ve** already **been** to the dentist this month. (= I don't need to go now)

b) This machine **has** often **broken** down recently. (= It may break down again at any moment)

c) We**'ve lived** here for ten years. (= We still live here)

2 **Have** you **eaten** any breakfast?
(= There is still time to eat)
Did you **eat** any breakfast?
(= It's too late now, it's past breakfast time)
I **spoke** to Jerry only five minutes ago.

3 A: Where's your father?
B: He**'s just gone** out.

A: You look tanned!
B: Yes, we**'ve just come** back from Greece.

4 a) **Have** you **ever had** any serious illness?
Has the document **ever been** published?
I**'ve never met** him.
The USA **has never had** a black president.

b) It's the **only** thing I **have** ever **regretted**.
This is **the most wonderful present I've** ever **received**.
This is the first time I've visited England.

5 a) **Haven't** you **had** a bath **yet**?
They **still haven't paid** me.

b) We**'ve had** this car **since** 1975.
Until now I haven't really **appreciated** it.
Have you **been** on holiday **this year**?

1 The *present perfect* (▶ 6.9) may be seen as a link between past time and present time. It is used in situations where an activity takes place either:
a) once;
b) repeatedly;
c) continuously;
but *always* during a period of time *beginning in the past* and *continuing up to the present*. In each case a link with the present is implicit.

2 If a speaker chooses to use the *simple past* (▶ 6.21, 11.6) this link with present time is broken and the activity is seen as *belonging only to past time* (even if this is the very recent past).

3 Because of its link with present time the *present perfect* is used to refer to recent activities, often in combination with **just** (▶ 11.34), **recently** or **lately** (▶ 11.21, 11.22).

4 a) The *present perfect* (often in combination with **ever** or **never**) is also used to refer to an *indefinite* past, meaning 'at any time up to the present'. In the examples it is implied that the situation or the action is *still* possible.

b) Notice the frequent use of the *present perfect* after **only,** *superlatives* and expressions like **this is the first time**.

5 Other time adverbs and prepositions which frequently accompany the *present perfect*:

a) indefinite time adverbs like **yet, already, still** (▶ 11.32, 11.33);

b) prepositions and adverbs which imply an unfinished period of time beginning in the past and continuing up to the present:
for, since (▶ 11.31); **so far, until now** (▶ 11.29); **today, this week, this year, in my life**.

The present perfect progressive

11.5

1 a) **Have** you **been drinking** whisky? You seem a bit drunk.
I**'ve been reading** 'War and Peace' for months.
She**'s been writing** letters since six o'clock.

Compare:
Have you **drunk** your whisky? Would you like some more?
I**'ve read** 'Oliver Twist' and now I want to read 'David Copperfield'.
She**'s written** three letters today.

b) I**'ve been learning** how to drive. (= The lessons aren't finished yet)
Who**'s been eating** my sandwich?
(= Some of the sandwich remains)

Compare:
I**'ve learnt** how to drive. (= Now I know)
Who**'s eaten** my sandwich? (= There's nothing left)

2 Some students **have been working** in a factory during the summer holiday.

3 She**'s lived** here since she was a child.
I**'ve been studying** English for two years.
He**'s been standing** there since two o'clock.

1 When the *progressive* aspect is combined with the *present perfect* (i.e. **have been** + **-ing** form/*present participle*), the connection with present time remains, but added to it there are two further implications resulting from the nature of the progressive aspect:
a) Attention is focussed on the *duration* of the activity. Compare the *present perfect simple* which is concerned with the *result* of an action and is less concerned with the time taken to achieve that result.

b) It is implied that the activity remains unfinished and may continue into the future.

2 The *present perfect progressive* is often used to refer to temporary activities.

3 Notice that some languages use a *present* tense where English uses the *present perfect* (simple or progressive) to refer to an action beginning in the past but still continuing.

NOTES: Some verbs are not often used in the progressive aspect (▶ 11.19). For the difference between **for** and **since** ▶ 11.31.

Past time

The simple past

11.6

1 Columbus **went** to America in 1492.
The train **left** at 9.35.

2 **Did** you **enjoy** the film?
He **worked** so hard that he **had** a nervous breakdown.

The *simple past* (▶ 6.21) is normally used to refer to a situation, a single action or a series of actions which took place in the past and where there is *no* attempt to establish a link with the present. A *definite moment* of time in which an action occurred may (**1**) be mentioned, or may simply (**2**) be understood from the context.

The past progressive

11.7

1 He **was reading** the paper at ten o'clock.
The doctor was busy – he **was examining** a patient.
Mike **was going** into a shop when we saw him.
It was a warm day and the beach was crowded. Some people **were sunbathing** and others **were swimming.** Some children **were playing** in the sand.

2 When the telephone rang I **was sitting** in the bath.
As the taxi **was moving off,** I realised I had forgotten my case.
When I came home my mother **was making** some tea. (= She had already started before I came home)
Compare:
When I came home my mother **made** some tea. (= First I came home and then she made some tea)

1 When the *simple past* is used an activity is seen as something *completed*. But we may wish to take a different perspective and look at an activity at one particular moment of its development *before* it is necessarily completed. If that particular moment is in the past we use the *past progressive* (▶ 6.6). The *past progressive* is therefore frequently used *to describe a scene* (compare the parallel use of the *present progressive,* ▶ 11.3).

2 The *simple past* and the *past progressive* may be used *together*. One action (viewed as *complete*) interrupts another action (viewed as it was *at the moment of interruption*).

NOTE: Some verbs are not often used in the progressive aspect (▶ 11.19).

The past perfect

11.8

1 He reached the station but the train **had** already **left**.
The Vikings **had discovered** America long before Columbus crossed the Atlantic.
Nobody **had paid** any attention to him before his novel was published.

2 Just before their arrival I **had prepared/ prepared** a meal.
After the passengers **had entered/entered** the plane took off.
I **knew/had known** him before he became famous.

3 We **HAD** hoped to start our own business but we never had enough money.

1 The relationship between past time and present time expressed through the *present perfect* (▶ 11.4) has a parallel in the past. We can establish a relationship between two past actions *in which one happens before the other*. In this case the *past perfect* (▶ 6.9) is used. It creates an effect of going further back in time.

2 When the sequence of events is made clear by the context or by the use of time conjunctions (e.g. **after, before**) the *past perfect* is optional.

3 The *past perfect* can be used to refer to an unrealised hope, intention, desire etc. **Had** is often stressed in such statements.

The past perfect progressive

1 We **had been waiting** for three hours when the doors finally opened.
The teams **had been playing** for only ten minutes before the storm broke out.
The engine **had been making** a lot of noise during the journey. Finally it broke down.

2 I **had been studying** English for two years when I took the exam.
I **had known** him for ten years when he got married.
It **hadn't rained** since October and the ground was hard.

1 The *past perfect progressive* (▶ 6.6) has the same function as the *present perfect progressive* (▶ 11.5) but it refers to one stage further into the past. It emphasises the aspect of *time duration* and may imply that the activity was *unfinished* at the time referred to.

2 Notice that in some languages a past progressive tense is used where English uses the *past perfect* (simple or progressive) to refer to an action beginning at one moment of time in the past and still happening at a later moment of time in the past.

NOTES: Some verbs are not often used in the progressive aspect (▶ 11.19). For the difference between **for** and **since** ▶ 11.31.

Used to and would

1 The house **used to stand** on the hill. (= Now it doesn't exist)
Before he got a car it **used to** take him two hours to get to work. (= Now he's got a car)

Compare:
He **was used to driving** in the city and arrived home quickly.
After a few years she **will be used to speaking** the language.
I**'m not used to going** to bed so late.

2 When he was annoyed he **would** take a deep breath.
Athletes from Ancient Greece **would** compete in the Olympic Games every four years.

3 a) I knew we **would** win that football match.

b) I asked them to come to the party but they **wouldn't**.

1 To describe a situation which was true in the past but is no longer true now, it is possible to use **used to** + *infinitive* (▶ 6.18) as an alternative to the *simple past*.

NOTE: This form, which can only refer to the past, must not be confused with **be used to** + **-ing** which means 'be accustomed to' and can be used to refer to past, present and future.

2 **Would** (▶ 6.15, 6.16) can be used as an alternative to **used to** to describe *habitual activity in the past*.

3 **Would** may function as a past form of **will** and can therefore be used for (**a**) 'future in the past' events (▶ 11.17), or (**b**) to describe willingness in the past (▶ 26.2).

Future linked to present

As the *present perfect* establishes a link between past and present time, so certain other structures set up a link between present time and future.

Be going to

11.11

1 A: What **are** you **going to do** this evening?
  B: I**'m going to stay** at home.
  After he has passed his exam he**'s going to go** to university.

2 The car is out of control – it**'s going to crash**.
  Aren't you taking a map? You**'re going to get** lost.

Be going to + *infinitive* expresses the future as it is influenced by the *present*. The origin of the future event lies in the present, perhaps in the form of (**1**) a *present intention* (▶ 26.8), or perhaps because of (**2**) *present circumstances*.

The present progressive for future events

11.12

We**'re going** to Hawaii next year.
First we**'re visiting** the Eiffel Tower and then we**'re having** a trip on the Seine.

If the future event is the result of something already definitely arranged, the *present progressive* can be used.

Be to

11.13

The Queen **is to visit** the new hospital.
The new ship **is to be launched** next week.
You**'re to take** these books to the secretary's office.

A future arrangement can also be indicated by the structure **be to** + *infinitive*. This structure is used in more formal English, and particularly in newspapers. It may also imply an element of obligation (▶ 24.4, 24.6, 24.9).

The simple present for future events

11.14

1 Next month **is** April.
  The plane **takes off** at three o'clock.
  The holiday **begins** next week.
  The new manager **takes over** on Monday.

2 a) **As soon as** the music **finishes,** we'll leave.
     Once the snow **falls** the skiers will start coming.
     The next time you **do** that you'll be punished.

  b) **If** you **come** with me I'll do it.
     There will be no point in going **unless** the shop **is** open.

1 In some cases future events may be considered, rightly or wrongly, as absolutely certain to take place. They are thought of as part of the fixed order of things or, at least, as part of a fixed plan or timetable. In such cases the *simple present* may be used.

2 The *simple present* is also used with reference to the *future* in other cases:
  a) in subordinate clauses after conjunctions of time like **when, until, as soon as, immediately, before, after, the moment, once, whenever, as long as, the first time,** etc. (▶ 11.40);

  b) in conditional sentences after conjunctions like **if, as long as, unless,** etc (▶ 20.7, 20.8).

Immediate future

11.15

> Let's go inside – it**'s about to rain**.
> She**'s on the point of handing** in her resignation.

Certain other structures may be used to refer to an immediate future: **be about to** + *infinitive*, **be on the point of** + **-ing** *form (verbal noun)*.

Future time

Future with **will/shall**

11.16

1 Their transport system **will be** the most modern in Europe.
When I retire I **shall live** in the country.
If you take that job you**'ll regret** it.
I think Spain **will win** the next World Cup.
You can sit at the back – nobody **will see** you.
I don't expect she **will phone** you again.
Compare:
John **will be** twenty-one next year.

1 To make a prediction about the future without seeing it as necessarily connected with the present we can use the modal verb **will** (or **shall** for the first person singular and plural) followed by the *infinitive without* **to**. **I/we will** is more common than **I/we shall,** especially in spoken English. The abbreviation **'ll** is commonly used for **will/shall** in speech and informal writing. Notice that the examples given here could also be expressed using the form **be going to** + *infinitive*. However, the use of **going to** would suggest stronger links with the present, e.g. there could be a greater sense of intention (▶ 11.11).

NOTE: **Will/shall** can also be used to talk about definite unavoidable events in the future.

2 You**'ll fail** the exam if you don't work harder.
If you break that glass I**'ll give** you a smack.

2 **Will/shall/'ll** are commonly used in conditional sentences before or after a clause with **if** + *simple present* (▶ 20.7, 20.8).

3 A: Tea or coffee?
B: I think I**'ll have** some coffee.
I think I**'ll phone** her now.
I promise I**'ll be** home early.

3 **Will** is used when speaking about a decision at the moment of making it. In this sense **will** is used to make promises (▶ 26.8) and threats (▶ 25.16).

4 Tim **will drive** her to the station. (= Tim **is willing to drive** her)
She **won't help** you. (= She **refuses to help** you)
They **won't work** this weekend.
Your guide **will explain** the details of the itinerary.

4 **Will,** besides having this role as an auxiliary verb for the future, is also used to express *volition* (▶ 26.2), i.e. when the subject of the sentence is a person, **will** may represent the *willingness* of the subject to carry out the action as well as the idea of the action as a future event.

5 a) Come at nine tomorrow – I**'ll be working** in the office.
In two years' time we**'ll** still **be living** here.

5 a) **Will** combined with the progressive aspect (**will be** + *present participle*) (▶ 6.6) may carry the usual implications of *duration* and *incompletion* (▶ 11.5).

b) The new manager **will be arriving** on Thursday.
She**'ll be bringing** all the documents with her.

c) Tim **will be driving** her to the station.
She **won't be helping** you.
They **won't be working** this weekend.
Your guide **will be explaining** the details of the itinerary.

b) This future progressive form is also often used to talk about something which has been arranged.

c) **Will** combined with the progressive aspect does not carry any overtone of *volition/willingness* and may therefore be used as a kind of *neutral* future.

Future in the past

11.17

1 I **was going to phone** you but I lost the number.
We went to bed early as we **were leaving** next morning.
We all had our roles – I **was to be** the driver.
The plane **was about to take off** when the message arrived.
Nixon **was on the point of resigning** – Ford **would be** the next President.
I didn't expect that **would work**.

2 She had told me that she **would be able** to come. (*not* **would have been able**)
If we had told her in time she **would have been able** to come.
The doctor said the operation **would take** place in two days.
(*Not* **would have taken**)
The operation **would have taken** place if a suitable donor had been found.

1 A *past* event may be viewed as *future* from a moment of time even further in the past. To convey this perspective, many of the *future* constructions already examined can be put into a *past* form.

2 In talking about future in the past the forms **would** and **would have** should not be confused.
The form **would have** is normally used to refer to an event which did not take place, and usually forms part of a conditional sentence (► 20.6, 20.7).

For reported speech ► 22.3.

Past in the future

11.18

1 He **will have finished** the job by six o'clock.
In one hour we **will have prepared** the meal and **eaten** it.
They **will** already **have left** by the time we get there.

2 Do you realise that in six months' time we **will have been living** in this house for twenty years?
I'm sure they'll be very thirsty. They **will have been working** outside in the sun all afternoon.

A *future* event may be seen as *past* from the viewpoint of a moment of time even further in the future.

1 In this case **will** is combined with the perfect aspect (**will have** + *past participle*, ► 6.9) to relate the two moments of time.

2 A future perfect progressive form (**will have been** + **-ing** form, ► 6.6) is also possible and carries the usual implications of the progressive aspect concerning *duration* and *incompletion* (► 11.5).

Verbs not normally used in the progressive aspect

11.19 The use of the progressive aspect focusses attention on the fact that an activity lasts over a period of time. This implies that the activity will not go on forever, that its *duration* is limited. But there are some verbs which, by their very nature, imply a permanent state:

Two plus two **equals** four.
Water **consists** of hydrogen and oxygen.

The use of the progressive in cases like these is impossible as it would contradict the essential 'permanent' meaning of the verb.

In a similar way the following groups of verbs refer to a state which, even though it may change, is considered essentially permanent. Therefore they do *not* normally appear in the progressive aspect.

1 He**'s** American.
Plants **need** water.
The car **belongs** to me.
I **have** three sisters.
These prices do not **include** the service charge.
Good health **depends** on many factors.

1 verbs which express the idea of *existence, possession* or some form of fixed relationship: **appear, be, belong to, consist of, contain, cost, depend on, exist, fit, have, include, involve, mean, need, owe, own, resemble, seem, weigh**;

2 I don't **understand**.
I **doubt** if I'll go.
I don't **remember** her name,

2 verbs referring to a *state of mind*: **believe, doubt, forget, guess, know, imagine, realise, recognise, remember, suppose, think, understand**;

3 She **hates** fish.
Do you **want** to do it?
We **prefer** to stay here.

3 verbs expressing an *opinion* or a *desire*; **hate, like, love, prefer, want, wish**;

4 I don't **hear** anything.
This wine **tastes** good.
Do you **see** him?
They **smelt** the smoke.

Compare:
Can you **see** him?
They **could smell** the smoke.

4 verbs referring to *physical senses* (verbs of perception): **feel, hear, see, smell, taste**. These verbs are often used with **can** in the present and **could** in the past, rather than the simple present or simple past.

Permanent states and temporary activities

11.20

1 a) I **think** it's an excellent film. (**think** = believe)
b) I**'ve been thinking** about your offer. (**think** = consider, reflect)

a) We **have** a flat in London. (**have** = possess)
b) We**'re having** steak for dinner. (**have** = eat)

1 Some of the verbs mentioned in paragraph 11.19 may be used not to refer to (**a**) a *permanent* state, but rather to (**b**) a *temporary* activity, which has limited duration in time. In this case the verb may appear in the *progressive* form.

2 a) I'm not **feeling** very well today.
   This holiday **is costing** us a lot of money.

  b) He**'s being** very generous.

2 It may also happen that for various reasons we wish to treat what is normally considered to be (**a**) a *permanent* state as (**b**) a *temporary* activity. The effect may be *ironic*.

Position in time

Indefinite time

11.21

We may wish to refer to past, present or future but without mentioning a specific time. The following table outlines some of the more common means of indefinite time reference.

Distant	PAST ← Near	— PRESENT —	Near → FUTURE	Distant
	recently		soon	
	lately	nowadays		
some time ago		these days		
once			in a while	
a long time ago				eventually
ages ago				after a long time

All of these expressions can be placed at the end of the sentence or, when given emphasis (▶ 18.2), at the beginning.
  Once, recently, soon, eventually may also be placed before the verb, but after the verb **be** or the first auxiliary verb (▶ position of adverbs 1.5).

11.22

1 Everybody has a television **nowadays**.
  These days people do their shopping in supermarkets.

1 **Nowadays** and **these days** can be used to refer to a *present situation* or *habitual activity*, i.e. the present in general, not just the present moment.

2 We've had some good weather **lately**.
  I haven't seen George **recently**.
  We have **recently** received a consignment from you.
  Have you seen any good films **lately**?

2 **Lately** and **recently** refer to the *past* but usually there is some link with the *present* because of *proximity in time*. They are therefore normally associated with the *present perfect tense* (▶ 11.4).

3 There used to be a field here **once**.
  Once upon a time there lived a king who had a beautiful daughter.
  They must be there now – the train left **ages ago**.
  A: We were here together **once**, do you remember?
  B: Yes, but that was **ages ago**.

3 **Once** is used to refer to a situation which *no longer exists*. Children's stories often begin with **Once upon a time**.
  Ages ago is used in informal English when the speaker wishes to emphasise *distance* in the past. These past time expressions are used with the *simple past, past progressive* or other past tenses (excluding the present perfect).

4 The doctor will be here **soon**.
The meeting will begin **presently**.
Henry II became king and **soon** established his authority.
They met at a party, **soon** fell in love and **eventually** got married.

5 Did you stay there **long**?
No, I didn't stay (very) **long**.
She lived in America **for a long time**.

6 A: Do you **ever** read westerns?
B: No, I **never** do.

A: Has she **ever** smoked?
B: Yes, she has occasionally.
I **hardly ever** go to parties now.
If you **ever** do that again you'll be sorry.

4 The time expressions referring to the *future* are used with the verb structures described in paragraphs 11.11–11.16.
In formal English **presently** is sometimes used with a similar meaning to **soon**.
The same expressions may also be used in *past* tense narratives to carry the events forward in time.

5 Notice that the adverb **long** is used in interrogative and negative sentences but not normally in affirmative sentences. The expression **for a long time** is used instead.

6 Questions referring to indefinite time may be made using **ever** which means 'at any time'.
Ever is used mostly in interrogative sentences but it can also appear in affirmative sentences after **if** and in certain sentences with negative implications, e.g. **hardly ever** (▶ 2.14). The negative form **not ... ever** has the same meaning as **never** but is not very commonly used.

Definite time: precise moments

11.23

1 a) **at: eight o'clock, breakfast, lunch, dinner, dawn, sunset, Christmas, Easter, night**

b) **on: Sunday (Sundays), Friday morning (Friday mornings), June 2nd**

c) **in: February, 1986, spring, the morning, the afternoon, the evening**

2 I met him **last week**.
The concert is **this Friday**.
At that time very few families had television.

1 To refer to *specific moments* of time the following prepositions are used:
a) **at:** before *clock times, moments during the day, festivals* and *weekends;*
b) **on:** before the *days of week* and *precise dates*. A plural form of the day suggests that the action is repeated regularly.
NOTE: **Today, tomorrow, yesterday** have no preposition.
c) **in:** before *months, years, centuries, seasons* and most *parts of the day*.

2 Prepositions are normally omitted before phrases beginning with **last, next, this, that, each, every,** (except **at this/that time/ moment, on this/that occasion**).

11.24

1 a) The building was put up ten years **ago**.
She left about five minutes **ago**.
In two hours' **time** we shall be landing.
We will have finished **in** half an hour.
You'll be at home **in** three hours **from now**.

1 A definite time reference may also be given by calculating the time period backwards or forwards from a specific moment.
a) If that specific moment is *now*, *past* time reference can be expressed using **ago** and a *future* time reference with the phrase **in ... (time)** or **in ... from now**. **Ago** always follows the period of time to which it refers.

b) In 1980 Sam entered the firm that his father had joined forty years **before**.
Frank left the party at midnight. Shirley had already gone home an hour **earlier**.
My mother is coming next Saturday and Dad will get here two days **after**.
I saw him first on Wednesday and we met again two days **later**.

2 a) I'll never forget that holiday last year. We had a really good time **then**.

b) Come back on Friday. The exam result should be out **then**.

b) If that specific moment is in the *past* or the *future*, calculating backwards or forwards can be made using **before/ earlier** or **after/later**. These words follow the period of time to which they refer.

For *sequence* words ▶ 11.42.

2 When a moment of time has been established further reference to it may be made by means of **then**. **Then** may refer to a time in either (**a**) the *past* or (**b**) the *future*. Similar expressions are **at that time** and **at that moment**.

For other uses of **then** ▶ 11.42.

Definite time: periods of time

1.25 We may take a different perspective on time and consider it not simply as a *succession of moments* but as a *period* extending from one moment to another. This perspective, drawing out the aspect of *duration*, is indicated by a different group of prepositions and adverbial phrases.

During

1.26

1 She came **in** the summer.

2 She often came to see me **during** the summer.

3 You'll have to do your homework **over** the weekend.
The couple behind me were talking **throughout** the film.
She kept on waking up **all through** the night.
We waited for him **all day long**.

1 In this example 'the summer' is treated as a specific time, almost like a date or an hour.

2 In this example the preposition **during** stretches 'the summer' into a period of time.

3 Other expressions which have the same 'stretching' effect are: **over, (all) through, throughout** and **all . . . long**.

Before, after

1.27

I enjoy the sense of excitement **before** a football match.
My children are always irritable **after** a long journey.

The prepositions **before** and **after** refer, respectively, to the period *preceding* or *following* the point of time mentioned.
For **before** and **after** as *conjunctions* ▶ 11.37.

Between, from

11.28

1 a) The office is open **between** 9.00 **and** 12.30.

b) The American Civil War lasted **from** 1861 **to** 1865.

c) He worked at IBM **from** the end of the war **until** last year.

2 I won't accept any excuses **from** now **on**. **From** October **on** the weather grew colder.

1 A period of time may be indicated by specifying when it begins and when it ends, using:
a) **between ... and**;
b) **from ... (up) to**;
c) **from ... (up) until/till**.

2 When the opening moment of a time period is given but no concluding moment, the expression **from ... on** may be used.

Until, so far

11.29

1 I lived in Paris **until** 1976.

2 There has never been a woman Prime Minister **until now**. (= But now there is one)

3 There has never been a woman Prime Minister **so far**. (= And there still isn't one)

1 **Until** (or, more informally, **till**) always refers to the terminating moment of a period of time.

2 **Until now** therefore implies that there is a *new* situation.

3 **So far** doesn't imply any change in the situation.

By, within, in

11.30

1 The contract must be signed **by** Friday. You should have the cheque **by** next week. I had to pay the fine **within** two weeks.

2 You can do that job **in** about an hour.

1 **By** and **within** are 'deadline' words referring forward to a *culminating future point of time*. **By** refers to the specific future *moment*; **within** (or sometimes simply **in**) refers to the *period* of time leading up to it.

2 **In** may also be used in a similar way to refer to a period of time necessary for an action.

Since, for

11.31

1 She lived in Paris **for** ten years.
A: Have you been waiting **for** a long time?
B: Yes, I've been standing here **since** eight o'clock.
The weather will remain warm **for** several days.
We've had that car **since** 1985.

2 I'll love you **for ever**. (**For ever** or **forever** = always)
Sit here **for the time being** (= for the moment, temporarily).

1 **For** refers to a *period* of time. **Since** refers to the *initial moment* of a period of time.
For may refer to a period of time in the *past* or in the *future*. **Since** can only refer to the *past*. When the period extends from a moment in the past up to the present, **for** and **since** are used with the *present perfect* (▶ 11.4).

2 In addition **for** is used in a number of idiomatic time expressions. Notice that **for ever** is often written as one word (**forever**).

Relationships in time

Actions finished and unfinished

Already, yet

1.32

1 a) We had **already** finished eating when he arrived.

   b) I'm sorry I haven't read the report **yet**.

   c) If you phone him before six, he won't have left **yet**.

2 a) The film **has already started**.

   b) By the time we get there the film **will already have started**.

3 a) Don't worry – the train won't have left **yet**.

   b) She hadn't **yet decided** what to do.

4 A: Have you taken your holiday **yet**?
   B: No, I haven't decided where to go **yet**.
   A: You're lucky – I've **already** had my holiday.

5 You know the story very well – have you **already** read the book?
   There's no light in the house – have they **already** left?

6 A: Does she know that **yet**?
   B: Yes, she **already** knows that.

1 **Already** and **yet** are closely associated with the *perfect aspect*. They reinforce the concept of an action taking place (or not taking place) before a certain moment of time. According to whether this moment of time is in the past, present or future, **already/yet** combine with (**a**) *past perfect*, (**b**) *present perfect* or (**c**) *future perfect* verbs.

2 **Already** normally appears immediately after the first auxiliary verb.

3 **Yet** usually appears at the end of the sentence (**a**). However, it is also sometimes placed before the past participle, especially with the past perfect (**b**).

4 Normally **yet** is used in *negative* and *interrogative* sentences and **already** in *affirmative* sentences.

5 **Already** may appear in *interrogative* sentences when the speaker has some reason to expect an affirmative response.

6 **Already** and **yet** can also be used with *present tense* verbs.

Still

1.33

1 He's fifteen years old and he **still** wears short trousers.
The house is **still** there after all these years.
Come back next year. I'll **still** be here.

1 The meaning of **still** is related to that of **already/yet** but it is used in cases where a situation or an activity continues longer than expected. It emphasises the sense of continuity.
Still is most frequently used in affirmative sentences. It is usually placed before the verb, but after the verb **be** or the first auxiliary verb.

2 He **still** hasn't finished it. (= I think he's taking a long time)

Compare:
He hasn't finished it **yet**. (= I expect he will soon finish)
He has **already** finished it. (= He finished it more quickly than I expected)

3 I don't smoke **any more**.
Eric is still in the factory but Stan doesn't work there **any longer**.
Credit cards will **no longer** be accepted.
By 1955 ration cards were **no longer** in use.

2 In negative sentences **still** has an emphatic meaning and is placed before the auxiliary verb. Compare the use of **still** in a negative sentence with **already** and **yet**.

3 **Not ... any more, not ... any longer,** and, more formally, **no longer,** can be considered opposites of **still**. They are used when a situation or an activity which was in operation in the past has now come to an end.
Any more and **any longer** are placed at the end of the sentence, **no longer** is placed before the verb, but after the verb **be** or the first auxiliary.

Just

11.34

1 A: Are you ready?
   B: Yes, we've **just** finished breakfast.
   The film had **just** started when I walked in.
   By the time you get here I will have **just** left.

1 **Just** refers to an action completed very recently in relation to a moment in past, present or future time. It is therefore normally used with *past perfect, present perfect* or *future perfect* tenses. It is placed before the past participle.

2 A: Are you ready?
   B: Yes, I'm **just** coming (now.)

2 In informal English **just** is often used as an alternative for **now** with *present progressive*.

Time conjunctions

While, as ·

11.35   **While** and **as** are used when two actions occur at the same time.

1 **While** I was doing the shopping she was cleaning the house.
Next week **while** you're lying on the beach I'll be working in the office.

1 **While** is often used with verbs in the *progressive form* when two actions take place at the same time and both take place over a period of time.

2 **As** the illness developed he gradually lost all his energy.
The days grew colder **as** the winter drew nearer.

2 **As** is used for two actions or situations which develop simultaneously, one depending on the other (▶ 16.4).

3 **While** he was checking the figures he noticed a mistake.
Look at the carvings on the door **as** you are entering the church.

3 Both **as** and **while** can be used when one short action takes place during a longer action. In this case **as** and **while** are followed by the progressive form.

4 **Just as** I got into the bath the doorbell rang. The bomb exploded **just as** he opened the car door.

5 You can stay with us **as long as** you like.

4 **As,** or **just as,** may also be used in sentences with simple verb tenses to refer to two sudden actions which take place at the same time (like **when** ▶ 11.36).

5 Notice that **as long as** may refer to *time* as well as to *condition* (▶ 20.10).

When

11.36

1 a) **When** the bell rang both boxers came out. **When** the champion hit him he fell down.

  b) **When** I arrived Alan was watching TV. Brazil were winning **when** the referee stopped the game.

  c) **When** I went to school we studied Latin. We had a beautiful house **when** we lived in Ireland.

2 **When** Brazil were winning the referee stopped the game. I arrived **when** Alan was watching TV.

3 **When** she had finished her homework she went to bed. I'll clean the kitchen **when** you have finished all the cooking.

4 **When** he saw the policeman come in he walked out. The audience applauded **when** the orchestra stopped playing.

5 **The moment** the bell rings the children run out of the classroom. We'll ring you **as soon as** we arrive. **Immediately** you hear the alarm you must leave the building.

1 **When** (like **while** and **as** ▶ 11.35) can be used to refer to two actions which occur *at the same time*. It may be followed by a simple verb form (i.e. not a progressive form) and refer to (**a**) two simultaneous sudden actions, or (**b**) a short action which interrupts a longer action, or (**c**) two actions which both take place over a long period of time.

2 **When** may also be followed by a progressive verb to refer to a longer action interrupted by a shorter one.

3 Unlike **while** and **as, when** may be used to refer to two actions occurring at different moments and expressed in different tenses. Here, **when** has the same meaning as **after**.

4 Similarly, if both actions are expressed in the same tense, **when** may indicate that one follows immediately after the other.

5 Other conjunctions used in the same way to refer to one action following immediately after another are: **as soon as, the moment, immediately**.

Once, before, after

11.37

Once he had learnt the language he felt at home. **After** the machinery had been repaired work restarted. **Before** I left home I had never done any cooking.

A clearer time interval between two actions can be established using **once, before, after**. For **before, after** as prepositions ▶ 11.27.

Whenever

11.38

> **Whenever** it rains the traffic gets chaotic.
> The police should be called **whenever** there's an accident.

Two activities which take place at the same time not once but repeatedly can be linked using **whenever**.

Since, until, by the time

11.39

> What have you been doing **since** I last saw you?
> Don't begin **until** you are given a signal.
> There won't be any seats left **by the time** we get there.

Since, until, by the time are conjunctions used with the same general meaning as the prepositions **since** (▶ 11.31), **until** (▶ 11.29) and **by** (▶ 11.30).

Time conjunctions/prepositions and verb forms

11.40

> **When** you **see** Jim tomorrow say hello from me.
> I'll read your book **immediately** I **finish** this one.
> **The moment** he **gets** home he'll switch on the television.
> The election results will be broadcast **as soon as** they **have arrived**.
> The trouble will begin **after** the match **has finished**.

All of the conjunctions mentioned may be used to link past, present or future actions (except **since,** which cannot refer to the future). However a verb form with **will** and **going to** is *not* normally used after these conjunctions. Therefore even when the reference is to future time the verb following the conjunction will have *present tense* form or, in some cases, *present perfect* form.

11.41

> 1 **After winning** the match, they reached the Cup Final.
>
>   Compare:
>   **After they had won** the match, they reached the Cup Final.
>   He read the contract carefully **before signing** it.
>
> 2 **Hearing** my mother's cry, I asked her what was wrong.
>
>   Compare:
>   **When I heard** my mother's cry, I asked her what was wrong.
>   **Having lost** all its business, the shop was obliged to close.

When the two verbs being linked have the same subject it is possible to use an **-ing** form either (**1**) *preceded*, or, in some cases (**2**), *not preceded* by a time preposition (▶ 6.25).

Sequence

11.42

1 (at a vending machine)
First of all you put in the money. **Secondly** you choose a drink, and **finally** you press the red button here.

2 (recipe)
Break two eggs into a bowl and **then** add a spoonful of milk. **Next** beat the mixture and **after that** add a little grated cheese.
I brushed my teeth; **after that** I went to bed.
Compare:
After I brushed my teeth I went to bed.

3 (recipe)
Pour the mixture into a pan which you have heated **beforehand**. Add the tomatoes which you have **previously** cut up.

4 If you fail you will have to take the exam **again**.
I saw her **again** last night.

1 To describe a *sequence* of actions, adverbs formed from ordinal numbers may be used (e.g. **first (of all), firstly, secondly**). The concluding action is introduced by **finally**.

2 Actions after the first can also be introduced by **then, next, after that, afterwards, later, subsequently**. **After that** must not be confused with the conjunction **after** (▶ 11.37).

3 To refer back to an earlier action we can use **previously, earlier** or **beforehand**.

4 **Again** is used to refer to an action which takes place a further time. It comes after the verb and the object.

Frequency

11.43

The *frequency* with which an event happens can be expressed using the adverbs in the table below. To ask about frequency the most commonly used question is **How often?** (▶ 2.10).

LESS FREQUENT						MORE FREQUENT
never	rarely seldom hardly ever	now and then occasionally	sometimes	frequently often	usually generally normally mostly	always

11.44

1 He used to visit us **now and then**.

People **normally** telephone us – they **hardly ever** write.
I **always** get up at six o'clock.
He is **often** late for work.
I have **never** read such an interesting book.
They are **always** out in the evening.

1 Adverbs of frequency are normally placed *before* the verb, but *after* the verb **be** or the first auxiliary verb. Longer expressions, like **now and then,** are usually at the *end* of the sentence. Other expressions with the same meaning as **now and then** are **now and again** and **from time to time**.

2 Take the tablets **three times a day**.
The phone rang **every ten minutes**
(= at intervals of ten minutes).
I take a bath **every other day** in winter.
I've been to Rome **twice,** in 1965 and in
1975.

3 The news was broadcast **hourly**.
The magazine is published **monthly**.
The light flashed **at five second intervals**
(= every five seconds).
She visited the prison **at intervals of two
months**.

2 A more specific indication of frequency can
be given using the structures:
a) **(ten) times a (week)**;
b) **every (three) (months)**;
c) **every other (week)** (= on alternate
weeks).
Notice the use of **once** and **twice** (*not* **one
time, two times**).

3 Other adverbs of frequency are made from
nouns and adjectives referring to units of
time: **daily, weekly, hourly, monthly, yearly,
annually**.
Frequency may also be indicated in certain
expressions using the noun **intervals**.

Measurement of time

Clock time

| 2 o'clock | quarter past 2 | half past 2 | quarter to 3 |

11.45

1 What**'s** the time?
What time **is** it?

2 It's six **o'clock**.
Compare:
It's five minutes past six.

3 It's (a) **quarter past** ten (= 10.15).
It's **half past** ten (= 10.30).
It's (a) **quarter to** eleven (= 10.45).

4 It's eleven **minutes past** seven (= 7.11).
It's twenty-one **minutes past** eight (= 8.21).
It's three **minutes to** nine (= 8.57).
It's ten **minutes to** seven (= 6.50).

5 It's twenty-five **(minutes)** to eight.
It's ten **(minutes)** past nine.

6 It's **five twenty** (= 5.20).
It's ten **forty-six** (= 10.46).
I took the **ten-fifteen** (train) to London
(= 10.15).

1 A moment of time is always considered
singular.

2 The phrase **o'clock** is only used for a time
which coincides exactly with the hour.

3 The quarter hour intervals are normally
referred to using **quarter past, half past,
quarter to**. **A** is often included before
quarter past/to.

4 All times until half past the hour are referred
to as **minutes past**. After the half hour, times
are referred to as **minutes to** the following
hour.

5 In referring to five-minute intervals the word
minutes can be omitted.

6 In some contexts (e.g. radio time checks,
station announcements etc.) a different
system is normally used. The hours and
minutes are simply read as numbers.

7 The train leaves at seven **a.m.** (= seven in the morning.)
The meeting is at seven **p.m.** (= seven in the evening).

7 **a.m.** (ante meridiem) refers to the twelve hours from midnight until the following midday.
p.m. (post meridiem) refers to the twelve hours from midday to the following midnight.

The date

11.46

1 January **the tenth,** March **the eighteenth** (British English)
the tenth of January, **the eighteenth** of March (British English)
January **tenth,** March **eighteenth** (American English)

1 To express the date *ordinal number*s are used (▶ 9.21). In spoken British English the number is always preceded by the definite article **the.** In American English **the** is usually omitted. Notice the two alternative ways of referring to the date in British English.

2 1756 = **seventeen fifty-six**
1983 = **nineteen eighty-three**
1907 = **nineteen hundred and seven**

2 In speech the year is expressed by two consecutive numbers.

3 March 1st 1986
1st March 1986
March 1 1986
1 March 1986

3 Notice the different ways of writing the date.

4 a) 10.1.1985 = **the tenth of January** nineteen eighty-five

b) 10.1.1985 = **October first** nineteen eighty-five

4 If the date is given only in figures:
a) in British English the sequence is: *day, month, year;*
b) in American English the sequence is: *month, day, year.*

5
Sunday	**January**
Monday	**February**
Tuesday	**March**
Wednesday	**April**
Thursday	**May**
Friday	**June**
Saturday	**July**
	August
	September
	October
	November
	December

5 Names of the *days of the week* and *months* are always written with *capital letters.*

6 Julius Caesar was assassinated in 44 **BC** (or **B.C.**).
Augustus Caesar died in 14 **AD** (or **AD** 14).
The French Revolution took place in 1789.

6 **BC** (or **B.C.**) = (before Christ) is usually written after the relevant year. **AD** (or **A.D.**) (= *Anno Domini*, i.e. after the birth of Christ) can be written before or after the year, and is only used when there is a possibility of confusion.

For the use of prepositions ▶ 11.23.

12 Space

This chapter is concerned with the language relevant to the question **Where?**. It deals with the use of place prepositions to describe a relationship in space. These prepositions can be divided into two main groups: those used to indicate *position* and those referring to *movement* from one position to another. The chapter also examines the use of adverbs to express ideas related to space.

Position in space

At, in, on

12.2

The three prepositions most frequently used to refer to position are **at, in, on.**

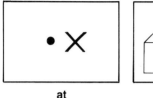 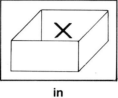 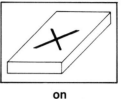 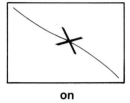

| at | in | on | on |

At

12.3

1 I saw her **at** the window.
They waited **at** the entrance.
Does this train stop **at** all stations?
We turned off the motorway **at** Preston.

2 a) We won't be **at** home tonight.
I met her **at** John's (house).
I bought this painting **at** Harrods.
Did he get his hair cut **at** the new barber's?

b) My friends live **at** 94 Kew Road, Richmond.

c) I think she's **at** school.
Is she still **at** the office?
Did you meet **at** the party or **at** the cinema?

1 The preposition **at** is used in connection with a place which is thought of as a *point* in space without considering its dimensions of length, width and height.

2 In particular **at** is used:
a) to talk about people's homes or business premises;
b) with precise addresses;
c) with places of study, work and entertainment.

In

12.4

1 Is there anything to drink **in** the fridge?
Jack is upstairs **in** his room.
Do you keep your car **in** a garage?

2 a) Do you want to take a walk **in** the park?
I think Dad's **in** the garden.
He set up the tent **in** a field.

1 The preposition **in** is used in connection with a place which is thought of as possessing *length, width* and *height* and therefore able to be entered.

2 In particular **in** is used to refer to:
a) places which, although not completely enclosed, have a wall, fence or hedge around them;

b) We had a marvellous holiday **in** Norway.
Napoleon was born **in** Corsica.
He lived **in** London for many years.

b) large areas (e.g. countries, deserts, large islands, towns);

NOTE: **On** is used for small islands (▶ 12.5).

c) The bank's **in** Victoria Street.

c) a street, but not a precise address;

d) I read it **in** today's paper.
You'll find her number **in** the telephone directory.

d) newspapers, magazines and books;

e) There was a strange green light **in** the sky.

e) the universe, the sky.

3 We stopped **at** Coventry on the way to Birmingham.

3 For towns both **at** and **in** may be used, but from a different perspective.

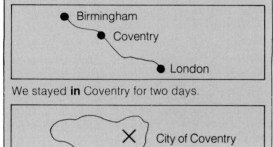

We stayed **in** Coventry for two days.

On

12.5

The preposition **on** is used in the following cases:

1 Your magazine's **on** the table over there.
Look – the key's **on** the floor.
Let's sit **on** the grass for a while.
There's some tomato **on** your shirt.

1 in connection with a place which is thought of as a two-dimensional surface area;

2 The station's **on** the main line to Glasgow.
The village lies **on** the Austrian border.
There's a nice pub down there **on** the river.

2 in connection with a place which is thought of as a point along a line;

3 a) The answers are **on** page 92.

b) The shoe department is **on** the second floor.

c) It's a beautiful fishing port **on** the Black Sea.

d) The pilot's already **on** the plane.
Compare:
She sat **in** the car until the rain stopped.

e) Napoleon died **on** St Helena.

f) In Britain you must drive **on** the left.

3 in particular to refer to:
a) a page;
b) floors in a building (but we say **in** the basement);
c) permanent location next to a lake or the sea;
d) large forms of transport, e.g. planes, trains, but not cars (**in** is also possible sometimes);
e) small islands;
f) the positions **right** and **left**.

Other place prepositions

12.6 Other commonly used prepositions are:

above; below; over; on top of; under; underneath; beneath
among; between
opposite; in front of; behind; at the front of; at the back of
inside; outside
beyond
beside; next to; by; near; far from
at the top of; at the bottom of

There is a house **in** a field. A man is standing **outside** the house **by** the door. A woman is **inside** the house **at** the window. There is a bicycle **under** the window. **In front of** the house there are some flowers. A cat is sitting **on** the grass **among** the flowers. There is a horse **behind** the house and a bird sitting **on top of** the chimney. The house is **between** two trees. There are some clouds **in** the sky **over** the field and **above** the clouds there is a plane.

Above, below, over, under, on top of

12.7

1 The lamp **over/above** that table is broken.
There was a shelf **under/below** the mirror.
She put a cloth **over** the cake because of the flies.
There's the cat **under** your chair.
Mexico City is 7,000 feet **above** sea level.
Clouds were floating **below** the top of the mountain.

2 I left the newspaper **on top of** the television.
We put a fairy **on top of** the Christmas tree.
She wore a pullover **under(neath)** her coat.

3 We put the books **on top of** the cupboard, which was full.
Your shirt is on the shelf **at the top of** the cupboard.
His office is **at the top of** the building.
Write your signature **at the bottom of** the page.
We saw some fish swimming **at the bottom of** the pool.
There is a pipe **under** the swimming pool to take away the water.

1 Both **over/under** and **above/below** indicate a difference of level and they are often interchangeable.
However **over** and **under** can be used to express the idea of covering or hiding whereas **above/below** are only concerned with relative levels and can be used to relate two points which are distant from one another in space.

2 **On top of** may be used instead of **on** to suggest direct physical contact with a surface area which is limited in size. The opposite of **on top of** is **under(neath)**.

3 Notice the difference between **on top of**, **under** (referring to external positions) and **at the top/bottom of** (referring to internal positions).

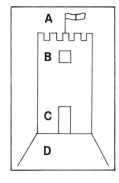

The flag (**A**) is **on top of** the tower.
The window (**B**) is **at the top of** the tower.
The door (**C**) is **at the bottom of** the tower.
The hill (**D**) is **under** the tower.

Among, between

12.8

The accident happened **between** Manchester and Leeds.
Mrs Moore was sitting in the bus **between** her two children.
A number of policemen were standing **among** the spectators.
It was a small village **among** the hills.

Between indicates an intermediate position with reference to two other points.

Among indicates position in a space with reference to an indefinite number of other points.

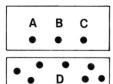

B is **between A** and **C**.

D is **among** the other points.

Lake Constance lies **between** Germany, Switzerland and Austria.

Between is sometimes used to refer to more than two people or things when each of them has a clear separate identity.

Opposite, in front of, behind

12.9

1 I couldn't see the film because the woman **in front of** me was wearing an enormous hat.
He was standing **in front of** them in the queue.
A stranger sat down **opposite** her at the table and stared into her eyes.
There's a cinema just **opposite** the school.

1 **Opposite** emphasises a 'face to face' relationship:

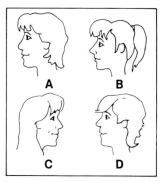

A is **in front of** B.

C is **opposite** D.

2 A tree had fallen across the rails **in front of** the train.
The first-class carriages are **at the front of** the train.
At the back of the office was a small cupboard.
The children hid **behind** a tree.

2 Notice the difference between **in front of**, **behind** (external positions) and **at the front/ back of** (internal positions).

A is **in front of** the bus.
B is **at the front of** the bus.
C is **at the back of** the bus.
D is **behind** the bus.

Beyond

12.10

I could see a mountain **beyond** the river.
We noticed differences in the people the moment we went **beyond** the frontier.

Beyond indicates a position more distant than the point of reference given.

Next to, near, far from

12.11

1 Is the school **next to** the library?
Wouldn't you like to have a house **beside** the sea?
I want to sit **by** you, not **next to** her.
The sofa is **beside** the television.

Compare:
The sofa is **at the side of** the room.

1 **Next to, beside, by,** all indicate an immediately adjacent position.
Notice that **at the side of** refers to internal position (compare at **the top/bottom of** ▶ 12.7, **at the front/back of** ▶ 12.9).

2 The school is **near** the library but not **next to** it.
I want to have the table **close to** the wall but without touching it.

3 A: Do you live **far from** your office?
  B: Yes, my house is **a long way from** the city centre.
   Let's go to the park. It isn't very **far from** here.
  A: You said Oxford was **close to** London but it takes an hour by train.
  B: It isn't **far from** London. An hour is nothing.

4 I felt very **close to** my sister after our parents died.
We are **far from** satisfied with your behaviour.

2 **Near** and **close to** both indicate a position of proximity, not necessarily immediately adjacent.

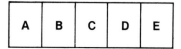

A is **next to** B.
A is **near** C.

3 The opposite of **near** is **far from** or **a long way from**.
Far from (and also the adverb **far**) are mainly used in negative and interrogative sentences. In affirmative sentences **a long way from** is normally used.
Near/close to and **far/a long way from** are relative terms.
What seems **near** to one person may appear **far** to another.

4 **Near/close to** and **far/a long way from** may refer to a psychological as well as a physical sense of distance.

For similar distinctions of physical/psychological distance see **here/there** ▶ 12.18; **this/that** ▶ 8.16–8.18.

Movement in space

12.12

He stepped **in front of** the bus.
The horse jumped **over** the gate.
Come **near** me.
He kicked the ball **between** the goal posts.
The shark swam **under** the boat and appeared on the other side.

The prepositions discussed in 12.2–12.11 refer essentially to position in space. However, depending on the context, they can also indicate a sense of *movement* when used with verbs of movement.

To, at, into, onto, towards, as far as

12.13

1 a) I hope I can go **to** Ireland next summer.
   Shall we go **to** the cinema?
   They came **to** the wrong conclusion.

  b) Please take me **home**.
   Compare:
   The little girl took the kitten **to her home**.

2 a) Finally we arrived **at** the hotel.

   Compare:
   They arrived **home** very late.
   We arrived **in** London that evening.

1 a) **To** is the most commonly used preposition to refer to the 'destination' (real or metaphorical) of a movement.

  b) Notice that **to** is not used with the word **home** used on its own. (However **to** is used if **home** is defined in some way.)

2 a) The preposition **at** is normally used with the verb **arrive** (except before **home** used on its own) but **in** can also be used with towns and countries.

b) Stop shouting **at** me.
Mummy, he threw a stone **at** me.
Compare:
Shout **to** me when you're ready.
Throw the ball **to** me.

3 a) He walked **into** the room without asking for permission.
She put all the clothes **into** the suitcase.
The glass fell **onto** the floor.
The cat jumped silently **onto** the shelf.

b) He ran **towards** the door but the guard stopped him.
We jumped onto a tram going **towards** the city centre.

c) Can you give me a lift **as far as** the station?
She walked **as far as** the edge of the woods.

b) **At** is used when somebody is the subject of abuse or an attack (especially with the verbs **laugh, shoot, throw, shout**).

3 There are other prepositions which refer to a 'destination':

a) **Into** and **onto** combine the idea of movement with the *in* and *on* concept (▶ 12.4, 12.5).

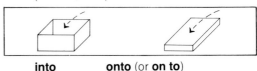

into   onto (or on to)

b) **Towards** refers to the direction of a 'destination' but the destination point itself is not necessarily reached.

c) **As far as** refers to a 'destination', drawing attention to the idea of the distance involved.

Other prepositions of movement

12.14

Other prepositions that refer to movement are:

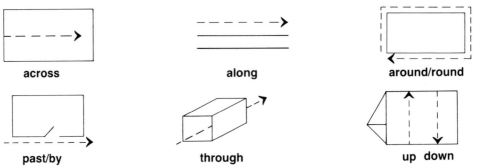

across   along   around/round

past/by   through   up down

You have to drive **across** the town to get to the station.

We cycled **along** the road for miles without seeing anyone.

We walked **around** the outside of the house looking at the damage.

The porter walked **past** the first three rooms, then stopped and went **into** the fourth.

She drove **by** the supermarket but didn't stop to buy anything.

The train went **through** the tunnel and reappeared on the other side of the mountain.

The children ran **up** the hill and rolled **down** the other side.

From, out of, off

12.15

1 They got the information **from** the
   newspaper.
   Has she come back **from** work?
   How far is the underground station **from**
   here?

2 Get **out of** this room immediately!
   He took a notebook **out of** his pocket.
   The cat jumped **off** the table and **onto** a
   chair.
   The boy pushed his friend **off** the edge of the
   swimming pool.

3 When the bus stopped he **got off** and **got
   into** a taxi.

1 Some prepositions that imply movement
   indicate the starting point of the movement
   rather than the 'destination'. The most
   common is **from.** The idea of 'movement'
   may be metaphorical.

2 **Out of** and **off** are the opposites of,
   respectively, **into** and **onto** (▶ 12.13).

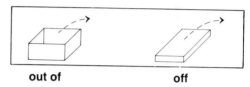

   out of   **off**

3 Notice the use of **get into/get out of** with
   small means of transport (e.g. car, taxi, lift)
   and of **get on/get off** with *large* ones (e.g.
   bus, train, plane, ship) (▶ 12.5).

12.16

There were houses **along** the river.
The orchard is **across** the field.
Some people were standing **around** the
fountain.

The prepositions discussed in 12.12–12.14,
usually refer to movement. However, depending
on the context, they may also indicate position
without necessarily implying movement.

NOTE: Position of place prepositions in the
sentence: for interrogative sentences ▶ 2.9; for
relative clauses ▶ 8.23, 8.24.

Adverbs of place and adverbial clauses

Adverbs and prepositions

12.17

1 a) Mr Jones is **in** the garden.
   b) Mr Jones isn't **in** tonight.

   a) She's looking **out of** the window.
   b) She's gone **out.**

   a) I saw her coming **down** the stairs.
   b) He slipped and fell **down**.

2 The man stopped for a moment and then
   walked **on**.
   Drive **on** until you come to the traffic lights.
   We stood on the bridge and watched a
   beautiful yacht sailing **by**.

1 Many of the prepositions discussed in 12.2–
   12.16 can also be used as adverbs referring
   to position or movement. In examples (**a**) the
   words in bold type are prepositions; in (**b**)
   they are adverbs or adverb particles (see
   Glossary for definitions).

2 **On** as an adverb of place has a different
   meaning from the preposition **on.** The adverb
   refers to a continuation of a movement or an
   action. The adverb **by** has a similar meaning
   to the preposition **by** in the sense of **past**
   ▶ 12.14.

3 She has a house in York and her mother lives **nearby**.
There were some menacing black clouds **overhead**.

4 Give me **back** the book when you've finished it.
After the meal they went **back** home.

5 She went **straight** home without stopping anywhere.
Be careful – there's a police car **ahead**.
Go **straight ahead**. You can't miss it.
Walk **straight on** as far as the bank.

3 **Nearby** and **overhead** are adverbs related to the prepositions **near** and **over**.

4 **Back** is an adverb which refers to a return movement.

5 The adverb **straight** refers to a direct forward movement; **ahead** refers to a forward position (they are often used together).
Straight on is used in the same sense as **straight ahead**.

For the use of verbs with adverbs and prepositions ▶ 7.1–7.7.

Here and there

12.18

1 Leave the letters **here** on my desk.
The newsagent's is **there**, next to the station.
This is my room **here**, opposite the bathroom.
Can you see those people **over there**?

2 Ask him to **bring** the documents **here** to my office.
Take all these things and put them away **there** in the cupboard.

1 The adverb **here** refers to a position considered to be near the speaker; **there** indicates a position considered to be at a distance from the speaker. There is a similar distinction between **this/that** ▶ 8.16 (and also between **near/far** ▶ 12.11).

2 **Here** is used with verbs implying movement towards the speaker (e.g. **come, bring**).
There is used with verbs implying movement away from, or at a distance from, the speaker (e.g. **go, take**).

Compound adverbs

12.19

1 Did you happen to see my atlas **anywhere**?
I'm sure I've searched for it **everywhere**.

2 a) He rushed **forward** as if he wanted to hit me.
The lift was moving **downwards**.
Car doors always open **outwards**.

b) Your room is **upstairs** on the left.
When the doorbell rang she rushed **downstairs**.

1 Compounds can be made of **where** and certain determiners: **somewhere, anywhere, nowhere, everywhere, elsewhere** (▶ 9.18).

2 a) Adverbs indicating the direction of a movement can be made using **ward(s)**:
backwards/forwards; downwards/ upwards; inwards/outwards; homewards.

b) The compounds **upstairs/downstairs** are also used to indicate place or movement.

For the position of adverbs in the sentence ▶ 1.5.
For emphatic sentences ▶ 18.2.

Subordinate adverbial clauses

12.20

1 Stay **where you are**.
You must find it **wherever it may be**.

2 I will go **wherever you tell me**.
Wherever you try to hide, the police will find you.

1 Another means of describing position is through a subordinate clause introduced by **where** or **wherever** (▶ 16.16).

2 In these clauses the verb is in the *present tense* if the verb in the main clause is in the *future* (compare time conjunctions ▶ 11.40).

13 Manner and means

13.1

This chapter is concerned with the language used to answer the question **How?**. It deals with the use of adverbs and adverb expressions to describe the *manner* in which something is done and it considers ways of talking about the method or means of carrying out an action.

Manner

Adverbs of manner: form

13.2

To describe the way in which an action is carried out adverbs are often used. These adverbs are called *adverbs of manner*. They are usually formed in the following way:

1 Lucy cooks **marvellously**.
(= She is a **marvellous** cook)
He drives **badly**.
(= He is a **bad** driver)
The children can swim **very well**.
(= They are very **good** swimmers)
She works **enthusiastically**.
(= She is an **enthusiastic** worker)

2 a) Why are you driving so **fast**?
You arrived **late,** didn't you?
We were used to working **hard**.
You'd better get up **early**.
The milk is delivered **daily**.

Compare:
b) This is the **fast** train.
You're **late** as usual.
We were used to **hard** work.
Let's make an **early** start.
I buy a **daily** newspaper.

3 Don't worry – it's a **friendly** dog.
She touched my arm **in a friendly way**.

4 Have you been there **lately** (= **recently**)?
We were **hardly** able to see the road
(= **scarcely**).

1 Most adverbs of manner are formed by adding the suffix **-ly** to the corresponding adjective.
For changes in spelling ▶ Appendix C. Notice that the adverb corresponding to the adjective **good** is **well** and that adjectives ending in **-ic** usually add **-ally**.

2 A limited number of adverbs (**a**) have the same form as the corresponding adjective (**b**). These include: **hourly, daily, weekly, monthly, yearly**.

3 Other adjectives which end in **-ly**, (e.g. **ugly, lovely, silly, lonely, friendly**) cannot be used as adverbs. An equivalent adverbial expression can be formed using **in a ... way**.

4 In some cases adding the suffix **-ly** to an adjective produces an adverb which has a completely different meaning.

For *comparative* forms ▶ 16.8.

Adverbs of manner: position

13.3

1 He plays **well**, doesn't he?
Speak **slowly**, please.
Listen **carefully**.

1 Adverbs of manner are usually placed after the verb which they qualify.

2 Mr Ferri speaks English very **well**.
Send us the goods **immediately**.

2 If a verb has an object the adverb comes after the object.

3 He was provoked **intentionally**.
He was **intentionally** provoked.

3 In a passive sentence the adverb of manner may come either before or after the past participle.

For more information about the position of adverbs ▶ 1.5.

Other ways of expressing manner

13.4

A description of the manner in which an action is carried out can also be given using:

1 She cried **like a child**.
He spoke **with great politeness**.
The soldiers obeyed the orders **without question**.
She acted **in a very natural manner**.
He stared at me **in a frightening way**.

1 adverb phrases formed by a *preposition* (+ *adjective*) + *noun*. Phrases using **like, with/without, in a** (*adjective*) **way** are common.

2 He went away **without saying a word**.
She turned away **as if hurt by the remark**.

2 phrases containing the present or the past participle of a verb;

3 Cook the chicken **the way I like it**.
They behaved **as I had expected**.
She cried **as a child does,** with floods of tears.

3 subordinate clauses introduced by **as, (in) the way**.

For **as if, as though** ▶ 16.7, 20.10.

Sentence adverbs

13.5

Fortunately I discovered that my cheque hadn't been lost.
I won't tell anybody about it, **naturally**.
The pupil, **wisely,** refrained from talking back.
The man, **surprisingly,** didn't react to the insult.
Hopefully she'll call back in an hour.

Compare:
She danced **naturally** (= in a natural way).
The emperor dealt with the problem **wisely** (= in a wise manner).
The man reacted **surprisingly** (= in a surprising way).

Some adverbs which, in their form, look like normal adverbs of manner have a very different function. They refer not to the verb but to the entire sentence and express a comment or the point of view of the speaker. Frequently, but not always, these 'sentence adverbs' are placed at the beginning or the end of the sentence. To avoid possible confusion of meaning they are not placed immediately after the verb. Commas are sometimes used to separate them from the rest of the sentence.
The use of certain adverbs, especially **hopefully,** as sentence adverbs is a fairly recent innovation in English and is still considered sub-standard by some speakers.

Adjectives and adverbs with verbs

13.6

1 I tasted the liquid **cautiously**.
She played the music **passionately**.
We examined the package **carefully**.

2 The liquid tasted **awful**.
The music sounded **magnificent**.
The package looked **suspicious**.

1 To describe the action of a verb, we normally use a verb followed by an *adverb*.

2 Sometimes a verb is followed by an *adjective* instead of an adverb (▶ 8.12). This happens when the adjective describes the subject of the sentence, not the action of the verb.
The verbs **look, seem, taste, feel, smell, sound** are often followed by adjectives in this way.

Means

13.7

1 Do you always travel **by** train?
I'll contact you **by** phone.
Peter earns his living **by** selling encyclopedias.
The little girl reached the switch **by** standing on a chair.

2 She reached the switch **without** standing on a chair.
The houses were built **without** using any wood.

3 Don't write **with** a pencil, write **with** a pen.
He drew the line **without** a ruler.

4 He used his knife **as** a lever to lift the stone.
The little boy used the chair **as** a ladder to reach the shelf.
She's using you **as** a spy to find out what's happening.

Compare:
I've found a job **as** a barman.
He was employed **as** a bank clerk.

1 The preposition **by** can be used to refer to a means of doing something or achieving some result.
By is followed by a noun or a verbal noun (**-ing** form).

2 **Without + -ing** form conveys the opposite meaning to **by**. Without is followed by **any,** not **some**.

3 The prepositions **with/without** refer to particular tools used to carry out a task.

4 **As,** used as a preposition, refers to the way in which something or somebody is used. Notice that with people, **as** may refer to the job which somebody does.

14 Degree

14.1 This chapter is concerned with the language used to indicate *different levels of intensity*. An examination, for example, may be described not simply as **difficult** but as **extremely difficult, rather difficult, a bit difficult,** etc. This function of the language is usually carried out by *adverbs of degree*.

Adverbs of degree and 'extreme' adverbs

14.2

Why are you driving **so** fast?   She speaks English **very** well.   The drink is **very** cold; in fact it's **too** cold.   Don't you think the work is **extremely** well done?   I'm **awfully** sorry.   I **totally** disagree.

Adverbs of degree (e.g. **so, very, extremely**) can be used to qualify other adverbs, adjectives or verbs. They increase or decrease the degree of intensity of the word to which they refer.

14.3

1 The show is **just** fantastic.
  Mrs Newton will be **absolutely** amazed.
  I was **utterly** disgusted by his bad manners.
  With all this noise it's **quite** impossible to hear what you're saying.
  It was **totally** unfair to blame him for the accident.
  That's **completely** false.
  This new technology is **entirely** unique.

2 The door number was **practically** invisible.
  Her performance was **virtually** perfect.
  It's **almost** impossible to understand what he says.
  The bottle was **nearly** empty.

3 I **absolutely** refuse to believe that.
  Her manners **utterly** infuriate me.
  I'd **just** love to see you.
  We had **almost** arrived.
  He's **virtually** finished now.
  I **quite** agree (= **completely**).

1 Even without being intensified certain adjectives automatically describe *extreme* positions (e.g. **perfect, superb, impossible, unique, terrible**). These adjectives cannot be measured in degrees; something is not more, or less, **superb**. However these extreme adjectives can be reinforced by certain extreme adverbs of degree. Some of the most common are: **absolutely, just, quite, utterly** (usually with negative adjectives); and, in some cases, **totally, entirely, completely.** For **quite** ▶ 14.4.

2 The adverbs **almost, nearly, practically, virtually** are less intense than **absolutely** but they are also sometimes used with 'extreme' adjectives. **Nearly** is weaker than the other three.

3 Many verbs can also be qualified by these adverbs of degree. They are normally placed before the verb, but after the verb **be** or the first auxiliary verb.

NOTE: This use of **quite** is different from **quite** with gradable adjectives (▶ 14.4).

Gradable adverbs

14.4 Most adjectives can be considered in terms of degree; something may be more, or less, **expensive** for example. The following table contains some of the most common adverbs of degree which are used to qualify adjectives.

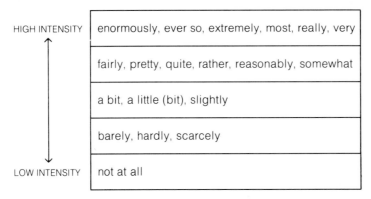

HIGH INTENSITY	enormously, ever so, extremely, most, really, very
	fairly, pretty, quite, rather, reasonably, somewhat
	a bit, a little (bit), slightly
	barely, hardly, scarcely
LOW INTENSITY	not at all

1 a) She's **ever so** careful.
    That was a **really** nice meal.

   b) It was **most** kind of you to invite me.

   c) It's a **very, very** good film.
       It's a **very** good film **indeed**.

2 a) His behaviour was **somewhat** curious.
       My car is **pretty** old.

   b) The exam turned out to be **rather** easy.
       I'd brought my raincoat but the weather
       was **rather nice**.

   c) What you say is QUITE TRUE.
       (= **absolutely**)

       No, that's QUITE IMPOSSIBLE.
       (= **absolutely**)

       The job was quite SIMPLE.
       (= **rather**)

       He speaks quite SLOWLY.
       (= **rather**)

   d) That was **quite a good meal**.
       It's **quite a long way** to walk.
       She had **rather a nasty experience**.
       It came as **rather a shock**.

3 The photograph is **slightly** out of focus.
   She's becoming **a little** deaf.

1 a) **Really** and **ever so** are more often used in
       informal English.

   b) **Most** (= **very**) is only used in formal
       English (in this sense).

   c) **Very** may be further intensified by
       repetition or by placing **indeed** after the
       word or phrase to which it refers.

2 a) **Somewhat** is only used in formal English
       and **pretty** is only used informally.

   b) When **rather** is used with a positive
       adjective or adverb it often expresses an
       element of surprise, implying that the
       speaker had expected something worse.

   c) Notice that **quite** has two different
       meanings. When used with 'extreme'
       adjectives it means **absolutely** (▶ 14.3).
       In this case **quite** is given stress in the
       spoken language. When **quite** has the
       same meaning as **rather** it is not given
       stress.

   d) An alternative structure is possible with
       quite and **rather: quite/rather + a(n)**
       (+ *adjective*) + *noun*.
       This structure is more natural than **a quite
       good meal** etc.

3 **A bit, a little, slightly** suggest a low degree
   of intensity. **A bit,** and also **a little bit,** are
   characteristic of informal English.

4 It's **hardly** the best restaurant in the town.
(= It's one of the worst)
The music was **scarcely** audible.

5 The concert was**n't** enjoyable **at all**.
The waiter was**n't at all** polite.
She ca**n't** type well **at all**.

4 **Barely, hardly, scarcely** are often used with positive adjectives to give a negative impression (▶ 2.14).

5 **Not at all** is used to give an emphatic negation of the adjective or adverb to which it refers. **Not** forms part of the verb phrase and is usually reduced to **n't; at all** can go either before or after the adjective or adverb. For adverbs of degree with comparatives and superlatives ▶ 16.8.

Adverbs of degree and verbs

14.5

1 a) I **quite** enjoy playing cards.
I can **barely** understand what he says.
You can't leave now – the meeting has **scarcely** begun.

b) Now it's **really** going to be difficult.

Now it **really** is going to be difficult.

c) We didn't want that **at all**.

1 a) Many of the adverbs of degree mentioned in 14.4 are also used with verbs: e.g.
really, quite, rather, slightly, barely, hardly, scarcely, not at all. They normally go before the verb, but after the verb **be** or the first auxiliary verb.

b) **Really** can be made more emphatic by being placed before **be** or an auxiliary verb, which is then given stress.

c) **At all** goes after the verb and the object if there is one.
For other adverbs of degree with verbs ▶ 14.3.

2 I don't like her **very much**.
She goes to discos **a lot**.

2 The intensity or frequency of some verbs can be emphasised by using expressions of quantity (▶ 9.5–9.17).

So, such

14.6

1 The painting is so beautiful!
(= very beautiful)

His story was so funny!
(= very funny)

The weather was so cold!
(= very cold)

1 **So** can be used as an adverb of degree, suggesting a high degree of intensity, in a similar way to the adverbs described in 14.4. In this case the sentence with **so** is usually followed by an exclamation mark and **so** is often stressed.

2 I was **so** tired **that** I went straight to bed.
The bus was **so** crowded **that** we walked.

2 **So** is also used with **that** to express cause and effect (▶ 15.6).

3 It's such a beautiful painting!

It was such a funny story!

It was such cold weather!

She has such beautiful eyes!

3 The word **such** can be used to convey a similar meaning to **so** but it forms part of a noun phrase and cannot be followed only by an adjective. In sentences of this type **such** is often stressed and there is an exclamation mark at the end.

4 We had **such** a good time **that** we want to go back again.
The film created **such** a scandal **that** it was banned.

4 **Such** is also used with **that** to express *cause and effect* (▶ 15.6).

Too, enough

14.7

He's **old enough** to drive a car
He isn't **too young** to drive a car.

Compare:
He isn't **old enough** to drive a car.
He's **too young** to drive a car.

The soup is **too hot** to drink.
It isn't **cool enough** to drink.

Compare:
The soup isn't **too hot** to drink.
It's **cool enough** to drink.

Too and **enough** are adverbs of degree. **Too** expresses the idea of *excess*, **enough** the idea of *sufficiency*. They are complementary in meaning. An affirmative sentence with **too** qualifying one adjective or adverb expresses the same meaning as a negative sentence with **enough** qualifying the opposite adjective or adverb.
Notice that **enough** comes after the adjective or adverb which it qualifies.

For **enough** as a quantifier ▶ 9.5, 9.6, 9.11.

Adverbs of degree and quantity

14.8   **So** and **too** can qualify the quantifiers **much, many, little, few** producing the following combinations:

1 a) He earns **so much** money that he doesn't know how to spend it.
I'm afraid I've drunk **too much** wine.

b) I liked the film **so much** that I'd gladly see it again.
You've been studying **too much** recently.

1 **So much, too much** can operate both as (**a**) quantifiers and (**b**) adverbs.

2 a) They always have **so little** time to relax.
I can't go on reading – there's **too little** light.

b) You work **so little** and yet you're always so tired.
You practise the piano **too little** – that's why you can't play very well.

2 **So little, too little** can operate both as (**a**) quantifiers and (**b**) adverbs.

3 There were **so many** people in the shops that you could hardly buy anything.
I've had **too many** personal problems recently to be able to concentrate on work.
There were **so few** advance bookings for the concert that it was cancelled.
There were **too few** clients for the business to expand.

3 **So many, too many, so few, too few** can operate as quantifiers before plural nouns.

NOTE: See also *cause and effect* ▶ 15.1– 15.7.

15 Cause, effect and purpose

15.1

English, like any other language, has several ways of indicating the link between *cause* and *effect*, in other words of relating someone or something (seen as the *cause* or the *reason*) to an event (seen as the *effect*, the *result* or the *consequence*). This chapter examines the most important ways in which this is done. It also considers how to express the purpose of an action and how to describe the action of causing something to be done (using *causative* structures).

Cause and effect

Use of verbs

15.2

The link between *cause* and *effect* can be indicated using the verbs in the following table:

CAUSE		EFFECT
Dangerous driving	causes gives rise to brings about leads to results in	road accidents.

1 The bad weather **caused** all sorts of problems.

2 The introduction of computers **has led to** extensive industrial reorganisation.
The closure of the factory **resulted in** the loss of many jobs.
The oil crisis **gave rise to** a period of depression.
Bad management **brought about** the strike (*or* **brought** the strike **about**).
Bad management **brought** it **about**.

3 a) Problems **were caused** by the snow.
The strike was **brought about** by bad management.

b) The loss of jobs **resulted from** the closure of the factory.

4 This song **makes** me feel very happy.
The journey **made** him tired.

1 **Cause** is more widely used than the other verbs in the table.

2 In more formal English the verbs **give rise to, bring about, lead to, result in** are also used. Notice that **bring about** is a phrasal verb (▶ 7.1–7.7) and so the object (the effect) can be put either before or after the adverb particle. If the òbject is a pronoun it must be placed before the adverb particle.

3 a) **Cause** and **bring about** can be used in passive structures to focus on the *effect*.
b) We can also focus on the effect by using the verb **result** with the preposition **from**.

4 The verb **make** can also be used to link cause and effect (▶ 15.11).

Use of nouns, adjectives, prepositions

15.3

1 Your telegram **is the cause of** the confusion.
The heavy traffic **is the reason for** the delay.
You **were responsible for** the quarrel.

1 A *cause-effect* relationship may be expressed by using the verb **be** followed by certain nouns or adjectives with prepositions: **be the cause of, be the reason for, be responsible for**.

2 The increase in crime **is due to** unemployment.
This discovery **is the result of** years of research.

3 We stayed at home **because of** the weather.
He was admired **because of** his originality.

4 The flight will be delayed **owing to** the late arrival of the incoming aircraft.
On account of the strike all payments will be postponed.
Due to her illness they changed their plans.

5 He began to shout **out of** excitement at the good news.
We've lost our way **through** your stupidity.
He did it **from** a sense of duty.

2 **Be due to** and **be the result of** focus on the effect.

3 *Cause* may also be introduced by prepositions alone. The most commonly used is **because of**.

4 **Owing to, on account of, as a result of** have a similar meaning to **because of** but are used only in formal English.
Due to is not accepted in traditional grammar as a preposition but it is often used in this way.

5 The prepositions **through, from, out of** can be used in certain cases, usually in the expression of emotion or sentiment.

Use of conjunctions

15.4

He felt very ill so he called a doctor.	
He called a doctor because he felt very ill.	
As Since	he felt very ill, he called a doctor.

The *cause-effect* relationship can be expressed by means of conjunctions which introduce subordinate clauses.

1 a) She was hungry **so** she made a sandwich.
  b) She made a sandwich **because** she was hungry.

  a) The shop didn't attract enough customers **so** it closed.
  b) **As** the shop didn't attract enough customers, it closed.

2 I'm doing this **because** I enjoy it.
They enter politics **because** they're hungry for power.
The plane exploded **because** there was a bomb on board.

1 a) **So** introduces a subordinate clause which expresses the *consequence* of the main clause.
It contrasts with **because, since, as** which introduce subordinate clauses expressing the *reason* for the main clause (**b**).

2 **Because** tends to be used when the speaker thinks that the listener does not know the reason. **Because** therefore emphasises the reason, which is usually given after the main clause.

3 a) **As** he can't be at home now it's no use phoning him.
As she has forgotten her camera we won't be able to take any photographs.
Since you're so friendly with him why don't you go and meet him?

 b) **Since** computers have been introduced industries have had to be reorganised.

4 The princess was sad, **for** her father had died.
He sat down by the roadside, **for** he was tired.
Compare:
A: Why are you laughing?
B: Because you're so funny. (*not* **for**)

5 **The reason (why)** she left him was **that** he treated her so badly.
The reason (why) they lost the game is **because** their goalkeeper is no good.

3 a) **As** and **since** (used in more formal English) tend to imply that the listener already knows the reason and therefore give more prominence to the effect. They are more often placed at the beginning of the sentence.

 b) In some cases there is ambiguity because **as** and **since** may also refer to time (▶ 11.35).

4 **For** can express *reason*. It is not often used in spoken English. It is more characteristic of an old-fashioned or literary style. It cannot be used at the beginning of a sentence or in reply to a question.

5 **The reason (why)** can be placed at the beginning of the sentence and linked to the clause explaining the reason by **that** or **because**.

Use of linkers

15.5

Terrorist attacks have been predicted. **Consequently** security has been strengthened at Heathrow.
The price of raw materials has increased. **As a result** a fall in demand can be expected.
The person in question violated the rules of the club. **Accordingly** he has been expelled.
The Bank of England has lowered its rate of interest. **Thus** a similar reduction can be expected from other banks.

A number of words and expressions can be used to create a cause-effect link between *two separate sentences*.
Therefore, consequently, for this reason are used in formal English with a similar meaning to **so** (▶ 15.4). **As a result/consequence, thus, hence, accordingly** can be used in the same way.

Other ways of expressing cause and effect

15.6

1 She spoke **so** fast **that** I could not understand.
He's **such** a nice man **that** I'd do anything for him.

2 **If** you **boil** the egg too long it **gets/will get** hard.
If he **is** treated properly he **behaves** well.

1 *Effect* or *consequence* can be expressed through the following constructions: **so** + *adjective/adverb* + **that** and **such** + *noun phrase* + **that** (▶ 14.6, 14.8). The main clause provides the cause or the reason.

2 *Conditional clauses* (▶ 20.6, 20.13) can express a *cause-effect* relationship. The two verbs may be in the same tense.

3 **Evicted** from their home, the family had to stay with friends.
The president **having left** earlier than expected, we closed the meeting.

3 *Cause* or *reason* may be indicated by the use of participle phrases: the *past participle*, or the structure **having** + *past participle*. These structures are used particularly in formal English.

15.7 Particularly in spoken English, we can set up a cause-effect link in many other ways. The expressions that we can use are often not explicit but rely on the context of the conversation to make their meaning clear. They occur at different levels of formality:

1 A: I didn't see John at school today.
  B: Yes, ... he was sick last night **and** I kept him at home.
  A: Why didn't John go to school today?
  B: **Well, (you see)/The reason was that/ Because** he wasn't well last night.

1 neutral language;

2 A: That girl gets on my nerves: she's always so irritable!
  B: **Well, the thing is/It's like this**; **you see,** she's got serious family problems.

2 more informal language;

3 A: I was wondering why you haven't typed those letters, Miss Swanson.
  B: **If I could explain, Mr Johnson/The main reason, Mr Johnson, is that** it has taken me so long to contact all our agents.

3 more formal language.

Purpose

15.8

1 a) We went to the station **to see** Mary off.
To get better results, you should study harder.
They have set up new control systems **so as to improve** road safety.
You have to obtain special permission **in order to enter** the building.

  b) **Go and buy** me some bread.
Come and have a beer.
Stay and have dinner with us.
Try and repair it yourself.

1 a) The aim or purpose of an action can be expressed using the **to-**infinitive. Sometimes in more formal English it is preceded by **so as** or by **in order.**
  b) After the *imperative* of the verbs **go** and **come** a second imperative introduced by **and** is normally used instead of the **to-**infinitive. This is also possible with other verbs: **stay, stop, try, run**.

2 Computers are used **for processing** information.
Special machines exist **for controlling** industrial operations.
I went to the shop **for** some bread.

2 The purpose which something serves is often indicated by **for** + **-ing** form (verbal noun). **For** may also be used before other nouns.

3 I'm writing to Sheila **so that** she knows what to do.
Fred's bought a new house **so that** he **can** have more room for the children.
We stayed in a hotel close to the airport **so that** we **could** catch the early morning flight.
I'm sure she married him **so** that she **might** get her hands on his money.
They sold the company **in order that** they **should** have some ready cash available.

3 The purpose of an action can also be expressed through a subordinate clause introduced by **so that**, or in more formal English, **in order that**, followed by a modal verb (e.g. **could, might** or **should**).

Precaution

15.9

He never went out by day **in case/for fear that** he **should** be seen.
He never went out **in case** he **was seen**.
I'm taking out a new insurance policy **in case** an accident **should** happen.
I'm taking out a new insurance policy **in case** an accident **happens**.

In case and **for fear that** are used to refer to an action carried out as a *precaution* against something.

In case may be followed by a *modal* verb or by the *simple present* or *simple past*.

Negative purpose

15.10 A *negative purpose* can be expressed using the following structures:

1 He sent a telex **in order not to waste** time.
We took a taxi **so as not to be** late.

1 **so as not** and **in order not** followed by the **to**-*infinitive*;

2 I lived in the city centre **so that** I **shouldn't** be too far from my job.
She locked herself in her room **in order that** he **would** not disturb her.

2 **so that** and **in order that** followed by a *modal* verb in the *negative* form;

3 I lived in the city centre **to avoid being** too far from my job.
She locked herself in her room **to avoid being disturbed** by him (= to **prevent him from disturbing** her).

3 **avoid** + **-ing** form *(verbal noun)*, or **prevent** + *noun/object pronoun* (+ **from**) + **-ing** form.

Causative: to have something done

15.11

1 I **had my car repaired** last week.
You paid him for that? You should **have your head examined**.
I **get my trousers dry-cleaned** every month.

1 The structure **have** + *noun/object pronoun* + *past participle* is used to describe the action of causing something to be done. In informal English **have** is often replaced by **get**.

2 I'll **have the computer check** the lists.
I hate studying but my father **made me do** my homework.
The sergeant **made the soldiers march** for three hours.
I **got the secretary to pass on** the message.

2 A different structure can be used to mention the person (or thing) that actually carries out the action: **have/make** + *noun/object pronoun* + *infinitive without* **to**. **Make** is used to describe an order which is imposed on someone against his/her will. In informal English **get** can be used followed by the **to-***infinitive*.

16 Comparison and contrast

16.1
This chapter deals with the language used to describe something by *comparing* it to another thing or to a number of other things. Adjectives and adverbs adopt particular forms for this purpose but certain prepositions and conjunctions may also be used to carry out this function. In addition the chapter considers ways of comparing facts or ideas and, in particular, the language used to point out *contrasts* between those facts or ideas.

Comparison

Comparative and superlative of adjectives: introduction

16.2

1 The film was **more exciting** than the book.
English is **less difficult** than Chinese.
Cats are **more independent** than dogs.
The history exam was **easier** than the other three exams.

1 The *comparative* form of an adjective is used to describe someone or something in relation to another person or another thing. One is viewed as separate from the other.
A comparison may involve more than two people or two things but they are divided into two groups.

2 The tiger was **the most impressive** animal in the zoo.
This is **the least comfortable** hotel in the town.
What is **the most difficult** language in the world?
Cats are **the most independent** animals.
The history exam was **the easiest** of all.

2 The *superlative* is used to describe someone or something in relation to the other members of the same group. The subject is itself part of the group, not separated from it.

Comparative and superlative of adjectives: form

16.3

Adjective	Comparative	Superlative
tall heavy	taller heavier	tallest heaviest
tired intelligent	more tired more intelligent	most tired most intelligent

There are two ways of forming the comparative and superlative of adjectives:

1 long–long**er**–long**est**
tall–tall**er**–tall**est**
Sheila is **taller** than you but she isn't **the tallest** in the class.

1 If the adjective consists of only one syllable we usually add **-er** to form the comparative and **-est** for the superlative. Notice that the number of syllables depends on the pronunciation, not the spelling (e.g. **nice** is one syllable). In some cases the addition of these suffixes causes changes in the spelling (▶ Appendix C).

2 interesting – **more** interesting – **most** interesting
I find physics **more interesting** than chemistry but for me **the most** interesting subject of all is maths.

   a) bored – **more** bored – **most** bored
      tired – **more** tired – **most** tired

   b) clever–clever**er**–clever**est**
      gentle–gentl**er**–gentl**est**
      narrow–narrow**er**–narrow**est**
      easy–easi**er**–easi**est**

   c) good–**better**–**best**
      bad–**worse**–**worst**
      much–**more**–**most**
      little–**less**–**least**
      She had very little money, **less** than any of the others.
      Compare:
      She was a very little girl, **littler** (= **smaller**) than any of the other children.

   d) Her behaviour made me **more sad** than angry.
      I was **more angry** than frightened.

2 If the adjective consists of two or more syllables it is usually preceded by **more** to form the comparative and **most** for the superlative.
However, notice the following points:

   a) Past participle adjectives require **more/ most**.

   b) Many two-syllable adjectives (especially those which end in **-er, -le, -ow, -y**) usually add **-er/-est**.

   c) Some very common adjectives of quality and quantifiers have irregular, comparative and superlative forms.

   NOTE: When **little** is used as a quality adjective and not as a quantifier its comparative and superlative forms are respectively **littler** and **littlest**. But **smaller** and **smallest** are much more common.

   d) When two adjectives are compared, **more** is used.

Characteristics of comparative structures

16.4

1 James is younger **than** his sister.

2 a) I was more relaxed than **him**.
     He got more annoyed than **me**.
     He speaks English better than **me**.

   Compare:
   b) I was more relaxed than **he was**.
      He got more annoyed than **I did**.
      He speaks English better than **I can**.

3 We climbed **higher and higher** and we grew **more and more afraid**.

4 **The more** he spoke, **the less** we understood.
  The older parents get, **the more difficult** they become.
  Compare:
  As the journey continued, we grew increasingly tired.

1 The comparative is followed by **than** to introduce the other element in the comparison.

2 If a personal pronoun follows **than** it takes an object form (**a**). (However, if the personal pronoun is itself followed by a verb it takes a subject form (**b**) (▶ 5.3).

3 The repetition of a comparative after **and** suggests gradual progression.

4 When two actions develop simultaneously they can be linked using **the . . . the** with comparative forms.

   A similar effect can be obtained using the conjunction **as** (▶ 11.35).

Characteristics of superlative structures

16.5

1 **The** most unusual scene was the last one.

1 The superlative is almost always preceded by the definite article.

2 It's the most interesting **of** all the programmes.
It's the most beautiful city **in** Europe.

2 The prepositions most commonly used after the superlative are: **of** and (especially with reference to places) **in.**

3 This is the most original gift **(that) I've ever been given**.

3 The superlative is often followed by a relative clause.

NOTE: For **most** as adverb of degree ▶ 14.4.

Less, least

16.6

Draughts is **less complicated** than chess.
I think history is **the least interesting** subject.
The subway is safe during the day but **less safe** at night.

Less and **least** are the opposites, respectively, of **more** and **most** and follow the same rules for formation and use.

NOTE: **Less** and **least** (unlike **more** and **most**) are used with *all* adjectives, even those with one syllable.

Similarity: **as** and **like**

16.7

1 a) The elephant seemed **as high as** a house.
For me, English is **as difficult as** Chinese.

b) The English team isn't **so/as good as** the Scottish.
It isn't **so/as cold as** it was last week.

c) She isn't **as tall as me**.

Compare:
She isn't **as tall as I am**.

1 a) To indicate similarity or equality we can use **as** + *adjective* + **as**.
b) In a negative sentence we can use either **not as . . . as** or **not so . . . as**.
c) For the use of personal pronouns after the construction **(not) as/so . . . as** compare pronouns after **than** (▶ 16.4).

2 They were playing **like** children.
She sang just **like** an angel.
They look **like** beggars.
It sounded **like** an explosion.

2 **Like** is also used as a preposition to express similarity. It means 'similar to'. It is often used with verbs related to perception.

3 a) You must approach this problem **(in the same way) as** you did the previous one.
She walks **(in the same way) as** her mother used to.

b) He always gets drunk **just like** his father does.
I can't do it **like** you can.

3 a) **As** is used as a conjunction meaning 'in the same way'.
b) In formal English **like** cannot be used as a conjunction. However, in colloquial English **like** or **just like** is often used instead of **as,** as a conjunction.

4 He always speaks **as though** he was more intelligent than everybody else.
You looked **as if** you had seen a ghost.

4 **As if** and **as though** combine the idea of comparison with that of manner (▶ 13.4) or condition (▶ 20.6).

Comparative and superlative of adverbs

16.8

1 Can you get to school **more quickly** than I do?
Can't you play **less noisily**?
I will give the cake to the child who asks for it **most politely**.
Compare:
He behaved **most politely**.

2 He drove fast but the police drove **faster**.
He drove **fastest** of all.
You've always worked **harder** than me.
She used to wake up **earliest** of all.
The letter came **sooner** than we expected.
She always stays **longest** at parties.

3 a) well–**better**–**best**
badly–**worse**–**worst**
much–**more**–**most**
little–**less**–**least**
far–**farther**–**farthest**
   further–**furthest**

b) In order to reach the hotel we had to drive **farther/further** than expected.
In his speech the President went **further** into the question.
Further developments have occurred in the Middle East crisis.

4 She ran **as fast as** the wind.

---

1 Adverbs ending in **-ly** have comparative and superlative forms with **more/less** and **most/least**.
Notice that **most** sometimes has the same meaning as **very** (▶ 14.4).

2 A few short adverbs have the same form as the corresponding adjectives and form the comparative and superlative using **-er** and **-est** like those adjectives.
Soon (which cannot be used as an adjective) also takes **-er/-est**.

3 a) Some common adverbs and quantifiers have irregular or alternative comparative and superlative forms.
For **little** as an adjective of quality ▶ 16.3.
b) Both **farther** and **further** may refer to distance. Only **further** can be used in the more abstract sense of 'additional' or 'more profoundly' or 'more advanced'.

4 **As ... as** is used to indicate similarity or equality with adverbs.

Comparison of quantity

16.9

1 I certainly earn **less** money than you.
I smoke **more** than my brother.
Of all the people I know he eats **most**.
I've got **fewer/less** friends than you.
You should eat **more** fruit and **less** chocolate.

2 Take **as much time as** you want.
There were almost **as many people** outside the stadium **as** there were inside.
Do you really smoke **as much as** I do?

3 If you're finished your tea you can have **more**.
There are **more of us** than there are of them.

---

1 In comparisons of quantity **more/most** and **less/least** are placed before the nouns, or after the verbs, to which they refer. With plural countable nouns **fewer/fewest** are used (although **less/least** are also sometimes found in informal English).

2 To indicate equality of quantity the construction **as much ... as** is used with verbs and uncountable nouns, **as many ... as** with plural countable nouns.

3 **More** and **most** are grammatically similar to other quantifiers and can be used in similar constructions, as pronouns and with **of** (▶ 9.6).

Adverbs of degree with comparatives and superlatives

16.10

1 The damage is **no worse** than we had imagined.
It's **a little quicker** if you go by train.
Your flat is **much bigger** than I expected.
I feel **a lot better** today.
Your car is **far more expensive** than ours.

2 Has she grown **any taller**?
It doesn't look **any bigger** to me.

3 The house was **even more beautiful** than I had hoped.

4 It isn't the fastest car **at all**.
She's **by no means the most efficient** secretary we've got.
Renting a small flat is **much the best** solution.
This is **by far the most valuable** painting in the collection.

1 The following quantifiers and adverbs of degree are commonly used with comparative forms: **no, a little, a bit, rather, somewhat, much, a lot, far**.

NOTE: **Very** cannot be used with comparatives.

2 **Any** can be used for emphasis in interrogative and negative sentences.

3 **Even** can be used to emphasise comparative forms (▶ 16.14).

4 The following adverbs of degree are commonly used to emphasise superlative forms: **not . . . at all, by no means, much, by far**.

Contrast

While, whereas

16.11

1 **While** most MPs favour the policy, a minority is strongly opposed to it.
Susan is friendly **whereas** her husband is more reserved.

2 **On the one hand** we must fight inflation but **on the other hand** we want to create new jobs.
It hasn't been a success but **don't forget** it only started a month ago.
She isn't very clever but **there again** she works very hard.

3 A: He's very generous.
B: Yes, but **on the other hand** he isn't very friendly.

A: He's very generous.
B: No, **on the contrary,** I find him rather mean.

1 Two different aspects of a subject can be brought together and compared using the conjunctions **while** or **whereas**. These words may be placed at the beginning of the sentence or between the two statements that are being contrasted.

2 The expressions **on the one hand** and **on the other hand** are used to contrast two different points of view.
Expressions used in informal English with a similar meaning to **on the other hand** are: **there again, don't forget, it's also true that** (▶ 27.15).

3 **On the other hand** must not be confused with **on the contrary**. **On the other hand** accepts that the alternative view is also true. **On the contrary** is used for contradiction. It denies the truth of the alternative view.

Though, although, even though

1 **Though** he was ill, he went to work.

Although it was warm, she wore a coat.
She wore a coat **even though** it was warm.

2 It was warm; she wore a coat, **though**.

3 He'll come **even though** it's snowing.
(= It is snowing)
He'll come **even if** it is snowing.
(= It may not be snowing)
Even though you're late it doesn't matter.
(= You are late now)
Even if you're late it doesn't matter.
(= You may not be late in the future)

1 When two ideas are clearly in contrast with each other they can be linked using the conjunctions **though, although, even though**.
These conjunctions can be placed at the beginning of the sentence or between the two contrasting ideas.

2 In spoken English **though** can also be placed at the end of a sentence.

3 **Even though** must not be confused with **even if**. **Even though** refers to two facts or two real situations which are in contrast.
Even if refers not to facts but to hypothetical situations.

Other ways of expressing contrast

He was ill	but/yet	he went to work.
He was ill.	Still All the same Even so However Nevertheless	he went to work.

1 I told him not to do it, **but** he just ignored me.
I don't really like discos; **still** I'll come if you want me to.
I realise they're poor; **all the same** they shouldn't steal.
A new government took power. **However** the economic situation continued to deteriorate.
Conditions were difficult. **Nevertheless** the work continued.

1 The linking words in the table must be placed between the two contrasting ideas. Different forms of punctuation can be used with these linking words.
But and **yet** are conjunctions, and are used with a comma or no punctuation mark.
The others may be preceded by a full stop or a semi-colon.
Still, all the same, even so, are used in informal English. **Yet, however, nevertheless** are used in written or formal English.

2 a) **In spite of the fact that** they had bought new players, the team had no success.
Despite the fact that I had studied hard all year, I failed the exam.

2 a) Another means of contrasting ideas is to use the expressions **in spite of the fact that** or **despite the fact that**.

b) We couldn't work the machine **in spite of following** all the instructions.
Despite studying hard all year, I failed the exam.

c) They decided to go on holiday **despite** the expense.

b) If the subject of two verbs is the same, **despite** or **in spite of** may be followed by the **-ing** form (verbal noun) of the subordinate verb.

c) **Despite** and **in spite of** may also be followed by other types of noun.

Even

16.14

1 All the newspapers reported the wedding – **even** 'The Times'.
This restaurant is **even** better than we expected.
There was no public transport; there weren't **even** any taxis.

2 Some parts of the country are cold **even** in July.
He's a polyglot – he **even** speaks Swahili.
There isn't **even** a lion in that zoo.
She can't **even** ride a bike.
I hadn't **even** thought of that.

1 The adverb **even** is used to suggest a contrast with what we would normally expect.

2 **Even** usually comes before the word to which it refers. When **even** refers to a verb it comes before the verb, but after the verb **be,** a modal auxiliary or the first auxiliary in a compound verb.

Contrast and condition

16.15

1 We'll fly **even if** it's expensive.
They'll join us **even if** they don't like the place very much.

2 a) **It doesn't matter how** important he is, I don't like him. (= **Even if** he is very important, I . . .)
No matter where you go, you'll have the same problem. (= **Even if** you go far away from here, you'll . . .)

b) **Whether** you like it **or not,** I'm going to buy it. (= **Even if** you don't like it, I'm . . .)

c) I'll finish the job **anyway** (**even if** he doesn't pay me).

d) I'd buy a car **in any case** (**even if** I couldn't afford it).

1 **Even if** combines the idea of *contrast* with that of *condition.*

2 Certain other expressions produce the same effect:
a) **it doesn't matter/no matter** + *question word;*
b) **whether . . . or not;**
c) **anyway;**
d) **in any case.**

16.16 Compounds of **ever** are also used as conjunctions which combine the idea of contrast with that of condition.

1 **Wherever** he goes they will find him (**even if** he goes a long way).	1 **Wherever** refers to place.
2 **Whatever** you do, don't forget to phone me (**even if** you are very busy).	2 **Whatever** refers to things.
3 I don't like him, **whoever** he is (**even if** he is very important).	3 **Whoever** refers to people.
4 Don't hesitate to call me, **whenever** you feel like it (**even if** it's very late).	4 **Whenever** refers to time.
5 **Whichever** player they buy they won't win the championship (**even if** he's very good). **Whichever** holiday he chooses, he'll complain (**even if** it's enjoyable).	5 **Whichever** refers to people or things where the choice is restricted.
6 a) **However** you do it, the result will be the same (**even if** you do it very well). b) **However** stupid he is, he wouldn't do that (**even if** he is very stupid).	6 a) **However** refers to manner or means. b) **However** may also be used in front of an adjective.

17 Inclusion and exclusion

17.1

1 **As well as** a dog there was a cat, a canary **and** a monkey.

2 She was the **only** one who understood.

3 It was a good film **apart from** the music.

4 We can go to an Indian restaurant **instead of** a Chinese.

This chapter looks at the various ways in which the language (**1**) joins different elements together or (**2**) restricts choice to a limited number. It also considers how the ideas of (**3**) exclusion and (**4**) alternatives can be expressed.

Inclusion

17.2

The following table lists the most common ways of adding elements together in English.

He speaks	French **and** Russian. **both** French **and** Russian. French **and also** Russian. **not only** French **but also** Russian. French **and** Russian **too/as well**. French **in addition to** (speaking) Russian. French **as well as** (speaking) Russian. French **besides** (speaking) Russian.

1 Napoleon was born in Corsica **and** died on St Helena.
Bring me a bowl **and** a spoon.
I need a saw, a hammer **and** some nails.

2 The sports field is for **both** boys and girls.

3 It's made of plastic and **also** leather.
The shop **also** sells classical records.
He is **also** very shy.
She **not only** loses her temper **but** she **also** gets violent.

4 Did you see the accident **too**?
Yes, I saw it **as well**.

5 I lost my passport **as well as** my money.
Besides damaging the doors they also broke the windows.
In addition to the fact that you disobeyed me you also told a lie.

1 **And** can be used to join two or more words, phrases or clauses. If there are more than two, **and** is only used before the last one; the other items are separated by commas.

2 **Both** is used to combine two things or two groups of things (▶ 9.14).

3 **Also** normally precedes the word to which it refers. If it refers to a verb it is placed immediately before the verb, but after the verb **be** or the first auxiliary verb. The expression **not only . . . but also** is a more emphatic form.

4 **Too** and **as well** are used in informal English and normally come at the end of the sentence.

5 **As well as, in addition to** and **besides** may be followed by a noun or **-ing** form (verbal noun). By adding the phrase **the fact that** they may also be followed by a clause containing a subject and a verb.

6 a) It isn't a particularly nice dress; **besides** it's very expensive.
It's too expensive and, **what's more, I** don't like it.
They didn't do the work properly; **on top of that** they made a mistake on the bill.
She doesn't know many people; **also** she's very shy.

b) The government's policy was unpopular. **Moreover** it wasn't even supported by all the ministers.
The weather was bad for the journey. **In addition** they had problems with the car.

6 a) **Besides** may also be used to establish a link between two separate clauses or sentences. In this sense it is used to put forward an additional argument to reinforce what has already been said. It is placed at the beginning of the second clause. Other linking expressions which can be used in the same way are: **what's more, as well, on top of that, also**.

b) In more formal English **moreover** and **in addition** have the same function.

So, neither/nor

17.3

1 a) Mike works in Leeds and **so does Phil**. (= Mike works in Leeds and Phil does too)
The pubs have closed down and **so have the restaurants**. (= The pubs have closed down and the restaurants have too)
The food tasted horrible and **so did the wine**. (= The food tasted horrible and the wine did too)

b) She reads 'The Guardian', **as** do all her friends.
The living room was very dirty, **as** was the kitchen.

1 Two clauses can be linked using other structures if the subjects of the two clauses refer to the same verb:

a) **So** can be placed at the beginning of the second clause. It is followed by the auxiliary verb used in the first clause and by the subject of the second clause.
If there is no auxiliary in the first clause, **do/does/did** appear instead.

b) In more formal English **as** may be used in a very similar way but without **and**.

2 a) I don't smoke and **nor does my wife**.
The Americans won't participate and **neither will the Russians**.
The unions don't agree with the policy and **nor does the government**.

b) He didn't believe me and **you didn't either**.
Billy can't swim and **Lucy can't either**.

2 a) When the first clause is negative **neither** or **nor** are used instead of **so**. Since they are already negative the verb following them is in the affirmative form (see also ▶ 2.13).

b) There is an alternative negative structure in the second clause: *subject + negative auxiliary verb* + **either** (i.e. **not either** is used instead of **neither**).

Else, more, another

17.4

1 I've spoken to Jenny. Who **else** should I tell?
Bread and sugar – do you want anything **else**?
He said he was sorry. What **else** did he say?
Barry and Mike are coming and somebody **else** too.

1 **Else** is often used in the sense of 'in addition'. It follows the word to which it refers, usually a question word or a compound of **some/any/every/no**. **Else** expresses the concept of addition or inclusion of something different from what has already been mentioned.

2 Tell me when you've read those books and I'll give you **some more**.
Is there **any more** tea?
Two more customers entered the shop.

3 Can't you stay for **another** hour?
I'm staying for **another few** days.
Will you bring **another two** glasses?

2 **More** is used to express the idea of an additional number or increased amount of the same element. In this sense **more** is used after quantifiers (▶ 9.5, 9.6) and numbers.

3 **Another** may also express the idea of an additional quantity. It is normally used with singular countable nouns (▶ 9.4), but with a number or **few** it can be followed by plural nouns.

Including, even

17.5

1 a) Everybody was at the meeting, **including** Mr Jackson.
All European countries, **including** Britain, have signed the treaty.

b) Study the first ten chapters, **especially** chapter six.

2 He's read everything that Dickens wrote – **even** the travel books.
Nobody came to see him – not **even** his brother.

1 a) The word **including** is used to focus on particular elements which are included among a larger number.

b) A more emphatic sense of inclusion can be given using **especially, particularly, in particular**.

2 **Even** can be used as an emphatic way of expressing the idea 'without any exception'. **Even** often implies an element of surprise, indicating a contrast with what we would normally expect (▶ 16.14).

Restriction

17.6

1 a) There was **only** one bedroom in the flat (= no more than one).
Only Roosevelt has been President for four terms (= no one except him).
We **only** took some sandwiches and a bottle of water.

b) **Only** Livingstone survived (= he and nobody else).
Even Livingstone survived (= he and everybody else).

c) You're the **only** one who liked it.
She's an **only** child.

2 a) There are **just** five minutes left before the final whistle.

b) I **merely** mentioned her name and he exploded in anger.
We did almost nothing. We **simply** lay on the beach all day.

1 a) The word most commonly used to express the idea of *restriction* or *limitation* is **only**. When **only** refers to the subject it comes before it. In other cases it normally goes before the verb (but after the verb **be** or the first auxiliary verb) (▶ 17.14).

b) **Only** contrasts with **even** (▶ 17.5).

c) **Only** may also be used as an adjective.

2 a) **Just** can be used in a similar way to **only**.

b) The adverbs **merely** and **simply** are also sometimes used in this sense.

3 I'm afraid that's **all** that I know.
All you need is love.

4 Numbers were **limited to** five hundred for the opening ceremony.
Cars were **restricted to** using only one lane because of the crash.

5 We didn't take anything to eat **except for** some sandwiches.
Apart from that I don't know anything about him.

3 When followed by a relative clause **all** can have the meaning 'the only thing(s)'.

4 The expressions **limited to** and **restricted to** are used in more formal English. They may be followed by an **-ing** form (verbal noun).

5 Many of the expressions used to refer to exclusion (▶ 17.7) can also have the sense of restriction when used in negative sentences.

Exclusion

17.7 The idea of *exclusion* or *exception* can be expressed using the prepositional phrases in the table below. These expressions can also be placed at the beginning of the sentence (except **but**).

All the rooms were large	**apart from** **except (for)** **with the exception of** **but (for)** **excluding**	the kitchen.

1 a) **Apart from** French we never studied foreign languages.
All the American states **except (for)** New Hampshire had a Republican majority.

b) It's a good film **except for the fact that** the ending is weak.
Apart from the fact that you'd like to live in Tahiti, why have you applied for this job?
The flat is nice **except that** there's no balcony.

c) She did almost everything in the house **except** clean the ceilings.
They haven't done anything **except** watch TV.

2 a) Nobody **but** the President has the power to do it.
I'll do anything **but** that.
Everyone **but** Frank decided to go home.

b) You do nothing **but** criticise me.

1 a) **Apart from** and **except (for)** are the prepositions most commonly used to refer to exclusion.

b) By adding **the fact that** these two expressions can also be used as conjunctions. **Except that** can be used in the same way.

c) In certain cases (especially after **do** + **anything/everything/nothing**), **apart from** and **except** can be followed immediately by the *infinitive without* **to**.

2 a) **But** is used especially after certain quantifiers: **no, none, any, every, all** (and compounds of these words).

b) **But** can be followed by the *infinitive without* **to** in the same way as **apart from** and **except** (see **1c**) above).

c) **But for the fact that** you had telephoned I would never have known.
We would all have got lost **but for** his sense of direction.

3 During our trip, we found the museum a bit dull but we enjoyed everything **else**.
We could hear the river but **otherwise** it was very quiet.

4 **Excluding** Mr Jackson, everybody was at the meeting.
All the European countries, **excluding** Britain, have signed the treaty.

c) **But for** and the conjunction **but for the fact that** are used with a conditional meaning: 'if this hadn't happened' (▶ 20.11).

3 **Else** (▶ 17.4) and **otherwise** (▶ 17.8) can be used to mean 'apart from that', referring to something previously mentioned. **Else** follows the word it refers to.

4 The word **excluding** is used to focus on particular elements which are excluded from a larger number. It is the opposite of **including** (▶ 17.5).

Alternatives

17.8 Some of the more common ways of referring to alternatives are listed in the table below.

You can take	the train **or** the coach.	
	either the train **or** the coach.	
	the train **rather than** the coach.	
You can take the train.	**Or else** **Alternatively** **Otherwise**	you can take the coach.
You can take the train **or** you can take the coach **instead**.		

1 You can get there by BÚS, TRÁIN **or** UŃderground.
Would you like BÉER, WHÍSky **or** WÌNE?

1 The most common way of expressing the idea of alternative is by using **or**. If there are more than two alternatives presented, **or** precedes the final element in the list; the other items are separated by commas.
In lists of this type, in the spoken language, there is a tendency to use a rising intonation for each item except the last one, which is spoken with a falling intonation to indicate the end of the list (see Appendix A).

2 a) **Either** help me **or** go away.
Take **either** the pen **or** the pencil but leave me one of them.

b) **Either** Paris **or** Vienna **is** going to be the venue for the congress.
If you see **either** George **or** Jim will you give **him/them** a message?

2 a) **Either ... or** emphasises the fact that there are only two alternatives.

b) When **either ... or** refers to two singular nouns which are the *subject* of the sentence, the following verb is normally *singular*. However plural pronouns are sometimes used to refer to nouns joined by **either ... or**.

c) There are two rooms free. You can have **either**.

3 I would send a telex **rather than** a letter.

4 There are only two choices: pay them the money **or else** go to the police.
Eat your dinner; **or else** you won't get any icecream.
Please repair the television – **or else** give me back the money.
Compare:
If you do**n't** repair the television, give me back the money.

5 a) I want you to keep quiet. **Otherwise** I'll get very annoyed.
Keep quiet. I'll get very annoyed **otherwise**.

b) I could meet you at the office.
Alternatively, I could go to your house
Compare:
Use these machines carefully. **Otherwise** you could damage them.

c) **Either** can also function as a pronoun.

3 **Rather than** can also express an idea of *preference* (▶ 26.12).

4 **Else** can be used in the sense of 'in addition' (▶ 17.4) or 'as an alternative'. It is often used after **or** as a way of reinforcing the sense of alternative.
The expression **or else** can be used at the beginning of a clause, in the sense of **otherwise**. Compare the use of **if not/ unless** (▶ 20.11) to convey a similar meaning.

5 a) **Otherwise** has a similar meaning to **or else** and may also be used in a conditional sense, meaning **if not**. It can be placed at the beginning or at the end of the sentence (see also ▶ 17.7, 20.13).

b) **Alternatively** means 'as an alternative'. It does not have a conditional meaning and so cannot always replace **otherwise**. **Alternatively** is used in more formal English. It is normally placed at the beginning of the sentence.

Other, another

17.9

1 Try some **other** sandwiches if you don't like these.
Don't go to that pub – go to the **other** one.
We lost one match but won all the **others**.
Which do you prefer – this wine or the **other**?

2 **Some** countries have free elections, **others** don't.
Some people say we should ban smoking completely, **others** disagree.

3 I had seen the western already so I went to see **another** film – a musical (= a different film).
Compare:
I've seen too many films today. I don't want to see **another** one (= any more films).

1 The adjective **other** expresses a sense of alternative, referring to something different from what has already been mentioned. **Other** is often followed by **one(s)** but can also be used on its own as a pronoun. Notice the plural pronoun form **others**.

2 **Others** is often used in contrast with **some**. In the spoken language **some** is stressed in such sentences (/sʌm/).

3 **Another** (▶ 17.4) may also be used to express the idea of an alternative.

Instead (of)

17.10

1 I don't like fish – let's have chicken for dinner **instead**.
He didn't go to university. He found a job **instead**.

2 I bought 'Newsweek' **instead of** 'Time'.
Instead of just sitting here why don't we do something?

1 **Instead** implies the rejection of one alternative in favour of another. It is normally placed at the end of the sentence.

2 The preposition **instead of** precedes the word to which it refers.

Rather

17.11

1 I'm interested in reading the book **rather than** seeing the film.
You should have walked out **rather than** listen to that nonsense.

2 They**'d rather** work here in the office **than** in the factory.
She **prefers** to work in the morning **rather than** in the afternoon.
Many people **prefer** being paid in cash **to** receiving a cheque.

1 **Rather than** is also used to reject one alternative in favour of another. It can be followed by an **-ing** form or by an *infinitive without* **to**.

2 To express preference for one alternative it is possible to use the verbs **prefer** and **would rather** (▶ 26.12).

On the other hand

17.12

You can pay by cash or, **on the other hand,** by cheque.

On the other hand can also be used to express the idea of an alternative.

Use of stress, intonation and word order

17.13

I only like WATCHing football
(– I don't like playing it).

I only like watching FOOTball
(– I don't like watching tennis).

Sally can DRIVE too
(– not only type but also drive).

SALly can drive too
(– not only Jim but also Sally).

In the spoken language, stress and intonation play a fundamental role in clarifying meaning, particularly in the case of concepts like *inclusion, restriction, exclusion* and *alternative*. Through stress and intonation, emphasis can be placed on specific elements within the sentence (▶ Chapter 18 and Appendix A).

17.14

I like watching **only** football.
Sally **too** can drive.

In the written language, the context normally helps to clarify the meaning but, where there is possible ambiguity, the relevant adverb can often be placed *immediately before* (or *immediately after*) the word to which it refers.

18 Focus and emphasis

Devices of focus and emphasis

18.1

In the spoken language it is possible to use the voice itself to place greater *emphasis* on certain words. This can be done through *stress, intonation* (▶ Appendix A) or significant *pauses*. In this way a sentence containing exactly the same words may take on different meanings according to which words are emphasised:

TOM flew to London. (= Tom, not somebody else)

Tom FLEW to London. (= He took a plane, not a train or a coach)

Tom flew to ... LONdon! (= Can you believe that?)

In the written language the same type of effect may be produced by changing the physical characteristics of the writing – using capital letters, underlining, different styles of writing or print:

Get OUT of here!
The Thames is the longest river in Britain.
There are *four* different possibilities.
Chapter 1 introduces the topic of the book.

However the language itself also provides means of placing emphasis. This chapter looks at how the grammatical organisation of the sentence, or the inclusion within it of certain emphasising words, may draw attention to one particular element in that sentence.

The principal ways in which *focussing* and *emphasising* are carried out are through:
1 the word order of the sentence;
2 adjectives and adverbs;
3 emphatic pronouns;
4 auxiliary verbs;
5 focussing language;
6 exclamatory language;
7 passive structures.

Word order

18.2

1 a) The journey takes five hours.
    Alex stayed in bed all day.
    It was a marvellous film.
    He said his name was Lenny.
    Her dress cost £500.

    Compare:
  b) Five hours the journey takes.
    All day Alex stayed in bed.
    A marvellous film it was!
    Lenny, he said his name was.
    £500 her dress cost!

1 Any change in the normal word order of a sentence (▶ 1.4–1.6) will have the effect of attracting the attention of a listener or reader. Within the sentence an important position is at the beginning because it is at this point that the listener or reader is usually introduced to the 'subject matter' of the sentence. For this reason the grammatical 'subject' (**a**) normally comes first.
If another element is placed at the beginning it takes on greater importance (**b**). This type of sentence is common in informal English.

2 a) Under the tree **sat a beautiful girl**.
   High up in the mountain **lived an old man**.
   Here **comes the sun**!
   There **goes my bus**!
   Here**'s the postman**.

   b) Under the tree **she sat**.
   There **she is**!

3 a) **In no way can they** possibly help you.
   Rarely have I seen such a magnificent building.
   Not only does he waste his time but he also wastes my money.
   Only a month later **did I** start feeling better.

   Compare:
   b) They can't possibly help you in any way.
   I started feeling better only a month later.

2 a) If an expression of place comes first in the sentence, the subject and the verb are often *inverted* (however notice that the verb is not in an interrogative structure). After **here** and **there** this inversion is obligatory.
   b) When the subject is a pronoun there is no inversion.

   NOTE: For **there** as an 'empty' introductory word ▶ 1.4.

3 a) In formal written English negative or restrictive expressions (e.g. **rarely, seldom, never, no, (not) only, hardly**, etc.) may be emphasised by being placed first in the sentence. In this case there is an inversion of the subject and the auxiliary verb. When there is no auxiliary in the basic sentence **do** is added (▶ 6.13).
   b) In informal English such inversions are not normally used.

Emphatic adjectives and adverbs

18.3

1 The film was **great**!
   I like that group: they're **terrific**.
   I've got an **awful** lot of things to do.
   The concert was **terrible** – it was really boring.

2 That actress is **so** good!
   We had **such** terrible weather!
   So beautifully **did she** sing that I couldn't take my eyes off her.
   She's **such** a singer!

3 He's **really** nice.
   I'm **definitely** not coming to your party.
   The story was **terribly** boring.
   She drives **positively** dangerously.

4 Where **on earth** have you been?
   Why **ever** didn't you tell her?
   How **on earth** did you find it?
   What **the hell** did you do that for?

1 Many adjectives are used specifically to increase the effect of what is being said, either positively (e.g. **great, fantastic, tremendous, terrific**), or negatively (e.g. **awful, terrible, dreadful**).

2 **So** and **such** (▶ 14.6) may be used to emphasise adjectives, adverbs and sometimes also nouns. In formal English they may be placed at the beginning of the sentence with inversion of subject and auxiliary verb (▶ 18.2).

3 Other adverbs of degree (▶ 14.2–14.5) may also emphasise adjectives, adverbs and verbs (e.g. **really, absolutely, definitely, certainly, positively, terribly, awfully**, etc.).

4 Expressions like **ever, on earth** or **the hell** (very strong, indicating anger) may be added to the question word.

5 I don't like him **at all**.
They did no work **whatsoever**.
It's got nothing **whatever** to do with you.

5 **At all, whatsoever, whatever** are used to increase the force of a negative sentence.

For **whatever, whoever,** etc. see also ▶ 16.16.

Emphatic pronouns

18.4

1 I **myself** did it.
Henry **himself** said that.
She wrote to the President **himself**.

2 I did it **myself**.
Henry said that **himself**.
They built their house **themselves**.
She wrote to the President **herself**.

1 *Reflexive pronouns* (▶ 5.6–5.8) can be used to emphasise a noun or another pronoun by being placed immediately after it.

2 An emphatic pronoun which refers to the subject of the sentence is often placed at the end of the sentence instead of after the subject.

Auxiliary verbs

18.5

She **DOES** know my name (even if she says she doesn't).

So you **DID** speak to him (even if you say you didn't).

They **DO** look miserable. (= They look very miserable)

The auxiliary verb **do** (▶ 6.13) can be introduced in affirmative sentences to emphasise the verb. In the spoken language **do** must be given emphatic stress when it is used in this way.
For emphatic **do** in imperatives ▶ 25.2.

Focussing on elements in the sentence

18.6

1 **It was Elizabeth** who phoned me.
It's the kitchen that's too small.
It was behind the supermarket that I parked the car.
It was the Russians who sent the first man into space.
It's the Jacksons who live across the road.

1 The pronoun **it** followed by the verb **be** can be used at the beginning of a sentence to focus attention on a particular word or phrase, which is normally followed by a relative clause (▶ 8.19). **It** may be used to focus on a plural as well as a singular noun. In the spoken language the word on which the attention is focussed would normally be stressed.

2 **What Charles wants** is a good wife.
What you need is a nice cup of tea.
A nice cup of tea is **what you need**.

2 A similar effect may be created using a clause beginning with **what** as the subject of the verb **be**. The sequence of clauses can also be reversed.

3 **Nixon was the one** who had to resign.
Margaret and Terry are the ones who should pay.

3 Another focussing structure involves the use of **be** with the pronoun **one(s)** (▶ 4.5). This structure is also normally followed by a relative clause.

4 a) A: Did you pass the exams?
   B: No, I failed in **both** French **and** English.

   b) A: Who was at the party?
   B: Almost everybody was there **except for** Margaret.

   c) A: Why did he kill her?
   B: **Only** the butler can tell us that.

   d) A: When could I come?
   B: I can give you an appointment on **either** Monday **or** Thursday.

4 Certain expressions related to the concepts of *inclusion, exclusion, restriction* and *alternative* also function as a means of focussing attention on particular elements in the sentence. The examples are related to:
   a) *inclusion* ▶ 17.1–17.5;
   b) *exclusion* ▶ 17.7;
   c) *restriction* ▶ 17.6;
   d) *alternatives* ▶ 17.8.

Focussing on ideas

18.7 Other expressions are used to focus more generally, on the *ideas* that are being discussed rather than on particular elements in the sentence.

1 In this lecture I intend to look at the role of the media.
With regard to television . . .
As far as radio **is concerned** . . .
As regards the newspapers . . .

1 When a speaker is dealing with more than one topic, certain expressions are used to focus attention on what each topic is, and to clarify when there is a change from one topic to another. Typical expressions used in this way are: **with regard to, regarding, as regards, as for, as far as . . . is concerned**.

2 This government has three major aims. **In the first place** we want to reduce taxation. **Secondly** we intend to expand the economy and **finally** we will strengthen national defence.

2 The sequencing of ideas allows us to focus on each one in turn. Many of the expressions used to sequence actions in time (▶ 11.42) can be used in this way.

3 The new power station is far too expensive and, **what's more**, it will damage the environment. **Besides** it isn't even necessary.

3 Other expressions are used to focus on additional ideas in turn, but at the same time to indicate that they are *reinforcing* the preceding idea (▶ 17.2).

4 It is true that the new power station is expensive. **However** it will eventually reduce the cost of energy. It will cause some damage to the environment. **On the other hand** it will create employment in the area.

4 It is also possible to focus on new ideas while, at the same time, indicating that they will be *in contrast with* the preceding idea (▶ 16.12, 16.13).

Exclamations

18.8

1 a) **What** dirty water!
   What beautiful flowers!
   What weather!

1 Exclamatory sentences are formed using:
   a) **what** (+ *adjective*) + *uncountable noun/ plural noun;*

b) **What a** nice day!
What an incredible adventure!
What a woman!

c) **How** nice!
How pleasant!

d) **How** she treats her husband!
How well she plays the piano!

2 a) **What** beautiful flowers **you've bought**!
What weather **we're having**!
What dirty water **to swim in**!

b) **What** a nice day **it is**!
What a woman **she is**!
What an incredible adventure **to have**!

c) **How** nice **this icecream is**!
How pleasant **to sit here** in the sun!

3 **What** a large house he lives **in**!
What strange people you work **with**!

4 **Wasn't it** exciting! (= How exciting it was!)

Isn't she a good cook! (= What a good cook she is!)

Aren't they lovely! (= How lovely they are!)

---

b) **what a/an** (+ *adjective*) + *singular countable noun*;
c) **how** + *adjective*;
d) **how** (+ *adverb*) + *subject* + *verb*.

2 In the first three cases in **1** above the exclamation is used on its own. But it may also be followed either by *subject* + *verb* or by the *to-infinitive*.
Notice that in all cases the word order is that of an *affirmative*, not an interrogative sentence.

3 Any *prepositions* are placed at the end of the sentence.

4 Sentences with a *negative-interrogative* structure are also used as exclamations (▶ 2.15). In this case these sentences do not function as questions. They are therefore spoken with falling intonation. In writing they are followed by an exclamation mark, not a question mark.

18.9

1 **Very good!** Your work is excellent!
What a shame! Are you sure you can't come?
Fine! I'll see you tomorrow then.
Nonsense! You know we can't afford it.
Poor Peter! He's lost his job.
If only she would listen to me!

2 a) **Aha,** this is just what I was looking for.

b) **Oh,** what a pretty garden!
Wow, that's great news!

c) **Ooh,** I like chocolate!

d) **Ugh,** isn't it ugly!

---

1 There are numerous idiomatic expressions which are used in informal English as exclamations.

For **if only** ▶ 26.7.

2 Informal English uses various exclamatory *interjections* to express different emotions such as:
a) (cautious) satisfaction;
b) surprise;
c) pleasure;
d) disgust.

Use of passive

18.10

The *passive* is not simply an alternative means of expressing what can already be expressed through an active sentence. Sometimes it is more natural and efficient to express the meaning through a passive construction.

For construction of passive verbs and sentences ▶ 3.1–3.8.

1 The traffic **has been paralysed** for hours.
The name of the new president **will be announced** tomorrow.
Several million people **were killed** in the war.
A window **has been broken** in the kitchen.
Ten people **were arrested** yesterday.

2 Medicines **should be kept** in a dry place.
Dogs **are not allowed** inside the shop.

3 Water **is heated** to 85°C.
When a solution of sodium chloride **is added** to one of silver nitrate, sodium nitrate and silver chloride **are formed**.

4 The picture was painted by **one of the most famous artists of the Renaissance**.
She was taught English by **Dr Roberts, who is the Chief Inspector for the whole of the northern province**.

5 A: Did Graham Greene write 'Heart of Darkness'?
B: No, **'Heart of Darkness' was written** by Joseph Conrad.

1 Sometimes we wish to draw attention to the result of an action or to the process involved in an action rather than to the agent of the action.
It may be that we cannot or do not want to mention the agent of an action, for example when the agent is unknown or made obvious by the context.

2 Passive structures can create an indirect, impersonal effect in giving *orders*, *prohibitions* and *instructions*, especially in formal written language.

3 Passives are often used to describe *experiments*, *processes* or *instructions*, especially in scientific and technical English.

In the three cases above the *agent* of the action (introduced using **by**) is usually omitted, creating an impersonal impression.

4 Sometimes use of the passive can improve the *style* of a sentence. This happens, for example, when the agent is described at such length that it would be clumsy to make it the subject of an active sentence.

5 A passive structure may also be chosen as a means of *focussing* on a particular noun by making it the subject and placing it at the beginning of the sentence.

19 Certainty and uncertainty

The language used to express feelings of *certainty* and *uncertainty* can be divided into a number of general areas, each representing a different level of conviction:

1 *Certainty* (in both a positive and negative sense):   I'm sure he is there/isn't there.
2 *Probability:*   He's probably there.
3 *Possibility:*   Perhaps he's there.
4 *Improbability:*   He probably isn't there.
5 *Uncertainty:*   I'm not sure if he is there.
6 *Lack of information:*   I don't know if he's there.

Certainty

Adjectives and adverbs

19.2 A number of adjectives and adverbs can be used to express the idea of certainty.

It is	obvious clear certain	(that) he is telling lies.
I'm	certain sure convinced positive	(that) he is telling lies.
He is	obviously clearly certainly definitely undoubtedly	telling lies.

1 It's **clear** that you don't want to help me.

2 a) **It's certain** that the match is taking place today.

  b) **Peter/He is certain** that the match is taking place today.

3 They're **sure to arrive** this evening.
(= It is certain that they will arrive)
Carol is **certain to be** there.
An encyclopedia is **bound to have** that information.

4 **Obviously** he's doing it for money.
You've seen the film, **naturally**.
Of course she knows how to drive.

1 Some adjectives (e.g. **obvious, clear**) can only be used impersonally.

2 **Certain** can be used either (**a**) impersonally or (**b**) qualifying a noun or personal pronoun.

3 **Certain, sure** and **bound** can be followed by the **to**-*infinitive* form to indicate *certainty*.

4 The adverbs given in the table can also appear at the beginning of the sentence.
Of course and **naturally** also indicate certainty and may be placed either at the beginning or at the end of the sentence.

5 **Surely** they haven't arrived yet. It's much too early.

5 Notice that the adverb **surely** expresses *surprise*, not certainty.

Other ways of indicating certainty

19.3 Other typical ways of indicating certainty include the following:

1 We all **know** who took the money.
  I **know** she saw me.

1 the verb **know** used in the affirmative;

2 There's **no doubt** at all that space exploration will continue.
  I **don't doubt** that the Republicans are going to win the election.

2 negative expressions with **no doubt/don't doubt**.

Modal verbs: **must, will, can't, couldn't**

19.4 Some modal verbs indicate positive or negative certainty.

That	must will	be Mary on the phone.
It	can't couldn't	be Mary. She's away on holiday.

1 a) She **must** be very tired after working so hard all day.
      It **must** be about two o'clock. (= Not long ago it was half past one)

1 a) **Must** (▶ 6.15–6.18) expresses a feeling of *certainty as a logical conclusion*. The reason for coming to this conclusion may be stated or may be understood from the context.

   b) That noise **has got to** stop sooner or later. (= It can't go on forever)
      A: Who's that at the door?
      B: That **will** be the postman. He always comes at this time.

   b) **Have got to** (▶ 6.10) and **will** (▶ 6.15–6.18) express the same idea but are not used so frequently. **Have got to** is more forceful and more dogmatic than **must**. **Will** is less forceful, more casual.

2 a) He left here two hours ago, so he **must/ will have arrived** by now. (= It **is** certain that he has arrived)
      You **must/will have paid** a lot of money for this painting. (= It **is** certain that you paid a lot of money)

2 To express the same type of certainty about the *past* we must distinguish between two situations:
   a) a *present certainty about a past event*: **must** (or sometimes **will**) + *past infinitive* without **to**;

   b) He was driving so fast that there **had to be** an accident. (= Under those circumstances it **was** certain that there would be an accident)

   b) a *past certainty*: **had to** + *infinitive*.

19.5

1 You **can't/couldn't** be that tired. We have only walked a mile!
She **can't/couldn't** be seventy yet. She is still working.
It **can't/couldn't** be so late already. (= It must be earlier)

2 a) Mrs Mariner **can't have received** your gift yet. It takes two days for the post to arrive. (= There is *present* evidence that she has not received it)
Johnny **can't have gone** far. Look, his bike is still here. (= The evidence *is here* in front of us)

b) What I heard **couldn't have been** true. (= There *was* evidence that it was not true)
He **couldn't have stolen** the money. He was with me at the time. (= A situation *in the past* provided the evidence in his favour)

1 It is possible to use both **can't** and **couldn't** to express negative certainty about a present situation as a result of a logical conclusion. In this sense they can be considered as opposites of **must**.

NOTE: **Mustn't** cannot be used in this sense. It can only be used for *prohibitions* (▶ 24.11).

2 To express the same type of negative certainty about the past, we must again distinguish between two situations;
a) certainty based on *present* evidence:
can't + *past infinitive without* **to** (**couldn't** is possible, but less likely);
b) certainty based on *past* evidence:
couldn't + *past infinitive without* **to** (**can't** is not possible).

Probability

19.6   The following table lists some common ways of expressing a sense of *probability:*

I	expect suppose should think dare say/daresay	that he lives near here.
It is	likely probable	that it will rain.
He probably lives near here.		
There's a good chance that he'll do it.		

1 They're **likely to be** here this weekend.
The flight is **likely to be** cancelled.

1 In addition to the impersonal structures shown in the table, **likely** followed by the **to**-*infinitive* can also be used to qualify a noun or a personal pronoun.

2 **It is probable** that the Government will resign soon.
You'll **probably** find the newspaper in the kitchen.
In all probability the species will be extinct within twenty years.

2 **It is probable** is used in more formal English. In informal English, the adverb **probably** is much more commonly used. The expression **in all probability** is used in very formal English.

Other ways of indicating probability

19.7 Other common ways of expressing *degrees of probability* are:

1 I'm **almost sure** I saw it move.
He was **fairly certain** he had dialled the correct number.

2 I **wouldn't be (at all) surprised if** they got married.

1 using adverbs of degree (▶ 14.2–14.8) to reduce the force of some expressions normally referring to certainty;

2 colloquial expressions.

Modal verbs: **should, ought to**

19.8

1 The cigarettes **should** be on the shelf; I left them there.
If I start now I **should** finish this letter by six o'clock.
If I post it tomorrow it **ought to** reach her next week.

2 My letter **should have arrived.** I posted it two days ago.
Why didn't the airport information office tell you about the change of flight time? They **ought to have known** about any delays.

1 The modal verbs **should** and **ought to** (▶ 6.15–6.18) can be used to express probability in the *present* or *future*.

2 To express probability concerning a *past* event the following structure can be used:
should/ought to + *past infinitive*.
For **should/ought to have** as an expression of unfulfilled obligation ▶ 24.5.

Possibility

19.9

There's	a chance some chance a possibility some possibility	(that) the record will be successful.
It's possible		
Perhaps Maybe Possibly	the record will be successful.	

1 a) There's **a chance of going** to London tomorrow.
   There's **a possibility of rain** in Scotland.

   b) There's **a chance that** he will pass the exam.

   c) **He has a chance of passing** the exam.

2 **Maybe** we'll go and see the film.
   Possibly the noise will disturb the neighbours.

1 **Possibility** is used in formal English, **chance** in informal English.
   a) They can be followed by **of** + *noun* or **-ing** form (*verbal noun*).
   b) They can also be followed by a clause beginning with **that**.
   c) In addition, **have a chance** can be used with a personal subject.

2 The adverbs **perhaps, maybe, possibly** are normally placed at the beginning of the sentence.
   Maybe is more informal than **possibly** or **perhaps**.

Specific possibility: modal verbs **may, might, could**

19.10

The record	may might could	be successful.

1 a) Let's wait for him. He **may** be on his way now.
   This book **might** have the information.

   b) It **may** be foggy tomorrow.
   Take a scarf. It **could** get cold later on.

2 **Do you think** this book **might** have the information.
   Do you think it **may** be foggy tomorrow?

3 It **may not** be so late. (= It is possible that it isn't so late)
   He **may not** succeed, but he's going to try.
   The shop **might not** be open now.
   Compare:
   The shop **couldn't** be open now. It's already eight o'clock.

1 To express the *specific possibility* that something is (**a**) actually true *now* or (**b**) will actually happen in the *future* we can use **may, might** or **could**. **Might** and **could** express a rather more remote possibility.

2 **May, might** and **could** are not normally used to make a direct question about this type of possibility. Instead questions can be expressed using forms like **Do you think ...?**

3 **May not** and **might not** can be used to express *negative possibility*.

NOTE: **Could not** has a completely different meaning, expressing *negative certainty* as a result of logical conclusion (▶ 19.5).

Specific possibility in the past

19.11

1 My cousin took the train last night so he **may have arrived** by now.
   He **might have been** telling the truth but I didn't believe him.
   Why not? His story **could have been** true.

1 A similar type of *specific possibility* but with reference to the *past* is conveyed by **may/might/could** + *past infinitive without* **to**.

2 Some of you **may not have heard** the news so I'll tell you what has happened.
Don't worry! The boss **might not have seen** you coming in late.

Compare:
Don't worry! The boss **could not have seen** you coming in late. He was busy in his office when you arrived.

2 **May not have** and **might not have** can be used to express a *negative possibility* in the past.

NOTE: **Could not have** has a completely different meaning, expressing *past negative certainty* as a result of logical conclusion (▶ 19.5).

General possibility: modal verbs **can, could**

19.12

1 New York **can** be very dangerous at night.
Watching TV **can** get rather boring.
My brother **can** lose his temper quickly.
It **can** be very difficult to find a hotel in London.
Being a teacher **can** be very frustrating sometimes.

2 When I was at school the discipline **could** get very strict.
In the Middle Ages, travelling **could** be very dangerous.

1 Paragraphs 19.10–19.11 are concerned with *specific possibility*, something which may or may not actually happen *on a particular occasion*. There is another type of possibility, *general possibility*, which is linked to a general situation and not to a particular occasion. The modal verb **can** is used to express this second type of possibility.

2 To express this type of *general possibility* in the *past* we can use **could**.

Improbability

19.13

I	don't expect don't suppose don't think shouldn't think	that	he lives near here.
	doubt if/whether		

It is	unlikely improbable	that it will rain.

There's not much chance that he'll do it.

1 It is **unlikely** that it will rain. (= It is **likely** that it will **not** rain)
I **don't expect** that they will come. (= I **expect** that they will **not** come.)

2 I **doubt if** I'll be ready on time.
I **doubt whether** we will ever discover the truth.

1 Because *improbability* corresponds to *negative probability*, it is often expressed through the negative forms of the structures used to express *probability* (▶ 19.6).

2 The verb **doubt** is usually followed by **if** or **whether** rather than **that**.

3 The Prime Minister is **unlikely to call** an election this year.
He's **unlikely to have** a car.

4 **It is improbable** that there is any form of life on Venus.

3 **Unlikely** can also be used, followed by **to-**-*infinitive*, to qualify a noun or a personal pronoun.

4 **It is improbable** is used in more formal English.

Modal verbs: **shouldn't, oughtn't to**

19.14

1 It **shouldn't** be difficult to translate this passage.
There **oughtn't to** be any more road works on the motorway tomorrow.

2 My letter **shouldn't have arrived** yet.

1 The modal verbs **shouldn't** and **oughtn't to** can be used to express improbability in the *present* or *future*.

2 **Shouldn't/oughtn't to** + *past infinitive* can express improbability concerning a *past* event.

Uncertainty

19.15

I	'm not	sure certain	if/whether she's Australian (or not).
	couldn't say (for sure) wouldn't like to say (for sure)		
There's some doubt (about)			
It's not	clear certain		where she comes from.

1 It's **not clear** whether he'll come or not.
I'm **not certain** if this is the right bus to Piccadilly.

2 There's some **doubt** whether they will reach an agreement.

3 I'm **not sure what** time we're leaving.
I **wouldn't like to say how long** it will take.

1 *Uncertainty* can be conveyed by using **not** + adjectives expressing *certainty* (▶ 19.2).

2 Expressions with **doubt** (▶ 19.3) are also used to express uncertainty.

3 These expressions of uncertainty can be followed by a clause beginning either with a **wh-**word (including **how**) or **if/whether**. Compare reporting interrogatives (▶ 22.6, 22.7).

Lack of information

19.16

I	(really) don't know have no idea haven't (got) a clue	if/whether the letter has been posted.
It's impossible for me to say		
It's no	use good	asking me	when the letter was written.

1 They **haven't got a clue** where to go. They're lost.
   It's no good asking me where your glasses are.

2 I **have no idea if** there's a direct flight to Chicago.
   I **really don't know how much** the ticket will cost.

1 A variety of expressions are used to convey the idea of 'not knowing'. **I haven't got a clue** and **It's no use/good asking me** are only used in informal English.

2 These expressions can be followed by a clause beginning either with a **wh-**word or **if/whether**.

   Compare reporting interrogatives (▶ 22.6, 22.7).

20 Unreal events and conditions

20.1 Sometimes we wish to talk about imaginary situations rather than events that have actually happened or are actually happening now. This chapter deals with ways of expressing such *unreal* events or situations. It looks at different means of presenting a hypothetical situation, the verb tenses used in referring to it and ways of expressing the conditions necessary for the realisation of an *unreal* event.

Hypothetical situations

Verb tenses in hypothetical situations

20.2 **(Let's) suppose, supposing** and **imagine** are expressions typically used to put forward a hypothesis. To convey the hypothetical nature of an event the verb tenses are different from those normally used:

1 Let's suppose (that) you **change** your job next year.
  Supposing he **doesn't get** here in time.
  Imagine (that) you **became** the Prime Minister.

1 If the hypothetical situation is set in the *future* the verb is in the *present tense* or, when the hypothetical situation is considered very unlikely to happen, in the *past tense*.

2 Let's suppose (that) you **changed** your job now.
  Suppose (that) we **lived** in the country.
  Imagine (that) dogs **could** talk.
  Let's suppose (that) he **were/was** right.
  Imagine (that) I **were/was** your father.

2 If the hypothetical situation is set in the *present* the verb is in the *past tense*.

  NOTE: In formal English, if the verb is **be**, it takes the form **were** (even after the pronouns **I, he, she, it**).
  In informal English **was** can be used.

3 Let's suppose (that) you **had changed** your job last year.
  Suppose (that) she **had failed** her exams in June.
  Imagine (that) Morocco **had won** the World Cup.

3 If the hypothetical situation is set in the *past* the verb is in the *past perfect tense*. This shows that the verb refers to an event which did not happen.
  Notice that the conjunction **that** would follow **(Let's) suppose** and **Imagine** in formal language or careful speech.

Summary table

20.3

Time reference	Degree of probability	Verb tense
future	possible	present (e.g. Suppose he **comes)**
present or future	improbable	past (e.g. Suppose he **came**)
past	impossible (i.e. the event didn't happen)	past perfect (e.g. Suppose he **had come**)

Desire, obligation and unreal events

20.4 Unreal events can be introduced by certain expressions indicating some form of desire or obligation.

1 **It's time we went** back home.
It's high time you started doing some work.

Compare:
It's time **for you to start** doing some work.

2 **I'd rather** you had been more truthful.

3 **If only** I were younger.
I wish I had met you before.

1 **It's (high) time** expresses a sense of urgency or irritation.
Forms like **it's time for us to go** are also possible but do not have the sense of urgency.

2 **Would rather/'d rather** expresses preference (▶ 26.12)

3 **If only** and the verb **wish** express desire or regret concerning something which is not easily attainable or something which has not occurred (▶ 26.7)

NOTE: These expressions cannot be used with a verb in the present tense.

Should

20.5 **Should** can sometimes have a hypothetical meaning. It can be used to refer to the *idea* of performing a certain action regardless of whether or not the action is actually carried out. It is used:

1 He **recommended** that we **should** see a lawyer.
My uncle **insisted** that he **should** pay for the meal.

2 **It's important** that the contract **should** be signed.
It's essential that everybody **should** arrive on time.

Compare:
He recommended that **we see** a lawyer.
It's important that **the contract be signed**.

1 after verbs of *ordering* and *suggesting* (▶ 25.10): **suggest, advise, recommend, propose, order, command, request, insist,** etc.;

2 after impersonal expressions of *obligation, importance,* etc. **it's important/vital/ essential/necessary,** etc. (▶ 24.4).

NOTE: In both cases **should** can be omitted without changing the meaning of the sentence.

Conditional sentences

20.6

If it's sunny I'll go for a walk.
I'll go for a walk if it's sunny.
If the engine got too hot it would switch itself off.
I'll take another chocolate if that's all right.

Conditional sentences deal with an event or a situation (e.g. **I'll go for a walk**) which is, or was, dependent on the fulfilment of a *condition* (e.g. **if it's sunny**).
Conditional sentences are hypothetical. Both the condition and the outcome are imaginary. The *condition-outcome* sequence can be reversed.

Types of conditional sentence

20.7 There are three basic types of conditional sentence which correspond to the three types of hypothetical situation presented in 20.2, 20.3:

1 **If I have** time **I'll finish** the work tomorrow.
He'll sing if everybody is quiet.
If they offer you the job **will you take** it?
She'll help you **if she is** able to.

1 A possible *future action* is dependent on a possible *future condition*. The verb in the main clause has a *future* form (usually with **will**). The verb in the conditional **if** clause has a *present tense* form even though it refers to the future.

2 **If I had** time **I would finish** the work now (but I don't have time).
He would sing if everybody were quiet.
If they offered you the job **would you take** it?
She'd help you **if she were** able to.

2 An imaginary *present or future action* is impossible, or very unlikely to take place, because it is dependent on a *condition which is not fulfilled*. The verb in the main clause takes the modal auxiliary verb **would.** The verb in the conditional clause has a *past tense* form. **Were** is often used instead of **was** (▶ 20.2).

3 **If I had had** time **I would have finished** the work yesterday (but I didn't have time so I didn't finish).
He would have sung if everybody had been quiet.
If they had offered you the job **would you have taken** it?
She'd have helped you **if she'd been** able to.

3 An imaginary action *in the past* didn't take place because it was dependent on a *condition which was not fulfilled*. The verb in the main clause takes the form **would have** + *past participle* (i.e. **would** + *past infinitive*). The verb in the conditional clause has a *past perfect* form.

Summary table: conditional sentences

20.8

Type	Time reference	Degree of probability	Verb tenses	
			Conditional clause	*Main clause*
1	future	possible	present (If I **am** free I **will** come.)	**will** + infinitive without **to**
2	present or future	improbable	past (If I **were** free I **would** come.)	**would** + infinitive without **to**
3	past	impossible (i.e. the event did not happen)	past perfect (If I **had been** free I **would have** come.)	**would** + past infinitive without **to**

Variations in patterns of conditional sentences

20.9 Variations are possible in the three basic patterns of conditional sentence shown in the table above:

1. If **he's working** I won't disturb him.
   If I did that **I'd be taking** a big risk.
   If **you had been standing** here you'd have seen the accident.

2. If I hurry I **can** catch the ten-thirty train.
   If you **must** ring your parents you **can** do it from here.
   If we had the time we **could** do a better job.

3. a) If they're studying **don't interrupt** them.

   b) If the temperature **rises** the water **evaporates**.

   c) If **you've found** a mistake we'll check it again.

4. If he **had followed** my advice he **would** feel much better now.

5. If Linda **should arrive/arrives** before six o'clock she won't find anybody there.
   If you **were to see/saw** her what would you say?
   If **by any chance** you pass the newsagent's, buy me a paper.
   If you **happen to** pass the newsagent's, buy me a paper.

1. *Progressive forms* may appear in both the conditional and the main clause.

2. *Modal auxiliary verbs* may appear in both the conditional and the main clause.

3. In *Type 1* conditional sentences:
   a) The *imperative form* may appear in the main clause.
   b) In sentences referring to general cause and effect the *present tense* may appear in both clauses.
   c) The *present perfect* may appear instead of the present in the conditional clause.

4. A combination of *Types 2 and 3* may occur in which the *past perfect* is used in the conditional clause and **would** in the main clause.

5. **Should** and **were to** may be used to express a condition which is considered less likely to be fulfilled.

   NOTE: The expressions **by any chance** and **happen to** may be added to give the same effect.

Alternatives to **if** in conditional sentences

20.10

1. My parents would buy me a flat **provided** (that) I got married.
   We'll go to the seaside **providing** it doesn't rain.
   I'll accept any job **as long as** I don't have to get up early.

2. **Suppose** you won a million pounds. What would be the first thing you'd do?
   Imagine Napoleon had won the battle of Waterloo. We would probably all be speaking French.

1. **On condition (that), provided (that), providing, so/as long as** are used to set *precise* conditions for the realisation of a certain action.

2. Instead of the condition and the outcome being contained in one sentence, they may be divided into two sentences. **(Let's) suppose, supposing, imagine, what if** may be used to present a *condition* (▶ 20.2, 20.3). The following sentence may then express the *outcome*.

3 I would never steal, **even if** I were the poorest man on earth.

4 He looked **as though** he had lost his temper. (= If he had lost his temper he would look like that)
You talk to me **as if** I were your servant. (= If I were your servant you would talk to me like that)

3 **Even if** combines the two notions of *contrast* and *condition* (▶ 16.15).

4 **As if,** and **as though,** which are used to make *comparisons,* also imply an element of *condition*.

Negative conditions

20.11

1 **Unless** my husband helps me I won't be able to clean the house.
If my husband doesn't help me I won't be able to do it.

2 a) **If it weren't for** my parents I would leave school. (= If my parents didn't prevent me . . .)

   b) **If it hadn't been for** your instructions we would have lost our way. (= If you hadn't provided instructions . . .)

   c) **If it weren't for the fact that** I'm so hungry I'd ask the waiter to take this steak away.

3 **But for** the rain we could sit in the park. (= **If it weren't for** . . .)
I wouldn't have survived **but for** the operation. (= **If it hadn't been for** . . .)
She would never have found out **but for the fact that** she had seen them together. (= **If it hadn't been for the fact that** . . .)

1 **Unless,** like **if . . . not,** expresses negative conditions.

2 a) The expression **if it weren't for** + *noun* can also be used to replace a negative conditional clause. The meaning is similar to a *Type 2* conditional sentence.

   b) **If it hadn't been for** + *noun* expresses the concept of negative condition with reference to the past, as in a *Type 3* conditional sentence.

   c) Both **if it weren't for** and **if it hadn't been for** can be used as conjunctions by adding **the fact that**.

3 In informal English **but for** + *noun* or **but for the fact that** + *clause* can be used instead of **if it weren't for** and **if it hadn't been for**.

Inversion in conditional sentences

20.12

We would have telephoned before **had we known** it was urgent. (= **If we had known** . . .)
Were the goods to arrive after the end of the month, we would cancel the order. (= **If the goods were to** . . .)
Should you want to contact me, call this number. (= **If you should** . . .)

In formal English when the verb phrase in a conditional clause contains the auxiliary forms **should, were to** (▶ 20.9) or the auxiliary verb **had,** the subject and auxiliary verb can be inverted and **if** can be omitted from the sentence.

Other means of expressing conditions

20.13

1 Come round **and** we'll talk about it. (= If you come round . . .)
Stop eating so much **or (else)** you'll get fat. (= If you don't stop eating so much . . .)
Take a map with you, **otherwise** you're sure to get lost. (= If you don't take a map . . .)

2 People **who are sensitive** can appreciate art. (= If people are sensitive . . .)

3 **In case of** emergency, please ring this number.
Compare:
In case someone attacks her she always carries a gun (as a precaution).
If someone attacks her she will shoot. (*not* **in case**)

4 Are you coming to the party? **If so,** will you bring some records? (= If you are coming to the party . . .)
I hope you're coming. **If not** I'll be very disappointed. (= If you're not coming . . .)

1 In sentences which function as *orders* or *suggestions*, **and** is often used to express a *positive* condition and **or (else)** or **otherwise** to express a *negative* condition.

2 Sometimes the idea of condition can be contained in a *relative clause*.

3 The expression **in case of** + *noun* is frequently used in public notices with the meaning **if there is**.

NOTE: **In case** + *clause* is used to express a *precaution*, not a condition (▶ 15.9)

4 **If so** and **if not** are used to avoid repeating words which have already been mentioned (▶ 4.8).

21 Asking questions and responding

One of the most important functions of a language is to provide the speaker with a means of *obtaining information* from other speakers. The way in which this is usually done is through *interrogative* structures (▶ 2.2–2.11). But we can also ask for information without using interrogative structures.

Questions

Questions and intonation

21.2

1 A: You LÍKE the play?
B: Yes, I do.
A: You're studying at uniVÉRsity?
B: Yes, that's right.
A: So she lived in PÁRis for a year?
B: Yes, she did.
2 A: He hasn't come HÓME yet?
B: No, he hasn't.
A: They don't WÓRK here any more?
B: No, they don't.

1 In the spoken language it is possible to ask questions *without* using interrogative structures. A sentence with an *affirmative* structure but spoken with rising intonation can be used as a question.
Notice that if this type of sentence is represented in written form it is followed by a question mark.

2 In the case of an *affirmative* sentence the speaker would normally expect to get an *affirmative* response. With a *negative* sentence the speaker would normally expect to get a *negative* response.

For more details about questions and intonation ▶ Appendix A6.

Polite questions

21.3

Sometimes we use the structure of *reported questions* (▶ 22.6) to avoid asking a direct question. This often happens out of politeness, when we wish to ask a question to a superior, or a stranger, or if the question is potentially embarrassing. The 'real' question is contained within the structure of:

1 I wonder if you could tell me what time the bus leaves.
I hope you don't mind my asking if you have ever been in trouble with the police.
2 Could I ask how much money you earn?
Would you mind telling me how old you are?

1 an affirmative sentence;

2 another question, more polite than the 'real' question.

Responses

21.4

1 A: Who told you that?
  B: **Mary told me (that).**
    Mary did.
    Mary.
  A: When did you ring me?
  B: **I rang you last night.**
    Last night.

2 A: Are you hungry?
  B: **Yes, I am./No, I'm not.**
  A: Has Robert failed his exam?
  B: **Yes, he has./No, he hasn't.**
  A: Does she get up early?
  B: **Yes, she does./No, she doesn't.**
  A: Didn't Andy go out?
  B: **Yes, he did./No, he didn't.**

3 A: Did Ann see John yesterday?
  B: **Yes, she saw him (at school).**
    Yes, she did.
    Yes.

4 A: Sue can swim very well.
  B: **Yes, she can.**
  A: You saw Carol last night.
  B: **I didn't.**
  A: I liked the film. It was very exciting.
  B: Yes, **it** really **was.**

5 a) A: Pauline lives in London now.
    B: **Really?**
    A: But she doesn't like it.
    B: **Oh?**
    A: She's thinking of emigrating to
      America.
    B: **I see.**
    A: Maybe she'll be happier over there.
    B: **Mm . . .**

  b) A: I saw Paul last night.
    B: **Did you?**
    A: He's married Jill, you know.
    B: **Has he?**
    A: Yes . . . but he can't find a job.
    B: Oh dear. **Can't he?**
    A: He wants to join the army.
    B: **Does he?**

1 In responding to a question it is not
necessary to repeat all the words contained
in the question. Longer answers tend to
sound more emphatic.

2 A response to a **yes/no** *question* is normally
limited to a *short response*, i.e. **yes** or **no**
followed by the personal pronoun which
corresponds to the subject of the question
and the auxiliary verb (with or without **not**).

3 A response to a **yes/no** *question* may consist
simply of **yes** or **no**. However these single
word responses usually sound too abrupt for
polite use.

4 Short responses may also be used to express
agreement or *disagreement* with something
which has been said. When there is no
auxiliary verb in the original sentence the
auxiliary **do** is used (▶ 27.14).

5 a) In everyday conversation a variety of
response expressions are employed to
demonstrate *surprise, pleasure, interest*,
etc. Sometimes they function simply as a
means of keeping the conversation 'alive'.
This is particularly true of telephone
conversations. If the listener doesn't make
these responses the speaker has no
encouragement to continue and
communication tends to dry up.
  b) *Short questions* with the same form as
question tags (▶ 2.11) are also used as
responses in this context.
A *negative short question* is the response
to a *negative sentence.*
Notice that for the responses in both a) and
b) rising intonation would tend to sound more
interested and involved (▶ Appendix A6).

22 Reporting

When someone reports what has been said by another person there is usually a time interval between the original utterance and the report. This presents no problem if the person reporting chooses simply to provide a *direct* quotation:

> ANN: I want to go home.
> Ann said, 'I want to go home.'

However if the reporting is done *indirectly* the time interval and change of speaker affect the tense and person of any verb which is reported:

> ANN: I **want** to go home.
> Ann said (that) she **wanted** to go home.

In *reported speech* there are three areas in which the original utterance may have to be changed:
a) *verb forms*;
b) *personal pronouns* and *possessive adjectives* and *pronouns*;
c) expressions connected with *time* and *place*.

NOTE: The use of the conjunction **that** in reported speech is optional.

Reporting speech without change of tense

1 a) The guide book says the cathedral **is** very interesting.

b) He's always asking me how much I **earn**.

c) Michael (phoning home):
'I'll be back late.'
Mother (to father):
'Michael says, he**'ll** be back late.'

2 She told me (that) the capital of Australia **is** Canberra.
The doctor said it **isn't** serious.
Compare:
'**I am** a student.'
He told me (that) **he is** a student.

3 'I don't want to go.'
He **has** already **said** he **doesn't want** to go.

1 Sometimes reported speech can be introduced by a verb in the *present* tense and then the verb tense in the original quotation remains *unchanged*. This often happens in the following cases:
a) reading and immediately reporting;
b) reporting a frequent remark;
c) reporting a conversation that is still continuing.

2 Particularly in *spoken* English tense changes are often not made in reported speech when referring to something that is still true at the time of reporting, and where there is no possibility of confusion over the meaning of the sentence.

NOTE: The form of the verb may change according to *person* (▶ 22.4).

3 Sometimes tense changes are not made in reported speech when the reporting verb is in the *present perfect*.

Reporting affirmative sentences

Changes in verb tenses

22.3 When reported speech is introduced by a verb in the *past tense*, the verb tenses in the original quotation are changed (but see 22.2 for reporting verbs in the present tense).

	Original quotation		Reported speech	
Present	'I drive' 'I'm driving'		he drove he was driving	
Past	'I drove' 'I have driven' 'I had driven' 'I was driving'	well.	he had driven he had driven he had driven he had been driving	well.
Modal auxiliaries	'I can drive' 'I may drive'		he could drive he might drive	
Modal auxiliaries in past form	'I could drive' 'I might drive'		he could drive he might drive	

(In 'Past' and 'Modal' rows, the middle column reads "He said (that)".)

1 'The meal **is** ready.'
He said (that) the meal **was** ready.
'**I'm** coming.'
He said (that) he **was** coming.

2 a) 'The train **left** at two o'clock.'
He said (that) the train **had left** at two o'clock.
'The match **has started**.'
He said (that) the match **had started**.

  b) 'I **was watching** TV.'
She said (that) she **had been watching** TV.

  c) 'I **had** already **seen** it.'
She said (that) she **had** already **seen** it.

3 'The manager **will** tell her.'
He said (that) the manager **would** tell her.
'You **can** go.'
She said (that) we **could** go.

1 *Present tense* verb forms (including present progressive) change to *past tense* forms.

2 a) *Past simple* and *present perfect* tenses change to *past perfect*.
  b) *Past progressive* forms change to *past perfect progressive*.
  c) *Past perfect* forms remain unchanged.

3 The same rule applies to modal auxiliary verbs, if they have a past form (▶ 6.15):
can → **could**
may → **might**
shall → **should**
will → **would**

4 'The film **should** be good.'
She said (that) the film **should** be good.
'The meal **had better** be ready.'
He said (that) the meal **had better** be ready.
'I **could** do it.'
He said (that) he **could** do it.

5 'The rules **must** be followed.'
She said (that) the rules **must/had to** be followed.
'I **must/will have to** leave soon.'
He said (that) he **must/had to/would have to** leave soon.

4 Modal verbs which do not have a past form or which are themselves past forms remain unchanged: **could, might, should, would, ought to, had better, used to** (▶ 6.15; **had better** ▶ 24.5).

5 **Must** can remain unchanged or be replaced by **had to** (or by **would have to** if **must** refers to the future in the original utterance).

Changes in personal pronouns and possessives

22.4

'**I** have left **my** umbrella on the bus.'
He said (that) **he** had left **his** umbrella on the bus.
Compare:
'**Colin** has seen **you**.'
He said (that) **you** (Colin) had seen **me**.

First and *second person personal pronouns, possessive adjectives* and *pronouns* change to the corresponding *third person* forms.

NOTE: If the reported quotation refers to either the speaker or the listener, the appropriate first or second person forms must obviously be used.

Changes in references to time and place

22.5

'The battle took place **here**.'
He said (that) the battle had taken place **there**.
'**This** is a wonderful place.'
He said (that) **that** was a wonderful place.
'I'll come back **tomorrow**.'
He said (that) he would come back **the following day**.
'The house was sold **last year**.'
He said (that) the house had been sold **the previous year**.
'We can **come** back **next week**. We will **bring** some of our records.'
They said (that) they could **go** back **the week after** and (that) they would **take** some of their records.

Expressions referring to time and place must be changed to reflect the distance (in both space and time) from the original utterance:
here → there
this, these → that, those
now → then
today, tonight → that day, that night
yesterday → the day before (or **the previous day**)
tomorrow → the day after (or **the following day**)
next week → the week after (or **the following week**)
last week → the week before (or **the previous week**)
a year ago → a year before
Verbs that imply a certain direction may also have to be changed, for example:
come → go
bring → take

Reporting interrogative sentences and imperatives

Reporting interrogative sentences

22.6

'Where are you going?'
She asked him **where he was going**.
'How much did it cost?'
He asked **how much it had cost**.
'Will there be enough time?'
He asked **if there would be enough time**.
'Do you smoke?'
She asked me **whether (or not) I smoked**.
'Has the post arrived?'
He asked me **whether (or not) the post had arrived**.

The changes described in paragraphs 22.3–22.5 are also made when reporting an *interrogative sentence*. Two additional characteristics of this type of reported sentence are:

a) Instead of **that,** a question word or **if/ whether** is used to introduce the reported speech.

b) The word order is the same as in an *affirmative* sentence (▶ 1.4).

22.7

1 '**Where** is Rob going tonight?'
She asked **where** Rob was going that night.
'**Who** is your sister leaving **with**?'
She wanted to know **who** my sister was leaving **with**.

2 'Will you be staying here long?' he said.
He wondered **if/whether** I would be staying there long.

3 She said, 'Did you come by train or by bus?'
She inquired **if/whether** I had come by train **or** by bus.
'Is Anne coming with you or not?'
He asked me **whether or not** Anne was coming with me.

4 I asked the attendant **where to park** the car.
She wants to know **how to say** this in English.

5 'Have you got **any** potatoes?' he said.
He asked (me) if I had got **any** potatoes.

1 If the original question is made with a question word (**wh-***question*) this word introduces the reported speech. In informal English, prepositions are placed at the end of the sentence.

2 If the original question requires the answer **yes** or **no** the reported speech is introduced by either **if** or **whether**.

3 If the original question requires a choice between two or more *alternatives* the reported speech is introduced by **if/whether . . . or** or **whether or not**.

4 In some cases interrogatives can also be reported by using the question word (but not **why**) followed by a **to-***infinitive* (▶ 6.28).

5 **Any** and its compounds (▶ 9.18) are not changed in reported questions.

Reporting responses

22.8

She said, 'Have you seen her?' and I said, **'No.'**
She asked me if I had seen her and I said (that) **I hadn't**.
He said, 'Are you still living in London?' and I said, **'Yes.'**
He asked me if I was still living in London and I answered that **I was**.

The response **yes** or **no** can be reported by using a personal pronoun and the appropriate modal or auxiliary verb (▶ 21.4).

Reporting imperatives

22.9

'Sit down.'
He **told us to sit down**.
'Don't smoke, please.'
She **asked them not to smoke**.
'Take the call, Miss Brown.'
He **asked Miss Brown to take** the call.
'Don't do it, Peter', I said.
I **told Peter not to do** it.

The *imperative* is transformed into reported speech by using a reporting verb (often **ask** or **tell**) followed by the *infinitive* or *negative infinitive* with **to** (▶ 6.27). The person or people addressed are referred to either by a *noun* or by a *personal pronoun* placed immediately after the reporting verb.

Use of reporting verbs

22.10

1 a) 'It's nine o'clock.'
    He **told me** (that) it was nine o'clock.
    He **said (to me)** that it was nine o'clock.

   b) 'It's about two miles away.'
    He **explained (to me)** that it was about two miles away.
    He **mentioned (to me)** that it was about two miles away.
    'I intend to resign.'
    The President **stated (to the reporters)** that he intended to resign.

   c) 'It's a very difficult job.'
    He **thought** that it was a very difficult job.
    'The window is broken.'
    He **supposed** that the window was broken.

2 'Is it raining?'
   He **wondered** if it was raining.
   He **wanted to know** if it was raining.
   He **asked (me)** if it was raining.

3 'Put up your hands.'
   He **told** them to put up their hands.
   He **instructed** them to put up their hands.
   'Please, take a seat.'
   He **asked** us to take a seat.
   He **requested** us to take a seat.

1 a) To report a *statement*, **tell** and **say** are the verbs most commonly used. **Tell** must be followed by an indirect object.
    Say is not followed by an indirect object but can be followed by **to** + *personal pronoun* or *noun*.

   b) Other verbs often used to introduce reported statements in the same way as **say** are **explain, mention, point out, reply, state**. All of these verbs can be followed by **to** + *personal pronoun* or *noun*.

   c) Verbs like **believe, imagine, suppose, think** can be used to introduce reported speech but cannot be followed by an indirect object or by **to** + *personal pronoun* or *noun*.

2 To report a *question* the most commonly used verbs are: **ask, enquire, want to know, wonder** + **if/whether**. Only **ask** can be followed immediately by an indirect object. For **ask** + **to**-*infinitive* used to report a *request* see **3** below.

3 Some of the most common verbs used to report an order are: **command, instruct, order, tell**.
    Ask and **request** (in more formal English) are used to report a request rather than an order.

4 'You'd better not drive so fast.'
The instructor **advised** me not to drive so fast.
'I didn't tell you.'
She **denied** telling me.
'I'll reserve you a room.'
He **offered** to reserve a room for me.
'Let's go out for a drink.'
She **suggested** going out for a drink.

4 We may also report what someone says without keeping so close to the original words used. The reporting verb itself may convey the *spirit* or the *intention* of the original utterance.
Some of the more common reporting verbs used in this way are: **admit, advise, agree, be sure, boast, complain, deny, encourage, insist, invite, offer, persuade, promise, refuse, remind, suggest, threaten, urge, warn**.

23 Ability

The following tables list the expressions most commonly used to indicate *ability*, together with the equivalent negative forms:

I can I'm able to I know how to	use a computer.
She's capable of passing this exam.	

I can't (cannot)			
I'm	not able unable	to	use a computer.
I don't know how to			
She's	not capable incapable		of passing this exam.

Use of can, could, be able to

23.2

1 Both of them **can** drive.
I **can** speak French but I **can't** speak German.
Can you type?
My wife **can't** cook.
I just **cannot** understand this book.

2 a) I **can't hear** you.

b) I **can't swim**.

1 The modal verb **can** (▶ 6.15, 6.16) is the most frequently used to express *ability* in the *present* or in the *future*.
Can is usually unstressed and pronounced /kən/ when it is used before a full verb. There are two negative forms: **can't** (/kɑːnt/) and, more emphatically or in the written language, **cannot** (/ˈkænət/)

2 Notice that **can** may refer to (**a**) 'absolute' ability (▶ 23.5) or (**b**) acquired skills.

23.3

1 a) She **could** speak French perfectly but she refused to answer.
He **could** play the piano when he was ten.

b) She **was able to** speak French perfectly but she refused to answer.
He **was able to** play the piano when he was ten.
Her French was poor but she **was able to** explain what had happened.
Believe it or not, I **was able to** repair my car yesterday.

1 To express *ability in the past* we use:
a) **could** + *infinitive without* **to** to refer to a general state of ability. It does not indicate that the ability was necessarily put into practice at a particular time. (For **could** ▶ 6.15, 6.16.)

b) **was/were able** + **to**-*infinitive* to refer either to general ability, like **could**, or to actual performance on a particular occasion.

2 I **couldn't/wasn't able** to repair my car yesterday.
Could she/**Was** she **able** to explain what had happened?

3 I **could** move that wardrobe if you helped me. I feel so lonely that I **could** cry.

4 a) You **could have lent** me some money but you were too mean.
He **could have won** the game with a bit more luck.
Could she **have gone** out without you seeing her?

b) I don't know how to type so I **couldn't have taken** the job.
Compare:
He **couldn't have understood**: he's too young.

2 In the negative or interrogative there is no difference in meaning between **could** and **was/were able**.

3 **Could** may also express *hypothetical* present ability.

4 a) **Could** + *past infinitive without* **to** expresses hypothetical ability in the *past*, implying that the hypothetical action did not take place or, in some cases, that we do not know whether or not it took place. I **could have done it** means 'I was able to do it but I didn't'.

b) **Couldn't** + *past infinitive without* **to** expresses hypothetical inability in the *past*, again implying that the action did not take place. **I couldn't have done it** means 'I wasn't able to do it and so obviously I didn't'.

NOTE: **Could have done** may also express *past negative certainty* as a result of logical conclusion (▶ 19.5).

23.4

1 I would like **to be able** to play a musical instrument well.
Have you **been able** to solve that problem yet?
He had to give up the journey as he **hadn't been able** to find his passport.

2 I **can/will be able** to do it tomorrow.

3 **I'll be able** to speak German after finishing the course.

1 **Be able** + **to**-*infinitive* is used to refer to ability in situations where there are no equivalent structures with **can/could** (e.g. when an infinitive or perfect tense form is necessary).

2 **Can** may sometimes refer to future ability. **Will be able** can also be used in the same sense.

3 **Will be able**, not **can**, must be used to refer to ability in the future which depends on another future event.

23.5

I **can't** hear any music.
Can you see that building over there?
He had a cold so he **couldn't** smell a thing.

Can and **could** are frequently used before verbs of perception (▶ 11.19). Such structures are more common than (e.g.) **I don't hear . . .** or **Do you see . . . ?**

Other ways of expressing ability

23.6

1 He **knows how to programme** a computer. Do you **know how to speak** Spanish?

1 The verb **know,** which implies mastery of a skill or a subject, cannot be followed immediately by an infinitive. The structure is: **know how** + **to-***infinitive.*

2 A two-year-old child isn't **capable of riding** a bicycle.

2 The adjective **capable,** meaning 'having the skill, power or potential to do something', is followed by **of** + **-ing** form (*verbal noun*).

3 a) Her French was poor but she **managed to explain/succeeded in explaining** what had happened.
After years of saving he **managed to buy** the nicest house in the village.
Did you **succeed in translating** that difficult passage?

3 a) **Manage** + **to-***infinitive* and **succeed in** + **-ing** form *(verbal noun)* have a similar meaning to **be able** (▶ 23.4), especially to express the idea that an action was (or will be) completed with difficulty.

b) Can you **manage** (to drink) one more whisky?

b) In spoken English **manage** may be followed by a noun instead of another verb in situations where the verb is understood from the context.

c) A: Shall I help you with your luggage?
B: No, thanks, I **can manage**.

c) **Manage** is often used in combination with **can**.

24 Permission, obligation and prohibition

Permission

Asking for and giving permission

24.1 The following table contains the most commonly used expressions to ask for, and to give, *permission* to do something. The more informal expressions are more likely to be used in asking for permission from people whom the speaker regards as equals. They generally indicate that the speaker is confident that permission will easily be obtained. The more formal expressions are *deferential* and are more likely to be used with people whom the speaker regards as superiors (e.g. the boss, the headmaster). They imply that the speaker is not confident that permission will easily be obtained.

INFORMAL				
Can I Is it OK/all right if I Could I (possibly) Do you think I could	use your car?	Yes,		sure. that's OK/all right. go ahead. of course/certainly (you can).
Do you mind if I use your car? Would you mind if I used your car?		No,		not at all. I don't mind at all.
I wonder if I could I was wondering if I could Would it be possible to May I Will you allow/permit me to Might I	use your car?	Yes,		of course (you can). certainly (you can). please do. of course (you may). certainly (you may).

FORMAL

1 **Can/could** I read your paper? – Yes, you **can**.
May/might we leave our coats here? – Yes, you **may**.
Could I come back tomorrow? – Yes, of course you **can**.
May I do it now? – Yes, certainly you **may**.

2 A: Do you **mind** if I sit here?
B: **No, not at all**.
A: Would you **mind** if I opened the window?
B: **No, I don't mind at all**.

Compare:
A: Do you **mind** if I take a cigarette?
B: Please do.

1 **Can, may, could, might** are all used to ask for permission and can refer either to the present or the future, depending on the context.
Can is the most colloquial and most commonly used form even though some conservative speakers consider it incorrect in this sense.
Might is a rarely used, extremely tentative way of asking for permission.
Can and **may** (but *not* **could** or **might**) can be used to give permission.

2 Notice that if someone asks for permission using **mind** a negative expression is used to grant it. (In practice an affirmative response can also be used to grant permission.)

3 **Will you permit** me to accompany your daughter to the ball?
Please allow me to carry that case for you.
Allow me to make a further point in the discussion.

4 **Will you let** me explain?
Let me have a look at it.
Please let Jimmy come to the park with us.

Martin and I are good with engines. **Let** us try to fix it. /let ʌs/

Compare:

Let's have a cup of TEA. /lets/

Let us PRAY. /let əs/

3 **Allow** and **permit** are used in formal requests for permission. They are followed by a noun or pronoun and the **to-***infinitive*. They can also be used in the imperative form and, in this case, they are more assertive, implying confidence on the part of the speaker.

4 In informal English **let** can be used in a similar way to **allow** (but notice that it is followed by a noun or pronoun and the *infinitive without* **to**). **Let** is an assertive, confident way of asking for permission, having some of the effect of an imperative. The assertiveness can be softened by using **please**.

NOTE: **Let** us /let ʌs/ (with the stress on **us**) is a request for permission from the person addressed. **Let's** /lets/ (or sometimes **let us** /let əs/ with no stress on **us**) is a suggestion which includes the person addressed (▶ 25.10).

Refusing permission

24.2 The following table lists some of the most common ways of *refusing* permission, from the more informal to the more formal.

Sorry but you can't I'd rather you didn't Actually you're not (really) allowed/permitted to I'm afraid I can't allow/permit you to I'm afraid you may not	look at the report.

1 a) You **may not** go yet.
  b) You **can't** go that way – it's a private road.
    You're not allowed to bring three bottles of whisky.

2 **I'd rather you didn't** use my typewriter. I need it myself.

3 **I can't let you** stay out so late.
  I won't allow you to trespass on my property.
  I won't let you borrow my books again.

1 In example (**a**), **may not** implies that it is the speaker himself/herself who is refusing permission (▶ 24.3). The other expressions (**b**) carry implications of more general obligation.

2 **I'd rather you didn't** (▶ 26.12) expresses a wish rather than an absolute refusal.

3 The expression **I can't let you** is used in informal English instead of **allow/permit**. If the speaker uses **I won't** instead of **I can't** the refusal is more forceful and there is an implication that it is the speaker himself who is refusing permission.

4 A: Can I borrow this record?
B: **Sorry** but you can't. **I'm afraid** I've already promised it to someone else.
Compare:
A: Could I read your newspaper?
B: No, you can't.
A: There's no need to be aggressive.

4 Notice the use of expressions like **sorry/I'm afraid** and **actually** to weaken the effect of the refusal (▶ 24.11).

Talking about permission

24.3

The expressions in the tables in 24.1, 24.2 are used to *ask for*, *give* and *refuse* individual permission on specific occasions. Some of these expressions are also used to *talk about permission* in general, (i.e. things that people are, or are not, allowed to do in general).

1 a) He **may** park here. (= I give him permission)
You **may** not use this dictionary. (= I refuse permission)

b) He **can** park here. (= It isn't against the rules)
You **can** borrow the books for two weeks. (= These are the rules)

2 a) They don't **allow people to make** any noise after nine.
The rules don't **permit you to bring** guests.
They don't **allow dancing** in this room.
The safety regulations don't **permit smoking** in the corridors.
They don't **let us do** anything in this school.

b) Until you are eighteen you won't **be allowed** to marry.
We've **been permitted** to play tennis on the lawn.

3 a) When I was a child I **could** not watch TV after eight o'clock.
Terry felt ill and was **allowed** to leave the examination room. (*not* **could** leave)
She **was allowed** to see her husband the day after the accident. (*not* **could** see)

b) If you were over eighteen you **could** see the film.

1 a) **May** is normally used when it is the speaker himself/herself who is granting or refusing permission (▶ 24.2).

b) **Can** is more often used to talk about permission in general because it does not carry this implication.

2 a) The verbs **allow, permit** and **let** are all used to talk about permission. **Allow** and **permit** are more formal. They can be followed either by a noun/pronoun with the **to**-*infinitive* or by an **-ing** form (*verbal noun*) when no person is mentioned. **Let** is followed by a noun/pronoun and the *infinitive without* **to**. (▶ 25.4).

b) **Allow** and **permit** (but not **let**) are commonly used in the **passive** form.

3 a) Referring to the past, **could** is used to talk about what was or was not permitted *in general*, but not to talk about one *specific occasion* (▶ 23.3). In this case **allowed** or **permitted** are used.

b) **Could** is also used in conditional sentences (▶ 20.7, 20.8).

Obligation

Expressing obligation

24.4 The following table lists a number of expressions indicating various kinds of *obligation* e.g. advice, moral and legal obligation, compulsion.

You'd better You should You ought to		see a doctor.	
You are	supposed meant expected required	to return the books by tomorrow.	
It's	essential necessary vital important	(for you) to that you (should)	fill in the form.
You are to examine the report carefully.			
You need to You must You have to You've got to		sign the contract.	
You are	compelled obliged	to wear a seat belt.	

I think you should see a doctor.
I'm afraid you have to fill in this form.

Expressions like **I think** and **I'm afraid** are often used to make the declaration of obligation sound more polite or less assertive.

Should, ought to, had better

24.5

1 She **should** go out more often.
They really **ought to** visit their parents occasionally.
You**'d better** wear a scarf.
You**'d better** go now; it's late.

1 **Ought to, should** (▶ 6.15, 6.16) and **had better/'d better** followed by the *infinitive without* **to** all express *obligation* in the sense of something that is good or right to do. But this 'obligation' is not compulsory. The speaker is expressing an opinion but is not imposing it. These expressions are therefore used to give suggestions or advice (▶ 25.10).
Had better can only be used to refer to the present or the future.

2 We haven't got enough bread. You **should have bought** more.
The police **ought to have** caught that murderer months ago.
It's disgraceful! His secretary **should have known** where he was.
Those parents **ought to have** been more careful with their children.

2 **Should/ought to** + *past infinitive* (**have** + *past participle*) refers to a past obligation or duty but only one which was *not carried out*. It therefore implies criticism.

Other obligation forms

The following expressions do not necessarily indicate suggestions or criticism. However, when referring to a person they do imply a clear requirement to carry out an action.

1 He**'s supposed** to tidy up his room every day.
You**'ll be expected** to take the exam after one year.
You**'re meant** to see the lawyer tomorrow.
I**'m supposed** to finish this job by the end of the month.
Compare:
It**'s supposed** to be a good film.

1 A passive structure with **suppose, expect, require, mean** followed by the **to-***infinitive* refers to a requirement imposed by other people.

NOTE: **Supposed** can be used to talk about other people's opinion rather than any requirement or obligation.

2 We **were supposed** to wear a uniform at the school.
The children **were expected** to say their prayers every night.
The assistant **was meant** to work until six o'clock.

2 When these verbs are used in the past they refer to a past obligation but without necessarily implying criticism for not carrying it out (▶ 24.5).

3 She **needs** to walk more often.
He **needed** to take all those medicines.
A primary school teacher **needs** to have a lot of patience.

3 **Need** followed by the **to-***infinitive* is used to express an obligation forced on someone by the circumstances in which he/she finds himself/herself.

4 **It's important for you to meet** the manager.
It's vital for him to arrive on time.
It's essential that you (should) take your passport.
It's important that Alan (should) be there.

4 Impersonal expressions indicating the importance of doing something, like **it's necessary/essential/vital/important,** can be constructed in two ways:
It's necessary for + *noun/pronoun* + **to do it**.
It's necessary that + *noun/pronoun* + **(should) do it**.

5 a) He **was to wait** in his room.
The teacher says you **are to do** these exercises.

b) This report **is to be examined** carefully.
All documents **are to be taken** to the registrar's office.

5 a) **Be** followed by the **to-***infinitive* can be used to express strong unquestioned obligation (but not future forms of **be**) (▶ 11.13).

b) The *passive infinitive with* **to** can be used to express the idea of obligation in a neutral, impersonal way, with either present or future reference.

Must, have to

24.7

1 He **must** stay at home in the evening. (= I don't want to see him go out so often)
You **must** come and stay with me.
I really **must** write to him.

You must GŌ. /məst/

You MUST go. /mʌst/

2 You **have to** stop when you see that sign.
Everybody **has to** pay tax.
When her husband died she **had to** go back to work.
If you lived on your own you **would have to** work much harder.
I don't like **to have to** get up so early.
When you get a train you**'ve got to** get a ticket first.

1 **Must** (▶ 6.15, 6.16) is used to refer to obligation in the present and also in the future. It often implies the authority of the person who is speaking or an emotional involvement on the part of the speaker. The speaker personally may want the action to be carried out. When **must** is used before a full verb it is usually unstressed and pronounced /məst/. It may be stressed for emphasis and is then pronounced /mʌst/.

2 **Have to** (▶ 6.10) does not usually carry the implication of personal involvement on the part of the speaker. It has a more objective sense than **must** and is therefore more likely to be used with reference to an external authority or an obligation caused by the circumstances (although **must** can also be used in this way, for strong emphasis). It can also be used to replace **must,** substituting for it in structures where **must** has no equivalent form. The form **have got to** (▶ 6.10) is commonly used in the present tense.

Compulsion

24.8

1 The diplomats **were obliged** to leave the country.
All students **will be compelled** to take an oral exam.
If the boy who broke the window doesn't come forward I **shall be obliged** to punish the whole class.

2 Visas are **compulsory** for travel to the Soviet Union.
Wearing seat belts in cars is now **obligatory**.

1 *Compulsion* is a very strong obligation which is enforced. Passive structures with **compel** and **oblige** are used to express this concept. The verbs are sometimes used in a rhetorical sense (i.e. the speaker really *wants* and *intends* to carry out the action).

2 The adjectives **compulsory** and **obligatory** are also used in formal English.

Asking about obligation

To ask if somebody is obliged to do something, the expressions listed in the table in 24.4 are used in their interrogative form.

Had I better Should I Ought I to	see a doctor?		
Am I	supposed meant expected required	to return the books?	
Is it	essential necessary vital important	(for me) to that I (should)	fill in the form?
Am I to examine the report?			
Do I (really) need to Need I (really)	fill in the form?		
Must I Do I have to Have I got to	sign the contract?		
Am I	compelled obliged	to wear a seat belt?	

1 a) **Do I need to** go?
   Do you need to make all that noise?

   b) **Need I** go?
   Need you make all that noise?

2 **Need** they **have come** so late? They woke everyone up.
   Need you **have spent** all that money? Now we have very little left.
   Compare:
   Did you need to spend a lot of money?

3 a) **Have** you **got to** do all this by yourself?
   Has he **got to** finish by midnight?

   b) **Do** you **have to** do all this by yourself?
   Does he **have to** finish by midnight?

1 In the present tense the interrogative structure with **need** can be either (**a**) that of a full verb or (**b**) that of a modal auxiliary verb (▶ 6.17). Modal auxiliary structures are used in formal speech.

2 **Need** as a modal auxiliary can be followed by the past infinitive (**have** + *past participle*) to ask about obligation in the past in very formal speech. It implies that the action referred to was *actually carried out* (▶ 24.10).
   The past tense of **need** does not carry this implication.

3 In the present tense interrogative structures with **have** can be made using either:
   a) **Have/has ... got to?** or
   b) **Do/does ... have to?** (▶ 6.10).

> 4 **Have** you **had to** repeat the exam?
> **Did** they **have to** call a taxi?

4 Other tenses are normally constructed using the full verb **have to**.

Absence of obligation

24.10 Some (not all) of the language used to express obligation (▶ 24.4). can indicate *absence of obligation* if used in a negative structure. Notice that in other cases, a negative structure may express a form of *prohibition* (▶ 24.11).

You don't have to You haven't got to You needn't You don't need to		pay for the drinks.	
You are not	meant to expected to required to	do all the cleaning.	
It's not necessary	(for you) to that you (should)		
You are not	compelled to obliged to	apply for this position if you don't want to.	
There's (really)	no need (for you) to no reason why you should	worry about the exam.	

1 a) I start work at nine, so I **don't have to** leave home until half past eight.
   They **won't have to** clean all the rooms after the party.
   I **didn't have to** walk all the way. Tom gave me a lift.
   I **haven't got to** work today; it's a holiday.
   You **don't need to** take your umbrella; it's going to be fine today.
   You **won't need to** take your tennis racket with you. They'll lend us one.

   b) She **needn't come** now; she can come later.
   You **needn't come** to the office tomorrow, Miss Barnes.
   Compare:
   She **mustn't** come now. We're not ready yet.

1 a) **Don't have to, haven't got to** and **don't need to** are roughly equivalent in meaning. All three indicate absence of obligation and tend to imply an external authority or external circumstances (▶ 24.6, 24.7).

   b) The form **needn't** tends to be more used when the speaker is in a position of authority and is giving permission not to do something. (▶ **must** 24.7).

   NOTE: **Must not** indicates prohibition (▶ 24.11, 24.12). It is not used to indicate absence of obligation.

2 a) She **needn't have called** a taxi; I could have taken her to the station.
Thanks very much for the flowers but really you **needn't have brought** me anything.

b) She **didn't need** to call a taxi; I took her to the station.
The holiday home had almost everything; we **didn't need** to take sheets or blankets.

2 a) **Needn't** followed by the past infinitive (**have** + *past participle*) refers to an action which wasn't necessary but which nevertheless took place.

b) **Didn't need** + **to-***infinitive* refers to an action which wasn't necessary and which probably (or certainly) didn't take place.

Prohibition

24.11

Prohibition can be seen as a *refusal of permission to do something* (▶ 24.2) or as an *obligation not to do something*. The following table lists a number of expressions used to indicate this type of negative obligation. Notice that some of them are the negative form of expressions used to express obligation. (▶ 24.4).

You'd better not You shouldn't You oughtn't to	drive so fast.		
You're not	supposed to meant to	leave your luggage here.	
It's	essential vital important	(for you) not to that you shouldn't	miss the train.
(Please) don't You mustn't You're not to	come in until I tell you.		
You are	forbidden to smoke prohibited from smoking	on buses.	
No smoking.			

1 **Actually,** you'd better not speak to him just now.
I'm afraid you're not meant to leave the room before the exam is over.
I think you're not supposed to walk on the grass.
You **shouldn't really** eat so much.
Compare:
You **really shouldn't** eat so much.

1 Expressions like **really, actually, I'm afraid** and **I think** are often used to reduce the force of the prohibition (▶ 24.2).

NOTE: When **really** is used before the auxiliary verb it strengthens the force of the statement.

2 **I don't think** you**'re supposed** to walk on the grass.
I don't think you **ought to** leave your bags here.

2 With **should, ought to, supposed to** and **meant to** we can suggest an even weaker prohibition by transferring the negative particle from these expressions to **I think** (so that **I think you shouldn't** becomes **I don't think you should**).

24.12

1 You**'d better not** buy that shirt if it doesn't fit you.
Colin **shouldn't** leave everything to the last minute.

1 **Had better not, should not, ought not to** suggest that it would be wrong or bad in some way to carry out the action mentioned. However, they do not indicate absolute prohibition and so are used to give suggestions or advice (▶ 25.10).

2 You **oughtn't to have gone** abroad with so little money.
Manchester United **shouldn't have sold** their goalkeeper.

2 **Shouldn't/oughtn't to** with the *past infinitive* (**have** + *past participle*) is used to criticise an action which was carried out in the past, mistakenly in the opinion of the speaker.

3 At a classical concert people **are not supposed** to applaud between the various movements.
It**'s important that** you **should not** cash this cheque before the end of the month.
You **must not** touch anything before the police arrive.
You**'re not** to eat any more sweets.

3 Many of the expressions used to refer to obligation (▶ 24.4) can indicate prohibition by being used in the negative form.

4 **Don't** make so much noise.

4 The negative imperative can also be used to refer to prohibition. (▶ 25.2)

5 a) Smoking is **forbidden**.
The children were **forbidden to enter** the kitchen.

5 a) **Forbidden** may be followed by the **to-**
infinitive.

b) **Parking** is **prohibited**.
We were **prohibited from importing** luxury goods.

b) **Prohibited** may be followed by **from** + **-ing** form.

c) **It is forbidden** to cross the railway lines.

c) An impersonal construction with **it** is possible with **forbidden** but not with **prohibited**.

6 **No trespassing.**
No smoking.

6 **No . . . -ing** is a way of indicating prohibition in the written language. It generally appears on notices in public places.

25 Influencing the behaviour of other people

25.1 This chapter is concerned with the language used to influence, or control, the behaviour of other people. How exactly this is done depends on the circumstances and the type of relationship between the people involved. This chapter looks, principally, at the different ways of giving *orders*, making *requests*, offering *suggestions* and *advice* and making *invitations*.

The behaviour of other people can also be influenced by *giving or refusing permission*, or by saying that someone is *obliged* to do something or *prohibited* from doing something, as well as by expressing a *desire* that someone should, or shouldn't, do something. This chapter is, therefore, very closely linked to the chapters on *Permission, obligation and prohibition* and *Feelings and attitudes*, and cross-references are frequently made to them.

Orders

The imperative

25.2

1 a) **Stand** up.
   Don't sit there.
   Don't be silly.
   Do not begin until you have read the instructions.

   b) (i) **DÒ** come in.

   (ii) **DÒ** try – it's very important.

   (iii) **DÒ** shut up – I'm trying to concentrate.

   DÒ be quiet.

2 a) **Please,** tell me what happened.
   Don't go now **please**.

   b) Don't hurt him, **will you**?

   c) Go and lie down, **why don't you**?
   Have a biscuit, **won't you**?

1 a) A direct order is conveyed by the *imperative* form of a verb (▶ 6.22). The negative imperative is used for an order *not* to do something. **Don't** is normally used in the spoken language; **do not** may be used in written instructions.

   b) There is an emphatic form for the affirmative imperative with **do** (▶ 18.5), which is always given stress when spoken. It may indicate attitudes like (**i**) politeness, (**ii**) urgency, or even (**iii**) irritation.

2 The authoritarian tone of an imperative may be softened by using certain expressions:
   a) **Please** is the most common.
   b) **Will you?** can be added to the end of the sentence.
   c) **Won't you?** or **Why don't you?** can be added to an affirmative imperative.

25.3

1 **Listen** to me, **Helen**.
   Please **don't speak** so quickly, **Mr Baker**.
   Simon, pass me the salt, please.
   Follow me, **boys and girls**.
   Ladies and gentlemen, give a big welcome to our guest singer.

2 **You,** get down off that table!
   You, clean up that mess!

1 In English no distinction is made between an imperative addressed to one person and an imperative addressed to a group of people. The subject (understood as 'you') need not be mentioned. If the subject is named it may appear either before or after the imperative sentence and is separated from it by a comma in the written language.

2 In addressing an imperative it is possible to use the pronoun **you** but this is normally considered impolite and aggressive.

3 Ticket holders this way. (= **Come** this way)
Over there. (= **Go** over there)
Out! (= **Get** out)

3 In written and spoken English the imperative verb is sometimes omitted when the meaning is clear.

Imperatives with **let**

25.4

1 a) **Let's take** a taxi.
Let's have a drink.
Let's go out for a meal.

b) **Let's not stay** in.
Don't let's stay in.

1 An imperative normally refers to a second person subject, whether singular or plural (▶ 25.3). However the construction (**a**) **let's** + *infinitive without* **to** can be considered an imperative for the first person plural. It conveys a suggestion rather than an order (▶ 25.10). Notice (**b**) that there are two negative forms for **let's: don't let's** and **let's not**.

2 Please **let Alex sit** in the front of the car.
Let me borrow your typewriter.
Let me give you some ideas about decorating the flat.
Let us help you to do the work. (*not* **let's**)

2 The construction **let** + *noun/object pronoun* + *infinitive without* **to** is usually a normal imperative form directed to a second person. **Let** in this case has a similar meaning to **allow** or **permit** (24.1). This structure is often used to make requests, suggestions or offers (▶ 26.3).

3 Just **let me have** another chance and I'll show them what I can do.
Please **don't let me** miss the train.

3 Sometimes the reference to a second person subject is very vague (perhaps to God or to good fortune) and then the effect is one of making a wish (▶ 26.6).

Other ways of giving orders and instructions

25.5

1 I **want you to call** there this afternoon.
We **want Mr Jenkins to move** to the Accounts Department.
I'd like you to take this to the Post Office.

1 Orders may be given without using a direct imperative. The speaker may express the *desire* that someone should do something (▶ 26.5). The construction is usually: **want/would like** + *noun/object pronoun* + **to-***infinitive*.

2 **No smoking.**
No trespassing.

2 In written, and sometimes also in spoken English a negative order can be expressed Using **No** + **-ing** form (*verbal noun*) (▶ 24.12).

3 You **must** show me your identity card.
You**'d better not** do that again.
You **can't** smoke in here.

3 Orders may also be transmitted by means of expressions referring to *obligation* (▶ 24.4), *prohibition* (▶ 24.11) and *refusal of permission* (▶ 24.2).

Requests

Asking someone to do something

In most cases it is more polite to *make a request* than to give an order. The following tables show some of the more common ways of making requests, from the more informal to the more formal.
See also: *asking for permission* (▶ 24.1); *expressing desire for someone to do something* (▶ 26.5).

Can you Will you Could you Would you	help me?	(▶ 6.15–6.18) modal verbs
Would you mind I wonder if you'd mind	helping me (?)	(▶ 24.1) **mind**

1 **Can't** you come? You know we want you to.
   Won't you give him the money? He does need it.
   Couldn't you apologise, just for my sake?

2 Close the door, **will you**?
   Tell him to come in, **would you**?
   Make some sandwiches, **could you**?

1 **Can, will** and **could** may also appear in the *negative* form, giving a sense of pleading and usually implying that the person addressed has already refused or is, at least, reluctant.

2 **Will you** and **would you, can you** and **could you** can also be placed at the end of the sentence to soften an *order* into a request.

Polite and formal requests

1 a) Could you **possibly** bring it tomorrow?

   b) **Would you do me a big favour** and let me borrow your car?

   c) **I was wondering/I wondered** if you'd mind postponing the meeting?

   d) If you're passing the chemist's you **might** get me some aspirins.
       Would you like to do some shopping for me?

2 **Do you think** you **could** send it tomorrow?
   I wonder if you **could** explain this incident.
   Could I ask you to be back by ten o'clock?
   I wish you would make less noise.

3 **If you'd** just take a seat. The doctor will see you in a moment.
   If you could just sign this form.

1 We can make a request sound more tentative and therefore more polite by using:
   a) the adverb **possibly**;
   b) different expressions with **do me a favour** placed before the request;
   c) the verb **wonder,** especially in the past tense;
   d) structures that are also used to express *suggestions* or *invitations* (▶ 25.10, 25.13).

2 More formal requests can be made using various structures. **Do you think** and **I wonder if** are normally followed by **could**. **I wish you would** may suggest irritation (▶ 26.7).

3 **If you will/would/can/could** is often used for routine requests, i.e. for things that are done habitually.

4 a) **Would you be so kind as** to send us your catalogue.
   Would you be good enough to inform me of the results.
   I would appreciate it if you could let me know as soon as possible.

   b) **I wonder if you would kindly** clean up the mess you've made.
   Would you be good enough to turn down that radio.

4 There are a number of other more complicated structures for making requests which are normally found only in (**a**) *written English* or (**b**) when a speaker is using them to create an *ironic effect*.

Accepting and refusing requests

25.8 The following tables show some of the more common ways of *accept*ing and *refusing* requests. The expressions are listed from the more informal to the more formal.

Accepting

Yes,	OK. sure. all right. of course. certainly.

Refusing tactfully

Sorry but I'd like to but Well, actually I'm afraid Unfortunately	I can't. it's rather difficult. it's not possible.

Refusing strongly

No,	I won't. I'm not going to. certainly not. I refuse. it's out of the question.

A: **Would you mind** show**ing** me your passport?
B: **No,** of course not.

Notice that we can use **No** to accept a request expressed using **mind** (▶ 24.1).

Asking someone for something

25.9 The following expressions are commonly used to *ask someone for something*. The order is from the least formal to the most formal. Typical responses are given, again in order of formality.

Asking someone for something

Can I have Could I have	some oranges (,please)?
I'd like some oranges (,please).	
Would it be possible to borrow your typewriter?	
I wonder if I could borrow your typewriter.	

Affirmative responses

Yes,	OK. sure. all right. of course. certainly.

Negative responses

Sorry but Well, actually I'm afraid Unfortunately	we haven't got any oranges. I need it myself.

1 A: **Could I have** two pounds of potatoes, please?
   B: Yes, of course. Anything else?
   A: Yes, **I'd like** some apples.
   B: Certainly.

2 A: **Would it be possible** to see your report?
   B: Yes, of course.
   A: **I wonder if I could** leave the office at four o'clock today?
   B: I'm afraid that would be rather difficult.

1 **Can/Could I have** and **I'd like** are used in situations where the speaker does not expect any difficulty in obtaining what he/she wants (e.g. in shopping).

2 **Would it be possible** and **I wonder if I could** are more polite forms, used in situations where the speaker is asking for a favour (▶ 25.7).

Suggestions and advice

Making suggestions and giving advice

25.10 Some of the most commonly used structures to make *suggestions* or give *advice* are contained in the following tables:

1

Let's go out for a walk.	
Shall we go out for a walk?	
What about How about	going out for a walk?

1 The most informal structures are:

a) **Let's** (▶ 25.4) and **shall we** + *infinitive without* **to;**

b) **What about/How about** + **-ing** form *(verbal noun)*. The use of **let's** and **shall we** means that the speaker will join in the action suggested. **What about/how about** do not necessarily have this meaning.

2

Suppose we buy/bought her a record? What if we buy/bought her a record?

2 **Suppose** and **what if** can be followed by a verb in the present tense or, for more tentative suggestions, in the past tense (▶ 20.2, 20.3).

3

Why don't you Why not	change your job?	
Have you (ever)	thought of considered	changing your job?

3 Various *interrogative* forms can also be used to make suggestions or to give advice.

4

If I were you, I would stay at home.	
Wouldn't it be a good idea	if you stayed at home? to stay at home?

4 We can also use conditional sentences (▶ 20.6).

5

I think you	should ought to had better	see a doctor.

5 Certain modal verbs that express a sense of *obligation* can also express suggestions or advice (▶ 24.4).

6

You could (always) Couldn't you	send a telegram?
You might try sending a telegram.	

6 Certain modal verbs expressing *possibility* may be used to express suggestions or advice (▶ 19.9).

7

I (would)	propose suggest recommend	(that) you (should) type the letter now. typing the letter now.
I would advise you to type the letter now.		

7 The verbs **advise, propose, suggest** and **recommend** are used in more formal English (▶ 20.5).

8

May Might	I suggest that we adjourn the meeting?

8 Modal verbs used to ask for *permission* (▶ 24.1) may be used to make a formal suggestion more tentative.

Asking for suggestions or advice

25.11 Many of the structures that are used to *make* suggestions or *give* advice can also be used to *ask* for suggestions or advice if changed into the interrogative form.

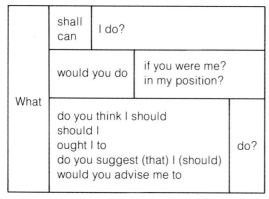

What	shall can	I do?	
	would you do	if you were me? in my position?	
	do you think I should should I ought I to do you suggest (that) I (should) would you advise me to		do?

Accepting and refusing suggestions or advice

Accepting

25.12

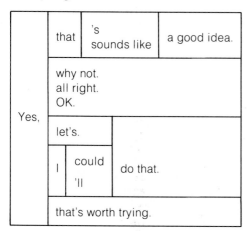

Yes,	that	's sounds like	a good idea.
	why not. all right. OK.		
	let's.		
	I	could 'll	do that.
	that's worth trying.		

Refusing

	I'd rather not. I'm not so sure about that.	
No, Actually,	I don't think that's such a good idea.	
	I doubt if that would	do any good. work.

Invitations

Giving invitations

25.13

(Do) join us tonight.		
Why don't you Will you/Won't you (How) would you like to Do you want to	join us tonight?	
How about Do you fancy/Do you feel like	joining us tonight?	
I was wondering/wondered if you'd like to stay Perhaps you'd be interested in staying	with us for a few days.	
May I invite you to stay with us for a few days?		

---

1 **Come** to our party.

   DO come to our party.
   Have dinner with us.

   DO have dinner with us.

2 **Why don't you** come to dinner on Saturday?
   How about coming for a meal on Saturday?

3 **Will/won't** you come and stay with us for a few days?

4 **(How) would you like/Do you want** to go to the cinema?
   Do you fancy/Do you feel like going to the cinema?

---

1 An *imperative* (▶ 25.2) may be used to make an informal, very direct invitation. The auxiliary **do** may be used for emphasis. In this case **do** is stressed.

2 Certain expressions used to make *suggestions* (▶ 25.10) may also be interpreted as invitations.

3 Modal verbs expressing *willingness*. (▶ 26.2) can be used to make an invitation.

4 Structures used to ask about *desire* (▶ 26.4) may also be used.

5 a) **I was wondering/I wondered** if you'd like to visit the museum.

   b) **Perhaps** you'd be interested in visiting the museum.

   c) **May I** invite you to my daughter's wedding reception?

5 More tentative, and more formal, invitations may be made using:
   a) the verb **wonder** and an indirect question (▶ 25.7);
   b) expressions referring to *possibility* (▶ 19.9);
   c) modal verbs used to ask for *permission* (▶ 24.1).

Accepting and refusing invitations

Accepting an invitation

25.14 The sentences contained in the table are amongst the more commonly used to accept an invitation and are in order of formality, starting from the more *informal* ones to the most *formal*.

Yes, thank you,	I'd love to. that would be nice. that sounds lovely. that's very kind of you. I'd be delighted to. I'll look forward to it.

Refusing an invitation

I'm afraid I can't. Sorry. I won't be able to, I'm afraid. Thanks all the same. What a pity – I've already arranged to go away this weekend.	
That's very kind of you but I'm awfully sorry but I'd really like to but	I'm afraid I'm going away this weekend.

Other ways of influencing behaviour

Warning

25.15

1 **Look** out! There's a car.
Mind your hand with that knife.
Be careful! You could fall off that wall.

2 **If you don't watch out,** you'll spill it.
I'm warning you, it's going to be cold.

1 Urgent warnings are usually in the form of an imperative (▶ 25.2).

2 Conditional sentences (▶ 20.6) and structures with the verb **warn** are also used.

Threatening

25.16

1 **If you want to see her alive,** don't tell the police.

2 **Don't speak** to me like that **or** I'll report you to the headmaster.

3 **I'll** murder you, I swear I **will**.

4 **You'd better** do as I say.

1 Threats may be in the form of conditional sentences (▶ 20.6).

2 They may also be expressed through clauses with **or** following an imperative form (▶ 25.2).

3 A threat is also often expressed through **will** (▶ 26.8).

4 It is also possible to use the expression **you'd better** (▶ 24.5).

Reminding

25.17

1 **Remember** to buy some sugar.
Don't forget to call at the library.

2 You **will** phone them, **won't** you?
You **won't** forget to lock the door, **will** you?

1 Reminding someone to do something usually takes the form of an imperative (▶ 25.2).

2 Sometimes *future structures* (*e.g.* **will/won't**) + *question tags* are used (▶ 5.10).

Persuading and encouraging

25.18

Go on – have a go!
Come on! Jump in!

Persuading and encouraging are also carried out using the imperative. The fixed expressions **Go on/Come on** are often used to add encouragement.

Complaining

25.19

1 The service is **too** slow.
You're not enthusiastic **enough** about the job.

2 I **don't like** your attitude.

3 **I wish** she wouldn't talk all the time.
If only you worked a bit harder.

4 **I'm afraid** his behaviour really isn't good enough.
I'm sorry but you haven't done it properly.

1 Complaints are often expressed through language indicating dissatisfaction. Adverbs of degree, especially **too** and **enough,** are commonly used (▶ 14.7, 14.8).

2 Expressions indicating dislike may be used (▶ 26.10).

3 Expressions of regret like **I wish, if only** (▶ 26.7) may also be used.

4 Expressions of apology (▶ 27.9) are often used to soften a complaint.

26 Feelings and attitudes

26.1 This chapter considers five main areas in the expression of feelings and attitudes: *willingness, desire, regret, intention and determination, liking and disliking.*

Willingness

26.2

I'll I would	(willingly) (gladly)	help him.
I'm	willing to ready to prepared to	

1 a) I'**ll** drive you to the station.
   He'**ll** post these letters for you.

   b) Don't worry, I'**ll** be back soon.
   They'**ll** go to university if they pass this exam.

   c) My boyfriend says he'**ll** give up smoking but I don't believe it.
   Alice'**ll** go to Scotland with me next summer.
   I'**ll** telephone you tonight.
   Will you give me a drink?

   d) I **won't** give up the idea of leaving.
   They **won't** listen to us, whatever we tell them.
   I'm afraid my car **won't** start this morning.

2 a) I said that I **would** drive her to the station.
   He said that he **would** post these letters for him.

   b) I asked her for her opinion but she **wouldn't** say anything.

   c) I **would** lend you some money if you asked me.
   The agency **would** find him a job if they could.

   d) **Would** you do me a favour?
   Would you open the door for me?

3 I like that girl: she's very **willing** to learn.
   I'm not **prepared** to put up with this treatment.
   Is he **ready** to accept all the extra work?

1 a) **Will**, usually contracted to **'ll**, can express the idea of *willingness* to do something.

   b) **Will** is also used to express the concept of *future* time (▶ 11.16).

   c) Sometimes there is a degree of ambiguity between these two meanings. **Alan will do it** may be simply a prediction about a future action or it may imply that Alan wants to carry out this action.

   d) In the same way, the negative form **won't** may be used to express a *lack of willingness*, a refusal to do something. It may refer to things as well as people.

2 a) **Would** may express willingness in the *past*, but only in subordinate clauses (e.g. in reported speech).

   b) **Wouldn't** may express *unwillingness* in the past.

   c) **Would/wouldn't** may also refer to a *hypothetical* state of willingness (▶ 20.7, 20.8).

   d) **Would** is often used as a more polite alternative to **will** in questions about being willing to do something (▶ 25.6).

3 The expressions **be willing/ready/prepared** followed by the **to**-*infinitive* are also used.

4 I would **gladly** help you.
She replied quite **readily** to all my questions.

4 The adverbs **willingly, gladly, readily** may also express or reinforce an idea of willingness.

Offering to do something

26.3

Shall I Can I	help you?
Would you like me to Do you want me to	
Let me help you, I'll help you,	(shall I?)

1 **Shall I** turn the television off?
Can I lay the table for you?
Should I go at once?

2 **Shall we** meet at the entrance of the cinema?
Shall we have a drink now?

3 **Would you like me to** carry your bag for you?
Would you like me to make you a cup of tea?
Do you want me to turn the television off?
Do you want me to start work now?

4 **Let me** call a taxi for you.
Let me open the door for you.
Let me type those letters for you, **shall I**?
Let me answer the phone, **shall I**?

5 **I'll** deliver the message.
A: Can somebody help me?
B: I **will**.
I'll take you to the doctor's, **shall I**?

1 **Shall/Can I** indicates *willingness* on the part of the speaker and at the same time asks whether or not the other person *wants* the speaker to carry out the action. Sometimes **should I** has the same effect.

2 **Shall we**, besides making an offer, also carries the implication that the speaker is *suggesting* a course of action (▶ 25.10).

3 **Do you want me to** and **would you like me to** are used to enquire about the other person's *desire* for something to be done by the speaker (▶ 26.5).
Would you like me to is more polite, more deferential and more clearly an expression of offering. **Do you want me to** may sound as much like a question as an offer to do something.

4 **Let me** + *infinitive without* **to** is a direct, informal expression of offering to do something. It is more assertive than the expressions in **1–3** above in that the speaker assumes that the other person will *accept* the offer. The speaker may go into action before there is any response from the other person. The addition of the tag **shall I?** has the effect of making the offer less assertive by calling for a response.

5 **Will** + *infinitive without* **to** is an assertive, enthusiastic way of offering to do something. Like **let me** it does not necessarily require an affirmative response from the other speaker. The tag **shall I?** softens the assertiveness.

Desire

26.4

I want I would like I would love I feel like I fancy I'm dying for	a cup of coffee.
I want I would like I would love I'm dying	to take a holiday.
I fancy I feel like	having a drink.

(hotel manager to guests)
I wish to welcome you to our hotel.

---

1 He **wanted** a new record player.
I don't **want** to talk about that.
What **would** you **like** to drink ?
Would you **like** to come for a walk?

2 a) I **would like to have taken** that job. (= I am sorry I didn't take it)
b) I **would have liked to take** that job. (= I was sorry at the time that I couldn't take it)

a) They **would love to have seen** that film.
b) They **would have loved to see** that film.

3 A: **Would** you **like** a banana?
B: Mm, yes please.
Compare:
A: Do you **like** bananas?
B: Yes, I do.

4 a) Do you **fancy** a sandwich?
I **feel like** go**ing** to the disco tonight.

---

1 **Want** and **would like** both express a sense of desire either *for something* or *to do something*.
Would like, which refers to present only (except in reported speech), is a more polite form and is therefore used more often in making invitations or offering.

2 Two structures with **would like** (and also **would love**) exist for talking about something in the *past* which we didn't do and which we think of with regret. Examples (**a**) indicate *present* regret about the *past*, while examples (**b**) refer to *past* regret.

3 **Would like**, as an expression of *desire*, must not be confused with the verb **like** meaning *be fond of, enjoy* (▶ 26.9).

4 a) **Fancy** and **feel like** are both used in informal English. They may be followed by a *noun* or **-ing** form (*verbal noun*).

b) I'**d love** a cold drink now.
I'**d love** to get some new clothes.
He'**s dying for** a cigarette.
They'**re dying** to see you again.

b) **Would love** and **be dying** are also used in informal English and suggest a more extreme form of desire. **Would love** may be followed by a noun or by the **to-**infinitive. **Be dying** may be followed by **for** + *noun* or by the **to-**infinitive.

5 a) I **wish** to raise another point in this debate.
(*extract from letter*)
We **wish** to make a complaint about the standard of service.

5 a) **Wish** is used in formal English. It is followed by the **to-**infinitive to express a desire to do something.

b) (*customer to shop assistant*)
I **wish** to speak to the manager.

b) **Wish** often functions almost as an imperative and can sound pompous or even aggressive.

c) I **wish** you a safe journey.
Compare:
I **want** a glass of beer.

c) I **wish** cannot normally be followed by a noun alone, except to express good wishes in a formal way (▶ 26.6). Compare the use of **want** + *noun*.

d) The fairy granted him three **wishes**.
Let's hope your **wish** comes true.

d) **Wish** is also a noun, normally used to convey a desire for something imaginary.

e) As he approached the princess his heart was filled with **desire**.
You may have whatever you **desire**.

e) **Desire**, as a noun and a verb, is used in a formal style.

Desire for someone to do something

26.5

I want I would like I would love I'm dying for	you to stay with us.

1 a) I **want you to know** what she told me.
Mrs Hall **would like her guests** to feel at home.
My parents **want me to go** to university.

1 a) To express a desire for someone to do something the following construction is used: *verb of desire + noun/pronoun + to-infinitive.*

b) I'**m dying for you to meet** her.

b) In colloquial English, **be dying for** is used in a similar way.

2 I **want you to type** these letters.
I'**d love you to come** and see me.

2 Notice that these expressions may function as *orders* (▶ 25.5) and *requests* (▶ 25.7).

Exclamations expressing wishes

26.6 Exclamations expressing wishes are constructed using:

1 God **save** the Queen! Long **live** the King! God **bless** you! Heaven **help** us all!	1 the *base form* of the verb, in a certain number of fixed expressions;
2 **May** all your dreams **come** true! **May** she never **regret** this decision!	2 **may**, meaning 'I hope that', followed by the *infinitive without* **to**;
3 I **wish** you good luck. I **wish** you every happiness. I **wish** you a Merry Christmas.	3 **wish + you** meaning 'I hope that you have', 'I want you to have', often expressed as a greeting or a kind of a blessing;
4 **Have** a nice time! **Enjoy** your evening out!	4 the **imperative** (▶ 25.2, 25.3);
5 **Let** him get home safely! Don't **let** me fail this exam!	5 the imperative form **let** which is not addressed to any particular person (or perhaps vaguely to God or good fortune) (▶ 25.4).

Regret

26.7

I wish If only	I were younger. you had more patience. she knew all this. we owned a car. you would tell me the truth. they could come here.

The above expressions of *regret* may also refer to *desires* which *cannot easily be fulfilled*.

1 a) I **wish** I **had** some money to lend him. I **wish** I **lived** in the country. They **wish** they **knew** where to find a house.	1 a) **Wish** followed by a verb in the *past tense* indicates a sense of *unhappiness* about the present situation by expressing a desire that it should be different. What is desired is practically *unattainable*. For the use of *past tense* to describe unreal events (▶ 20.2, 20.3).
b) I **wish** I **were/was** rich. I **wish** she **were/was** here with me.	b) Notice the use of **I wish I was**, and in more formal English, **I wish I were**.

2 I **wish** he **would** ring me more often.
   I **wish** you **wouldn't** interrupt me all the time.
   I **wish** you **could** write more neatly.
   Compare:
   I **hope** the Democrats **(will) win** the next election.

3 I **wish** I **had started** earlier.
   He **wishes** he **had grown** a beard.
   I **wish** I **hadn't mentioned** her mistake.
   They **wished** they **hadn't decided** to take the train.

4 **If only** I **had** more time.
   If only she **could** come and see us.
   If only I **had followed** his advice (but I didn't follow it).

2 **Wish** is followed by **would** or **could** if the realisation of the desire depends on the *willingness* or *capability* of somebody. **Wish ... would/could** is therefore used to express criticism of other people's behaviour or lack of ability.

   NOTE: **Wish ... would/could** cannot be used to express a hope about the future. The verb **hope** is used instead.

3 If the desire concerns a *past* event which *did not happen*, **wish** is followed by the *past perfect*. If, on the other hand, the past event *took place* and now the speaker regrets it, **wish** is followed by the *negative past perfect*.

4 The expression **if only**, followed by past or past perfect tense forms, can be used instead of **I wish** or **we wish** (▶ 20.4).

Intention and determination

26.8

I intend I aim I mean I'm going I'm determined	to finish	this job.
I shall/will	finish	
I insist on	finishing	

1 a) She **means** to come back as soon as possible.
      We **aim** to please our customers.

   b) He doesn't **intend** to work here for much longer. (= He intends not to work here)

   c) I'm sorry, I didn't **mean** to hurt your feelings.

   d) I **have no intention of** repay**ing** the money.

2 **I'm going to** make myself a strong coffee.

1 To express an *intention* to do something we can use the verbs **intend, aim, mean** followed by (**a**) **to**-*infinitive*. To express (**b**) a *negative intention*, or (**c**) *absence of intention*, the negative forms of these verbs can be used. The expression (**d**) **have no intention of** + **-ing** form (*verbal noun*) is also commonly used.

2 **Be going to** may also indicate intention (▶ 11.11).

3 We **are determined** to get our money back.
He **insisted on** pay**ing** the bill.

3 *Determination* to do something is expressed by **be determined** + **to-***infinitive* and sometimes also by **insist on** + **-ing** form *(verbal noun)* when the sense of determination meets opposition.

4 a) We**'ll** pay you tomorrow, don't worry.
I promise I**'ll** be there on time.

4 a) **Shall** and **will**, usually contracted to **'ll** (▶ 6.15), are used to make a promise. They may be accompanied by the verb **promise**.

b) I **shall** tell him frankly what I think.
I **shall** marry him.
You **will** always have your own way.

b) When they are not contracted **shall** and **will** may indicate determination. They may be stressed for greater emphasis. In this sense **shall** is used in the first person (**I/we**) and **will** in the other persons.

c) I **shan't** do that.
He just **won't** leave me alone.

c) **Shan't** and **won't** may express determined refusal.

5 You **shall** do as I tell you.
They want to sack me at the office but they **shan't** manage it.
He **shall** get what we owe him.

5 **Shall** used in the second and third persons indicates determination on the part of the speaker that something will or will not happen.

6 The police ordered that the night club **should** be closed for a month.
I urged that his friends **shouldn't** be invited.

6 This same idea of *determination* may be expressed by verbs of *ordering* and *suggesting* (▶ 25.10) followed by **should**.

Liking and disliking

Expressing likes

26.9 The following table lists some of the most common ways of expressing a liking for something. The order is from less enthusiastic to more enthusiastic.

I like	
I enjoy	westerns.
I'm fond of	
I'm keen on	playing tennis.
I love	
I'm mad/crazy about	

1 I **like** television.
I **enjoy** watching television.

1 All of these expressions can be followed by a noun or **-ing** form *(verbal noun)*. For use of the infinitive after **like, love** ▶ 6.36.

2 a) All the kids are **crazy about** ice cream.

   b) The Royal Family are all **fond of** horses.

3 We**'re quite keen on** going to the theatre.
  I **just love** Indian food.

2 a) **Mad/crazy about** is used only in informal English.

   b) The other expressions can be used in both formal and informal styles.

3 These expressions are frequently qualified by adverbs of degree. e.g. **quite, just, rather** (▶ 14.5).

Expressing dislikes

26.10 The expressions of disliking listed in the following table are in order of increasing strength.

I don't like/I dislike I can't stand/I can't bear I hate I'm fed up with/I'm sick of I detest/I loathe	hamburgers. driving in town.

1 I **don't like** cities.
  I **dislike** living in cities.

2 I've been working here for twenty years. I'm **fed up with** it.
  Why do you complain all the time? I'm **sick of** listening to you.

3 I **really can't stand** musicals.
  She **absolutely detests** her boss.

1 All of these expressions can be followed by a noun or **-ing** form (*verbal noun*). For use of the infinitive after **hate, like** ▶ 6.36.

2 **Fed up with** and **sick of** imply that the speaker dislikes something because he/she has been over-exposed to it. These two expressions are used in informal English.

3 These expressions are frequently qualified by adverbs of degree, e.g. **really, absolutely** (▶ 14.3).

Expressing indifference

26.11

1 I **don't mind** cold weather but I can't stand rain.
  She **doesn't mind** washing the dishes.
  I **didn't mind** going to school but I didn't really enjoy it.
  Compare:
  I **wouldn't mind** another drink. (= I would quite like one)

1 A negative structure with the verb **mind** can be used to indicate a position of neither liking nor disliking something. It can be followed by a noun or **-ing** form (*verbal noun*). It is normally used in the affirmative.

NOTES
Wouldn't mind is often used to express weak desire – often as a tentative form of request.
For **mind** in requests and permission ▶ 24.1, 25.6–25.8.

2 A: Would you like tea or coffee?
 B: I **don't mind**. (= I'll have either)
 They **don't mind** where they go on holiday provided it's sunny.
 She **won't mind** whether you pay by cash or cheque.

3 (Compare **2** above)
 A: Would you like tea or coffee?
 B: I **don't care**. (= I'm not interested in choosing)
 His parents **don't care** what he does. He's completely wild.
 I **don't care** if I never see you again.

4 The film was**n't bad** but the book's much better.
 The job's **all right** though I'm not crazy about it.

2 **Mind** can also be used as a polite way of expressing indifference. It can be followed by a subordinate clause introduced by a **wh-***word* (**where, when, how,** etc.) or **if/ whether**.

3 A negative structure with the verb **care** may be used in a similar way to **mind** in the previous point. It suggests *lack of interest*. **I don't care** is an impolite way of expressing indifference and may even sound aggressive.

4 The expressions **all right, OK** (sometimes written **okay**) and **not bad** indicate a neutral position of neither liking nor disliking something.

Expressing preference

26.12

I prefer	tea to coffee. watching TV to reading.
I'd prefer	a cup of tea rather than coffee. to watch TV rather than read.
I'd rather	have a cup of tea than coffee. watch TV than read. we watched TV.

1 I **prefer** summer **to** winter.
 Some people **prefer** water-ski**ing** to swimm**ing**
 I **prefer** to get up early **rather than** stay in bed.

2 A: Would you like a whisky?
 B: No, I**'d prefer** a soft drink **rather than** anything strong.
 I**'d prefer** to find a flat myself **rather than** pay an agency.
 The company **would prefer** to negotiate directly **rather than** use an intermediary.

1 The verb **prefer** is used for habitual preference, a constant or permanent state of mind. It is often used with the preposition **to**. A verb following **prefer** is normally in the **-ing** form (*verbal noun*). **Prefer** can also be followed by **to-***infinitive* + **rather than**

2 **Would prefer/'d prefer** expresses a spontaneous preference valid for one particular moment (compare **like** and **would like** ▶ 26.4). It is often used in response to an offer of something. **Would prefer** is often followed by **to-***infinitive* + **rather than** + *infinitive without* **to**.

3 I**'d rather** have a sandwich **than** a proper meal.
He**'d rather** be poor **than** make money dishonestly.
Would you **rather** come with me **or** stay at home?
They**'d** much **rather** go out **than** stay in the hotel.

4 She**'d rather** you **arrived** at nine instead of eight o'clock.
I**'d rather** the flat **were/was bigger**.

3 **Would rather/'d rather** also expresses desire in terms of alternatives. **Would rather** is normally followed by the *infinitive without* **to** and not simply by a noun.

4 If the subject of **would rather** is different from the subject of the following clause, the verb in the following clause is in the *past tense* (▶ 20.4).

For the use of **were/was** ▶ 20.2, 20.3.
For the use of the past tense to describe unreal events ▶ 20.2, 20.3.

27 Language of social situations and discussion

Language of social situations

Introducing yourself | Responses

27.1

Hello, I'm Sam Walker. (*informal*)	Hello/Hi, Sam. Nice to meet you.
How do you DO? My name's Peter Blake. (*formal*)	How do you DO, Mr Blake?

Notice that the expression **How do you do?** is used both as a means of introducing oneself and as a response. It is spoken with falling intonation.

Introducing other people | Responses

27.2

Carol, this is/meet Ann. (*informal*) Carol, do you know Ann? (*informal*)	Hello/Hi, Ann.
Mrs Baker, I'd like you to meet Gordon Burns. (*formal*) Mrs Baker, may I introduce you to Gordon Burns? (*formal*)	Pleased to meet you, Mr Burns.

Greetings | Responses

27.3

Hello/Hi. (*informal*)	Hello/Hi.	
How are you? How are you getting on/doing? (*informal*)	I'm fine, I'm very well, I'm not too bad,	thanks.
Good morning/afternoon/evening.	Good morning/afternoon/evening.	
Happy Christmas/New Year! Have a nice weekend/time/meal! Enjoy yourself!	Thanks very much! The same to you! You too! And you!	

Notice that **Good morning/afternoon/evening** are used at the moment of meeting someone.
Goodnight (▶ 27.4) cannot be used in this way. It is only used at the moment of leaving someone.

Saying goodbye and related expressions   Responses

27.4

Goodbye. Bye. (*informal*) Goodnight.	Goodbye. Bye. Goodnight.
Nice to have met you. (*formal*)	Yes, I hope we meet again.
Give my regards to your wife. (*formal*) Remember me to Sarah. Say hello to Sarah. (*informal*) Give my love to Sarah. (*informal*)	Yes, I will.
Hope to see you soon.	Yes, I hope so.
See you later/on Sunday. (*informal*)	Yes, see you.
Take care. (*informal*)	Yes, I will.
Don't forget to phone/write.	No, I won't. Don't worry.

NOTES

1 The above expressions are used at the moment of leaving someone. They may be combined in different ways. For example:

A: Nice to have met you. Goodbye.
B: Goodbye. Give my regards to Frank.
A: Yes, I will.

2 Notice that **Goodnight** is usually written as one word.

Complimenting   Responses

27.5

What a marvellous (meal)! That was such a good (meal)! That was one of the best (meals) I've ever (eaten).	I'm glad you liked it. It's nice of you to say so.

Congratulating   Responses

27.6

Congratulations! Well done! I was delighted to hear that (you passed the exam).	Thanks very much.
I'm so pleased for you. You deserve it.	Thanks. It's very kind of you to say so.

Thanking | Responses

27.7

Thanks (a lot). (*informal*) Thank you (very much). Thank you so much. (*formal*) It's really kind/nice of you. I'm very grateful to you. (*formal*)	That's all right. You're welcome. Not at all. (*formal*) Don't mention it. (*formal*) It's a pleasure. (*formal*)

Notice that in English these responses are not so commonly used as in many other languages. In many situations the person who is thanked will not respond verbally but may use a non-verbal gesture, for example, a smile, to respond.

Offering | Accepting

27.8

(Please) have a biscuit. DO have a biscuit. (*formal*) Would you like a biscuit? Do you feel like/fancy a biscuit? (*informal*) Would you care for a biscuit? (*formal*)	YES, PLEASE. THANK you. **Refusing** NO, THANK you.

NOTES
1 In the expression **Do have a biscuit** the auxiliary verb **do** would normally be stressed (▶ 25.2).
2 Notice that the expression **Thank you** (in this case usually spoken with falling intonation) indicates *acceptance* whereas **No, thank you** (spoken with falling/rising intonation for politeness ▶ Appendix 6) indicates *refusal*.

Apologising | Responses

27.9

I'm sorry. I'm afraid I've lost your book. I'm REALly sorry. I DO apologise. I seem to have lost your book. (*formal*)	Forget it. (*informal*) Never mind. Oh, that's all right. It doesn't matter. Don't worry about it.

NOTES
1 Notice that if adverbs like **really, terribly, so** are used with **sorry,** they are stressed.
2 If the auxiliary verb **do** is used with **apologise** it is stressed (▶ 18.5).
3 Notice that **pardon** (▶ 27.19) and **excuse me** (▶ 27.17) are not normally used for apologising. **I beg your pardon** is sometimes used for a spontaneous apology immediately after a small accident (for example, standing on someone's foot).

Speaking on the telephone

27.10

Person receiving the call	Person making the call
A: Hello, Edinburgh 56988.	B: Can I speak to Mark Roberts, please?
A: Speaking.	B: Oh, hello, Mark. This is Pete here.
A: Hello, Worldwide Insurance Company.	B: Could you put me through to extension 716, please?
A: Hold the line please. I'm trying to connect you.	B: Thank you.

Notice the use of **this** and **that** to identify people over the telephone (▶ 8.18):
> **This is Pete.** (*not* **I am Pete**)
> **Is that Paul?** (*not* **Are you Paul?**)

Writing letters

An informal letter

27.11

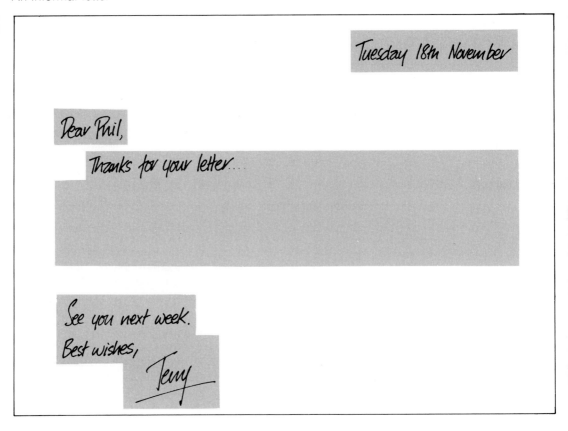

NOTES
1 Instead of **Best wishes** other expressions often used to conclude an informal letter are: **Yours**, **All the best**, **Love from**.
2 A comma is used after **Dear** (*Name*) but notice that the following word begins with a capital letter.

A formal letter

63 Grosvenor Road
Brighton
18th November 1988

(Mr A Blake)
Managing Director
ABC Industries

Dear Sir/(Mr Blake),

Thank you for your letter....

I look forward to hearing from you soon.

Yours faithfully/(Yours sincerely),

T. Butler

Terence Butler

NOTES

1 The expression **Yours faithfully** is normally used to conclude a letter beginning **Dear Sir** (i.e. when no individual is named personally).

2 A married woman may be addressed as **Mrs Blake** if **Blake** is the name of her husband.
An unmarried woman may be addressed as **Miss** (*Surname*).
Some women prefer to be addressed as **Ms** (*Surname*), a title which can be used for both married and unmarried women.

Language of discussion

Asking for an opinion

27.12

How do you like What do you think of/about How do you feel about What's your opinion of	American pop music?

1 **How do you like** London?
 How do you like living in London?

2 Do you like classical music?
 Are you fond of jazz?

3 I don't like Bartok. **Do you**?

 I'm sick of all this electronic music. **Aren't you**?

 I love African music. **What about you**?
 I didn't enjoy the concert, **What about you**?

1 The expressions listed in the table can be followed by a noun or an **-ing** form (*verbal noun*).

2 It is also common to ask for an opinion by forming a **yes/no** type of question using a verb expressing liking or disliking (▶ 26.9, 26.10).

3 Another means of asking for an opinion is to make a statement of opinion and follow it with a short question (▶ 21.4) or **What about you?** They are spoken with rising intonation and the pronoun **you** is stressed.

Giving an opinion

27.13

(Personally/Frankly/Honestly) I think (that) In my opinion, As I see it, If you ask me, It seems to me (that) As far as I'm concerned,	the concert was a disaster.

Frankly and **honestly** are normally only used to express a negative opinion.

Expressing agreement

27.14

Opinion	Agreement
I think the music is superb.	I agree/couldn't agree more. That's just/exactly what I think. Yes, exactly. Yes, I think so too. Yes, so do I. Yes, it is, isn't it?
I don't think the acting is very good.	No, I don't think so either. No, nor do I. No, it isn't, is it?

1 A: I found the film exciting.
 B: Yes, **so did I**.
 A: I didn't think the story was very original.
 B: No, **I didn't think so either./Neither did I**.

1 Expressions like **I think so too** and **so do I** are used to indicate agreement with an affirmative verb. **I don't think so either** and **nor/neither do I** indicate agreement with a negative verb. These expressions vary according to the tense of the verb they refer to (▶ 17.3).

2 A: Richard Gere wasn't very good in that film.

B: No, he wÁsn't, wÁs he?

A: The special effects worked very well.

B: Yes, they DÍD, DÍDn't they?

2 A common means of indicating agreement is to give a short response followed by a question tag (► 21.4). In this case the question tag would be spoken with falling intonation.

Expressing reservation

27.15

A: I think watching TV is a waste of time.

B: MAYbe			
TRUE		don't forget	
		there again	
In a way	but	don't you think	people need to relax (?)
Possibly		you must admit	
That may be so		on the other hand	

Notice that reservation is usually expressed by the use of falling–rising intonation.

Expressing disagreement

27.16

Opinion	Disagreement	
	I'm sorry, (but) I'm afraid Actually,	I can't agree with you there. I disagree. (*formal*) I don't think that's true. I'm not so sure about that.
	Really?/Do you really think so?	
	Emphatic disagreement	
The book is very well written.	No,	as a matter of fact in fact actually on the contrary	it's very badly written. it isn't.
	Are you serious?/You can't be serious! (*informal*) Are you joking?/You must be joking!(*informal*) Nonsense!/Rubbish!/Never! (*strong*)	

Notice the difference between **on the contrary** and **on the other hand** (► 16.11). **On the contrary** contradicts the previous statement. **On the other hand** accepts the truth of the previous statement but presents an opposing point.

Interrupting

27.17

SǑRry; ExcǓSE me; Hold on/Hang on a moment; (*informal*) Just a moment;	could I just say . . . ? I'd just like to say . . .

Notice that falling−rising intonation is typically used for politeness.

Clarification

27.18

The letter was badly written;	I mean or rather in fact in other words	it was almost illegible.

Asking for clarification

27.19

Statement	**Asking for clarification**
The whole ambience was suffused with angst.	Sorry?/Pardon?/I beg your pardon. Could you repeat that/say that again? I'm sorry, I don't understand. I'm afraid I didn't (quite) understand/catch what you said. What exactly do you mean by 'angst'? What? (*informal – often impolite*)

Appendix A
Stress and intonation

A1 *Stress and intonation* are features of the spoken language. *Intonation* refers to the way in which, in speaking, the tone of the voice rises or falls. *Stress* refers to the fact that certain parts of a word or a sentence sound more prominent than the other parts. The features of stress and intonation are interconnected. Intonation patterns are based upon the parts of a sentence which are stressed. Stress itself may be achieved through a change in intonation as well as by other means, such as speaking in a louder voice.

In this book a rising arrow ↗ over a word indicates that a *rise* in intonation begins on the stressed syllable and a falling arrow ↘ indicates a *fall* in intonation. The arrow ↗ indicates that the intonation *first falls and then rises*.

Stress

Word stress

A2 All English words of two or more syllables have stress on one of the syllables. In most dictionaries the stressed syllable is indicated by the symbol ' placed immediately before it. Stress may be on the first syllable:

after /'ɑ:ftə/   Friday /'fraɪdi/

or it may be on the second syllable:

before /bɪ'fɔ:/   today /tə'deɪ/

In longer words stress may be on the first, the second or a later syllable:

exercise /'eksəsaɪz/   potato /pə'teɪtəʊ/
interfere /ɪntə'fɪə/   education /edjʊ'keɪʃən/

Sentence stress

A3 Complete sentences also have their own typical stress (and intonation) patterns. Certain words are given more attention than others. These are the words that carry the most important information in the sentence and they tend to be *vocabulary* words: for example nouns, adjectives, full verbs. Other words are given less attention. They tend to be short *grammatical* words, words that occur repeatedly in sentence after sentence: for example articles, prepositions, auxiliary verbs. Usually the vocabulary words keep their stressed syllable when they are part of a sentence while the grammatical words may have no stress at all. In the following examples the words or syllables which are preceded by the symbol ' are those which would normally be stressed. The other words or syllables would normally have no stress.

'Kevin is 'looking for a 'new 'house.
Kev   look   new house

'What have you been 'doing to'day?
What   do   day

She 'put the 'cake in the 'oven.
        put   cake   ov

English is a *stress-timed* language. This means that the rhythm of English speech is based upon the stressed syllables, coming at regular intervals of time rather like a beat. The unstressed syllables between these beats have to be spoken comparatively quickly if the rhythm is to be maintained. This may give the impression that the speaker is swallowing rather than clearly pronouncing the syllables which are unstressed.

Each of the following sentences contains three stressed syllables. They would all be spoken with the same rhythm, and in roughly the same space of time, in spite of the fact that there are more unstressed syllables in the second sentence, and even more in the third.

He 'drove 'Jane 'home.

He has 'driven 'Catherine 'home.

He has been 'driving E'lizabeth to her 'home.

The fact that short grammatical words are usually unstressed when they form part of a sentence has an important effect on the pronunciation of these words. In many cases the pronunciation of the vowel changes because, in English, the vowel sound in most unstressed syllables tends to be the neutral vowel /ə/ or sometimes /ɪ/ or /i/. The result is that many of these short grammatical words have two pronunciations; one which is used when they are pronounced in isolation, or when they are stressed, and the other when they form part of a sentence and are unstressed. The following list shows how this affects some of the most common of these words.

	stressed	*unstressed*		
can	/kæn/	/kən/	as in:	He can do it.
been	/biːn/	/bɪn/		I've been working.
was	/wɒz/	/wəz/		She was eating.
some	/sʌm/	/səm/		I got some bread.
and	/ænd/	/ən(d)/ or /(ə)n/		Come and see me.
a	/eɪ/	/ə/		Here's a pen.
the	/ðiː/	/ðə/ or /ði/		Give me the paper.
				Give me the ink.
them	/ðem/	/ðəm/		I saw them.
to	/tuː/	/tə/		I want to do it.

For this reason some of these short grammatical words are abbreviated in the written representation of spoken English (for example **I'm, they're, we'll** instead of **I am, they are, we will**). Forms like **Rock 'n Roll, I wanna, I'm gonna** are also attempts to represent the actual sound of these expressions in colloquial English (**Rock and Roll, I want to, I'm going to**).

Main stress

A4

The stressed syllables of a sentence do not all have equal importance. If they did the rhythm of the language would sound very even. Instead one (or possibly more than one) of the stressed syllables is more prominent than the others because the speaker has decided that this part of the sentence is more important. This is the *main stress* of the sentence (also known as the *nucleus*) and it is on this syllable that the intonation pattern of the sentence is focussed. It is at this point that a significant rise or fall in intonation occurs. In the examples below the syllable with main stress is written in small capital letters.

Let's have a DRINK.

Do you want to COME?

There's a MESSage for you.

Haven't you SEEN it yet?

In longer sentences, and especially where there is more than one clause, there is usually more than one main stress.

When she SÁW you did she SPÉAK?

Even as a CHÍLD he was very QUÍet and also very SÉrious.

Emphatic stress

A5

Emphatic stress is used when we wish to focus attention on one particular element of a sentence, which may not be the element which would normally have main stress. Emphatic stress is given either by pronouncing the stressed syllable of a word even more forcefully than normal or by stressing a syllable which normally has no stress. Emphatic stress has an important effect on the meaning of a sentence, usually by introducing additional implications of contrast. The intonation pattern of the sentence is based upon the syllable with emphatic stress. In the following examples the syllable in large capital letters is the one with emphatic stress.

Kathy lives in DÚBlin.	(no emphatic stress: where Kathy lives is the important information)
KÀTHy lives in Dublin.	(Kathy, not Susan or another person)
Kathy LÌVÉS in Dublin.	(she is not there temporarily)
Kathy lives ÌN Dublin.	(not outside the city)
Kathy lives in DÙBlin.	(not Belfast or another city)

Intonation

A6

It is very difficult, perhaps impossible, to provide an accurate analysis of exactly how intonation functions in English because there is so much variation from one regional accent to another and even between one individual speaker and another. Here it is only possible to make some general observations about standard British English.

As we have seen (▶ A4) the intonation pattern of a sentence is based on the syllable(s) which have main stress. A significant change in the direction of intonation begins on these syllables. The three most important types of intonation in English are falling, rising and falling/rising. In the examples that follow the syllable with main stress is in small capitals.

1 Affirmative sentences normally end with falling intonation, which tends to indicate:
   a) *certainty*; simple statements of fact are pronounced with falling intonation.

   The milk's in the FRÌDGE.

   b) *completeness*; falling intonation indicates that a particular message or piece of information is concluded.

   The prince married the prinCÉSS and they lived happily ever ÀFter.

2 Rising intonation tends to indicate:
   a) *uncertainty or questioning*; most yes/no questions are spoken with rising intonation.

   Does she WÓRK here?

   Are you RÉADy?

   A sentence in affirmative form spoken with rising intonation can function as a question.

   A: You WÓRK here?   B: Yes, I DÒ.

   Notice, however, that questions beginning with **Wh-** words (**when, where, how,** etc. ▶ 2.2–2.10) normally have falling intonation.

   What's your NÀME?

   Where do you LÌVE?

b) *incompleteness*; rising intonation can indicate that the speaker has not finished what he/she wants to say. For example, in making a list, each item mentioned would be spoken with rising intonation until the last one, where falling intonation would show that this was the end of the list.

Could you get me some TEA, some COFFee and some SUGar?

Similarly in alternative (**either . . . or**) questions the first alternative is normally spoken with rising intonation while the second is given falling intonation, indicating that there is no other alternative.

Would you like TEA or COFFee? (you can choose either)

Rising intonation on the second alternative would imply that the list is incomplete and there are also other possibilities.

Would you like TEA or COFFee? (or something else)

3 A fall in intonation may be followed almost immediately by a rise. This falling/rising type of intonation may, like rising intonation, express a sense of incompleteness. In longer sentences where there are two clauses it is often used on the first clause to indicate that the sentence is going to continue.

If you WANT you can come WITH me.

When we finally GOT there the shop was CLOSED.

Both falling/rising and rising intonation are used to convey a sense of politeness. They may indicate interest in, or concern for, the person to whom we are speaking. They are used to convey politeness in, for example, making requests, invitations, offers, greetings, commands. In all these cases falling intonation might sound impolite.

I'll help you.

Sit DOWN.

Could you open the DOOR?

Compare:

Sit DOWN (= an order).

Come HERE (an order).

Conclusion

A7 The choice of different stress and intonation patterns completely transforms the meaning of what is said. The same words can be used and interpreted in radically different ways.

You LOVE him?   (Do you love him?)

YOU love him!   (I thought somebody else loved him)

You LOVE him?   (I thought you hated him)

You love HIM.   (He really is the one you love)

This grammar does not attempt to provide a complete description of how stress and intonation function in English. However it draws attention to features of stress and intonation at certain points where these features play a particularly important role in conveying meaning.

Appendix B
Pronunciation of word endings

Pronunciation of suffix -s

B1

1 The suffix **-s** is added to form:
   a) the plural of nouns;
   b) the third person singular of verbs in the simple present;
   c) the possessive of nouns.

2 It is pronounced /ɪz/ in words whose root form ends with the sounds /z/, /s/, /dʒ/, /tʃ/, /ʒ/, /ʃ/:

   a) wish /wɪʃ/ – wishes /wɪʃɪz/
   boss /bɒs/ – bosses /bɒsɪz/
   tax /tæks/ – taxes /tæksɪz/

   b) raise /reɪz/ – raises /ˈreɪzɪz/
   catch /kætʃ/ – catches /ˈkætʃɪz/

   c) James /ˈdʒeɪmz/ – James's /ˈdʒeɪmzɪz/
   Douglas /ˈdʌɡləs/ – Douglas's /ˈdʌɡləsɪz/

3 It is pronounced /s/ in words which end with unvoiced consonant sounds (except those in **2** above), i.e. the sounds /p/, /t/, /k/, /f/, /θ/:

   a) cup /kʌp/ – cups /kʌps/
   bit /bɪt/ – bits /bɪts/

   b) bite /baɪt/ – bites /baɪts/
   kick /kɪk/ – kicks /kɪks/

   c) Eric /ˈerɪk/ – Eric's /ˈerɪks/
   Elizabeth /iˈlɪzəbeθ/ – Elizabeth's /iˈlɪzəbeθs/

4 It is pronounced /z/ in words which end with any other sound (including vowels):

   a) dog /dɒɡ/ – dogs /dɒɡz/
   tree /triː/ – trees /triːz/
   car /kɑː/ – cars /kɑːz/
   toe /təʊ/ – toes /təʊz/

   b) need /niːd/ – needs /niːdz/
   free /friː/ – frees /friːz/

   c) Joan /dʒəʊn/ – Joan's /dʒəʊnz/
   Mary /ˈmeərɪ/ – Mary's /ˈmeərɪz/

5 Notice some particular cases:

   a) the change in the pronunciation of the vowel sound in **do** /duː/, **does** /dʌz/ and **say** /seɪ/, **says** /sez/;

   b) The sound /θ/ at the end of a word sometimes changes to /ð/:
   mouth /maʊθ/ – mouths /maʊðz/
   youth /juːθ/ – youths /juːðz/

   c) The sound /s/ at the end of a word sometimes changes to /z/:
   house /haʊs/ – houses /haʊzɪz/

Pronunciation of suffix -ed

B2

The suffix **-ed**, added to form the simple past and the past participle of regular verbs (► 3.21), is pronounced:

1 /ɪd/ in verbs which end with the sounds /t/, /d/:

   invent /ɪnˈvent/ – invented /ɪnˈventɪd/
   plant /plɑːnt/ – planted /plɑːntɪd/
   end /end/ – ended /endɪd/

2 /t/ in verbs which end with unvoiced consonant sounds (except /t/), /p/, /k/, /f/, /s/, /ʃ/, /tʃ/, /θ/:

   clap /klæp/ – clapped /klæpt/
   cook /kʊk/ – cooked /kʊkt/
   laugh /lɑːf/ – laughed /lɑːft/
   kiss /kɪs/ – kissed /kɪst/
   cash /kæʃ/ – cashed /kæʃt/
   match /mætʃ/ – matched /mætʃt/

3 /d/ in verbs which end with any other sound (including vowels):

   drag /dræɡ/ – dragged /dræɡd/
   play /pleɪ/ – played /pleɪd/
   span /spæn/ – spanned /spænd/

Appendix C
Spelling of word endings

In certain cases, when suffixes are added to nouns, verbs, adjectives and adverbs, there are additional changes in spelling. These changes can be considered in four groups:
1 An extra **e** may be added to the original word.
2 An **e** at the end of the original word may be omitted.
3 A final **y** may change to **i** or **ie** and final **ie** may change to **y**.
4 A final consonant may be doubled.

Adding **e**

C1

1 a) bus–bus**es**
   dish–dish**es**
   lunch–lunch**es**
   tax–tax**es**

 b) fix–fix**es**
   pass–pass**es**
   push–push**es**
   watch–watch**es**

   Compare:
   price–price**s**
   gaze–gaze**s**
   judge–judge**s**

2 hero–hero**es**
   potato–potato**es**
   tomato–tomato**es**

   Compare:
   a) radio–radio**s**
      video–video**s**

   b) photo (graph)–photo**s**
      kilo (gram)–kilo**s**

1 Words ending with the sounds /s, z, ʃ, ʒ, tʃ, dʒ/ add **e** before the suffix **-s**. This may affect:
   a) the plural form of nouns;

   b) the simple present tense of verbs (3rd person singular).

Exceptions:
words which already have a final **e** in the spelling.

2 Nouns ending in **o** add **e** before the plural suffix **-s.**

Exceptions:
a) nouns ending in *vowel* + **o;**

b) nouns which are abbreviated forms.

Omitting **e**

C2

1 a) late–lat**er**–lat**est**
   nice–nic**er**–nic**est**
   wise–wis**er**–wis**est**

 b) create–creat**ing**–creat**ed**
   like–lik**ing**–lik**ed**
   move–mov**ing**–mov**ed**

 c) arrive–arriv**al**
   molecule–molecul**ar**
   wide–wid**en**

1 Words ending in **e** normally omit **e** before suffixes beginning with a vowel.
   This may affect:
   a) the comparative and superlative forms of adjectives and adverbs (suffixes **-er, -est**);

   b) the present and past participles and the simple past tense of verbs (suffixes **-ing, -ed**);

   c) the formation of nouns, adjectives and verbs (e.g. suffixes **-al, -ar, -en**).

2 a) see–see**ing**
    agree–agree**ing**–agree**able**

    Compare:
    agree–agre**ed**
    free–fre**er**

  b) charge–charg**eable**
    notice–notic**eable**
    courage–courag**eous**

3 possible–possib**ly**
  simple–simp**ly**
  terrible–terrib**ly**

4 due–du**ly**
  true–tru**ly**
  whole–whol**ly**

2 There are some exceptions to the rule in
1 above:
  a) Words ending in **-ee** do not usually omit
    the final **e** (unless the suffix begins with
    e).

  b) Words ending in **-ce, -ge** do not omit **e**
    before **a** or **o**.

3 Adjectives ending in **-le** omit both letters
before the suffix **-ly** (to form adverbs).

4 The adjectives **due, true, whole** omit the
final **e** before the suffix **-ly**.

Changes involving **y**, **i** and **ie**

C3

1 a) ally–all**ies**
    baby–bab**ies**
    country–countr**ies**

  b) carry–carr**ies**
    fly–fl**ies**
    hurry–hurr**ies**
    try–tr**ies**

    Compare:
    boy–boy**s**
    say–say**s**

2 a) hurry–hurr**ied**
    rely–rel**ied**
    try–tr**ied**

  b) early–earl**ier**–earl**iest**
    lazy–laz**ier**–laz**iest**
    ugly–ugl**ier**–ugl**iest**

  c) crazy–craz**ily**
    sleepy–sleep**ily**

    Compare:
    shy–shy**ly**
    sly–sly**ly**

1 Words ending in *consonant* + **y** change **y** to
ie before the suffix **-s** This may affect:
  a) the plural form of nouns;

  b) the simple present tense of verbs
    (3rd person singular).

Notice that words ending in *vowel* + **y** do not
change **y** to **ie.**

2 Words ending in *consonant* + **y** usually
change **y** to **i** before all other suffixes, except
those beginning with **i** (see **3** below).
This may affect:
  a) the past participle and simple past tense
    of verbs (suffix **-ed**);

  b) the comparative and superlative forms of
    adjectives and adverbs (suffixes **-er,
    -est**);

  c) the formation of adverbs, with some
    exceptions (suffix **-ly**);

d) tidy–tid**iness**
carry–carr**iage**
deny–den**iable**
glory–glor**ious**

3 a) beauty–beaut**ify**
glory–glor**ify**
summary–summar**ise**

b) fly–fl**ying**
hurry–hurr**ying**
try–tr**ying**

4 die–d**ying**
lie–l**ying**

d) the formation of nouns and adjectives
(e.g. suffixes **-ness, -age, -able, -ous**).

3 a) Words ending in *consonant* + **y** usually
omit **y** before suffixes beginning with **i**
(e.g. **-ify, -ise**).

b) Verbs ending in *consonant* + **y** keep **y**
before the suffix **-ing**.

4 Verbs ending in **ie** change **ie** to **y** before the
suffix **-ing**.

Doubling of consonants

C4

1 a) thin–thi**nn**er–thi**nn**est
big–bi**gg**er–bi**gg**est
fat–fa**tt**er–fa**tt**est

b) fit–fi**tt**ing–fi**tt**ed
plan–pla**nn**ing–pla**nn**ed
stop–sto**pp**ing–sto**pp**ed

Compare:
2 a) quick–qui**ck**er–qui**ck**est
wish–wi**sh**ing–wi**sh**ed

b) sweet–swe**et**er–swe**et**est
gain–gai**n**ing–gai**n**ed

c) open /'əʊpən/
ope**n**ing–ope**n**ed
visit /'vɪzɪt/
visi**t**ing–visi**t**ed

d) raw–ra**w**er–ra**w**est
obey–obe**y**ing–obe**y**ed

3 travel /'trævəl/
trave**ll**ing–trave**ll**ed
Compare American English:
travel–trave**l**ing–trave**l**ed

1 Words ending with *a single stressed vowel +
single consonant* have the final consonant
doubled before the suffixes **-er, -est, -ing,
-ed**.
This may affect:
a) the comparative and superlative forms of
adjectives;
b) the present and past participles and the
simple past tense of verbs.

2 Notice that there is no doubling when:
a) the final consonant sound is written with
two letters;
b) the vowel preceding the final consonant
is written with two letters;
c) the vowel preceding the final consonant
is unstressed;
d) the word ends with the letters **-w** or **-y**.

3 The final letter **l** is doubled even when the
preceding vowel is unstressed (in British
English but not in American English).

Appendix D
Formation of words

Prefixes and suffixes

D1
English often uses *prefixes* and *suffixes* to create new words. A prefix is a part of a word which can be added at the beginning (e.g. **un**comfortable) and a suffix is one which can be added at the end (e.g. relation**ship**).

Suffixes mostly have a grammatical function. They are used to create different parts of a verb (e.g. **-ing** to form the present participle, **-ed** to form the past participle: work–work**ing**–work**ed**). They are used to create the plural form of nouns (e.g. cup–cup**s**) and the comparative and superlative forms of adjectives (e.g. long–long**er**–long**est**). Suffixes are also used to create new words (e.g. nouns from verbs: teach–teach**er** ▶ D3).

Prefixes mostly have a lexical, rather than a grammatical, function. They qualify in some way, or form the opposite of, the word to which they are joined (▶ D2).

Various prefixes and suffixes can be combined to create increasingly complex new words (e.g. de-**nation**-al-ise; dis-**courage**-ment; un-**employ**-able).

Prefixes and suffixes follow certain patterns and can help us to guess the meaning of unknown words. They also play an important part in helping us to understand new terminology which is constantly being developed, particularly in the field of scientific and technical English.

Common prefixes

D2

1 The **anti**thesis of love is hate.
The **bi**lateral agreement will become effective in January.
A **co**-educational school is for both boys and girls.
Be careful – there's a motorway **inter**change ahead.
The audience was soon bored by his **mono**tonous voice.
Any **over**time work must be authorised by the manager.
The shop was **re**decorated before being **re**opened.
The clothes marked **sub**standard were sold at a lower price.
The dangers of drug addiction must not be **under**estimated.

	Prefix	Meaning
1	**anti-**	against (**anti**social)
	bi-	two (**bi**lingual)
	co-	with (**co**operation)
	ex-	former (**ex**-officer)
	extra-	beyond (**extra**ordinary)
	inter-	between (**inter**national)
	intra-	within (**intra**venous)
	mono-	one (**mono**syllabic)
	multi-	many (**multi**racial)
	over-	too much (**over**work)
	pre-	before (**pre**fix)
	pro-	in favour of (**pro**-Arab)
	re-	again (**re**build)
	semi-	half (**semi**circle)
	sub-	below (**sub**title)
	super-	above (**super**natural)
	trans-	across (**trans**atlantic)
	under-	too little (**under**fed)

2 There are advantages and **dis**advantages in the project.
What you say in **in**formal situations is often **in**adequate on formal occasions.
He took a **non**-stop flight to New York.
Your behaviour is **il**logical, **im**moral and **ir**responsible.

2 The negative prefixes **de-, dis-, in-, non-, un-** express the opposite meaning of the adjective, noun or verb to which they are added.
The negative prefixes **il-, im-, ir-,** are used instead of **in-** in some cases (e.g. if the original word begins with **l, m** or **r**).

3 Some English sounds are often **mis**pronounced by foreigners.
A printing error is called a **mis**print.

3 The prefix **mis-** placed before verbs, and sometimes also nouns and adjectives, expresses the idea that something is done incorrectly.

Suffixes: formation of nouns

D3

1 Jane is a teach**er**; she teaches in a secondary school.
John learnt to swim a year ago and is now a good swimm**er**.
Machines that process words are called word process**ors**.
To receive the BBC World Service you need a good receiv**er**.

Nouns can be formed in the following ways:
1 by adding the suffix **-er/-or** to the base form of a verb. They refer to people who work in a certain profession or carry out a particular action, and to objects, machines or substances which are used for a particular purpose. The action or function carried out is indicated by the original verb.

2 On arriv**al** the tourists were taken to their hotel.
The priest made a strange impress**ion** on the congregation.
Pay**ment** will be made upon receipt of the invoice.

2 by adding the suffixes **-al, -ion, -ment** to certain verbs. Nouns formed in this way refer to the action expressed by the original verb.

3 You have all the free**dom** of movement you want.
Do you know the dens**ity** of this substance?
If you cook these vegetables they'll lose their good**ness**.

3 by adding the suffixes **-dom, -ity, -ness** to certain adjectives. Abstract nouns, referring to the quality expressed by the original adjective, are created in this way.

4 I don't know anybody in the neighbour**hood**.
He can rely on my friend**ship**.
Admission to the club is by member**ship** only.

4 by adding the suffixes **-hood, -ship** to other nouns. The abstract nouns created in this way are linked to the concept expressed by the original noun.

For spelling changes ▶ Appendix C.

Suffixes: formation of adjectives

D4

1 I met a blue-ey**ed** girl
(= a girl with blue eyes).
We need a skill**ed** worker
(= a worker with skills).
Three-wheel**ed** cars are not so common
(= cars with three wheels).

1 The suffix **-ed** can be added to a noun in order to make an adjective describing a particular characteristic or quality (in a similar way to the use of past participles as adjectives ▶ 8.12).

2 a) It was child**ish** of him to behave like that.
The monster in the film was a fish-**like** creature.
She is a very friend**ly** woman.
I like staying at home on a rain**y** day.

2 Many other suffixes can be added to nouns to form corresponding adjectives. In particular:
a) **-ish, -like, -ly, -y** which express comparison, resemblance or connection of some kind;

b) Is your watch water**proof**?
They fitted new sound**proof** windows.

c) She sent me a colour**ful** postcard of Venice.
What you are saying is absolutely meaning**less**.

d) English has a large scientif**ic** and technic**al** vocabulary.
Molecul**ar** biology is a relatively new branch of science.

3 The bedroom is small**ish** but it's all right for me.
The walls are painted a green**ish** colour.

4 Is this water drink**able**?
Don't you think this is an accept**able** offer?

b) **-proof,** which indicates ability to resist or protect from;

c) **-ful** and **-less,** which express, respectively, possession and lack of possession (in a general sense);

d) **-ic, -al, -ar,** which are often added to nouns, particularly in the field of technical and scientific English.

3 The suffix **-ish** added to adjectives sometimes gives a meaning similar to that of **rather** or **fairly** (▶ 14.4).

4 The suffix **-able/-ible,** added to verbs, forms adjectives which indicate the possession of the quality or the capacity implied by the meaning of the corresponding verb.

Suffixes: formation of verbs

D5

They want to wid**en** the road.
The first job is to class**ify** the stamps according to origin.
To summar**ise,** every effort must be made not to wors**en** the situation.
We are going to computer**ise** the accounting system.
All the training programmes should be regular**ised**.
They've privat**ised** British Airways.

The suffixes **-en, -ify, -ise/-ize** added to nouns or adjectives may form verbs which describe a corresponding action or process.
The inventing of all kinds of new verbs by means of the suffix **-ise/-ize** (e.g. computer**ise**, regular**ise**) is a feature of modern English which some speakers find ugly and disapprove of.

Compound nouns

D6

1 Compound nouns are very common in English. In their simplest form they are created by placing two nouns side by side so that the first noun qualifies the second almost in the same way as an adjective:
  a **television programme** (= a programme shown on television)
  winter sports (= sports practised in winter)

The order of the nouns is important. In interpreting the meaning we should always remember that the final noun is the one which provides the key information, and that the preceding word, or words, qualify it, i.e. they provide supplementary information.

2 It is difficult to make a distinction between compound nouns and cases where a noun is preceded by another noun functioning as an adjective (▶ 8.14). A compound noun is a 'close' combination – two words fused together to function as one. This is often indicated by the fact that the two words are written as one or are joined together by a hyphen (e.g. **bookshop, coat-tail**). However not all

compound nouns are joined together in this way and, in some cases, two or more written forms are acceptable (e.g. **earache/ear-ache**).

In the spoken language, compound nouns usually have the main stress on the first noun of the combination (for example: 'tea-cup, 'tourist guide, 'traffic lights) although there are also many cases where both nouns of the compound are given stress (for example: 'day 'trip, 'summer 'holiday, 'school 'hall).

3 a) Dial 100 for the **'telephone operator**.
   She works as a **'tourist guide**.
   Where can I find a **'tea-cup**?
   Compare:
   Would you like a **'cup of 'tea**?
   The **'milk bottle** is empty.
   Compare:
   He drank a **'bottle of 'milk**.

3 Compound nouns may be used to convey a variety of meanings:
   a) to express the *function* carried out by a person or the purpose with which objects, machines and substances are associated;

   b) I've got a car with a **'diesel engine** not a **'petrol engine**.
   The **'brake lights** came on when the car stopped at the **'traffic lights**.

   b) to distinguish one particular *variety* of something;

   c) Excuse me, where's the **'physics la'boratory**?
   Fiat is one of the largest **'car 'companies** in Europe.
   The pupils assembled in the **'school 'hall**.

   c) to express, in general terms, a link of some kind between two entities or the *possession* (in the widest sense of the term ▶ 10.1) of one entity by another;

   d) They went on a **'day 'trip** to Brighton.
   Did you have a nice **'summer 'holiday**?

   d) to indicate *time*;

   e) I like to have a **'window 'seat** on the plane.
   They met at the **'theatre 'door**.

   e) to indicate *position in space*.

4 He works as a **'car salesman**.
   Have you lost your **cigar'ette lighter**?

4 Notice that in compound nouns the first noun is normally singular even when the meaning is plural.

5 Do you know the **train dep'arture times**?
   This model is produced by a **motorcycle manu'facturing company**.

5 More complicated combinations involving more than two nouns are possible.

Appendix E
Principal irregular verbs

The verbs below are listed in their infinitive, past and past participle form.

to be	was	been
to bear	bore	borne, born
to beat	beat	beaten
to begin	began	begun
to bend	bent	bent, bended
to bet	bet, betted	bet, betted
to bite	bit	bitten
to blow	blew	blown
to break	broke	broken
to bring	brought	brought
to broadcast	broadcast, broadcasted	broadcast, broadcasted
to build	built	built
to burn	burnt, burned	burnt, burned
to burst	burst	burst
to buy	bought	bought
to catch	caught	caught
to choose	chose	chosen
to come	came	come
to cost	cost	cost
to cut	cut	cut
to deal	dealt	dealt
to dig	dug	dug
to do	did	done
to draw	drew	drawn
to dream	dreamed, dreamt	dreamed, dreamt
to drink	drank	drunk
to drive	drove	driven
to eat	ate	eaten
to fall	fell	fallen
to feed	fed	fed
to feel	felt	felt
to fight	fought	fought
to find	found	found
to fly	flew	flown
to forget	forgot	forgotten
to freeze	froze	frozen
to get	got	got, (USA) gotten
to give	gave	given
to go	went	gone
to grow	grew	grown
to hang	hung, hanged	hung, hanged
to have	had	had
to hear	heard	heard
to hide	hid	hidden
to hit	hit	hit
to hold	held	held
to hurt	hurt	hurt
to keep	kept	kept
to kneel	knelt	knelt

to know	knew	known
to lay	laid	laid
to lead	led	led
to learn	learnt, learned	learnt, learned
to leave	left	left
to lend	lent	lent
to let	let	let
to lie	lay	lain
to light	lighted, lit	lighted, lit
to lose	lost	lost
to make	made	made
to mean	meant	meant
to meet	met	met
to pay	paid	paid
to put	put	put
to read	read	read
to ride	rode	ridden
to ring	rang	rung
to rise	rose	risen
to run	ran	run
to say	said	said
to see	saw	seen
to sell	sold	sold
to send	sent	sent
to set	set	set
to sew	sewed	sewn, sewed
to shake	shook	shaken
to shave	shaved	shaved, shaven
to shine	shone	shone
to shoot	shot	shot
to show	showed	shown, showed
to shrink	shrank, shrunk	shrunk, shrunken
to shut	shut	shut
to sing	sang	sung
to sink	sank	sunk, sunken
to sit	sat	sat
to sleep	slept	slept
to slide	slid	slid
to smell	smelt, smelled	smelt, smelled
to speak	spoke	spoken
to spell	spelt, spelled	spelt, spelled
to spend	spent	spent
to spill	spilt, spilled	spilt, spilled
to spit	spat	spat
to split	split	split
to spoil	spoilt, spoiled	spoilt, spoiled
to spread	spread	spread
to stand	stood	stood
to steal	stole	stolen
to stick	stuck	stuck
to stink	stank, stunk	stunk
to strike	struck	struck, stricken
to swear	swore	sworn
to sweep	swept	swept

to swim	swam	swum
to take	took	taken
to teach	taught	taught
to tear	tore	torn
to tell	told	told
to think	thought	thought
to throw	threw	thrown
to understand	understood	understood
to wake	woke	woken
to wear	wore	worn
to weep	wept	wept
to win	won	won
to wind	wound	wound
to write	wrote	written

Appendix F
Punctuation and use of capital letters

Punctuation

F1 The punctuation marks are:

Full stop	.	Exclamation mark	!
Comma	,	Dash	–
Semi-colon	;	Hyphen	-
Colon	:	Brackets (parentheses)	( )
Question mark	?	Apostrophe	'
Inverted commas	(quotation marks)		
single	' '		
double	" "		

F2

She suspects I know where the money is.
(= She suspects that I know ...)
Compare:
She suspects, I know, where the money is.
(= I know she suspects where ...)

Punctuation marks are used to make a piece of writing clearer and easier to read. They may also affect the meaning of a sentence.

The full stop

F3

That's my sister. She's a student.
You can't import foreign currencies, **e.g.** (= **for example**) dollars or French francs.
Please write to:
The Consumers **Dept.** (= **Department**)
He lives at 14, Andover **Sq.** (= Square)

The *full stop* (.) is used at the end of a sentence. It can also be used in many abbreviations and shortened words.

The comma

F4

1 Students, **who are careless,** often forget to do their homework. (= All students are careless)
Compare:
Students who are careless often forget to do their homework. (= Only a restricted number of careless students forget to do it)

The *comma* (,) separates parts of a sentence. It is used to separate:

1 non-restrictive relative clauses (▶ 8.20);

2 Mr Brown, **a former colonel,** will deliver the speech.

2 nouns or noun phrases used in apposition (▶ 8.29);

3 **To my surprise,** she was wearing an evening dress.
I would, **if I were you,** leave him in peace.
You can, **however,** do as you wish.

3 words, phrases and clauses used *within a sentence* that stand apart from the main information conveyed;

4 You can have **tea, coffee, milk** or chocolate.

5 **Paul, give** me the paper.
  Look, ladies and gentlemen.

6 He said, **'Let's go.'**

7 **Fortunately,** the train hadn't left.

8 **If you need me,** just give me a ring.

4 items in a list (but usually not before **and** and **or** (▶ 17.2, 17.8);

5 imperative forms from the person addressed (▶ 25.3);

6 quoted speech.

7 initial adverb phrases (▶ 13.5);

8 a subordinate (especially conditional) clause from the main clause, when the subordinate clause comes first.

For the use of full stops and commas in numbers ▶ 9.20, 9.22.

The semi-colon

F5

1 The chapters deal with: **nouns; adjectives; adverbs; prepositions**.

2 The bus takes a long time to get there**;** it stops at a lot of places.

The *semi-colon* (**;**) can be used to separate:

1 items in a list (instead of a comma);

2 two main clauses which are closely related in meaning or significance, e.g. the second clause expands on or helps to explain the first.

The colon

F6

1 Please bring the following items**: passport; driving licence; two photographs**.

2 She said**: We're late**.

3 This is what you should do**: go and see a doctor**.

The *colon* (**:**) can be used to introduce:

1 a list of items;

2 quoted speech;

3 a second clause which continues the meaning of the first.

The question mark

F7

What's the time?
Compare:
He asked me **what the time was**.

The *question mark* (**?**) is used after *direct* questions, but not after *indirect* questions.

The exclamation mark

F8

1 **How beautifully** she sings**!**

2 **Watch out!**

The *exclamation mark* (**!**) can be used:

1 after an exclamation;

2 to make an imperative stronger or more urgent.

The dash

F9

> This book **– which I have just read –** has been a bestseller for years.

The *dash* (–) can be used, especially in informal writing, to show a break, e.g. to separate non-restrictive relative clauses (instead of a comma).

The hyphen

F10

> 1 I went to his party and **enjoy-ed** myself very much.
>
> 2 He has bought a **well-kept sixteenth-century** house.
> He is very much **pro-American**.

The *hyphen* (-) is used:
1 at the end of a line, when the word is split into two parts;

2 in compound words and after certain prefixes.

NOTE: Hyphens are often optional. Use a dictionary to check if a hyphen is usual in a particular word.

Brackets

F11

> 1 Shakespeare **(1564–1616)** will be treated separately **(see Chapter 21)**.
>
> 2 The substance has been tested **(using a special machine),** but the results are inconclusive.

Brackets (parentheses) **( )** can be used to indicate:
1 cross-references and periods of time, in more formal writing;

2 additional, often incidental, information.

Inverted commas

F12

> 1 **'Go to the baker's,'** she said, **'and get me some bread.'**
>
> 2 Gibbon called it **'the eighth wonder of the world'**.
> Have you seen **'Out of Africa'**?
>
> 3 If you don't wear jeans, you're **'out'** here.

Inverted commas (quotation marks) (' ' or " ") are used:
1 at the beginning and at the end of direct speech;

2 to quote words, including titles of books, films, etc;

3 to indicate that a word is used in a new or unusual sense.

The apostrophe

F13

> 1 Where**'s** Tom? I ca**n't** find him.
>
> 2 This is Mary**'s** room, and that's my parent**s'** room over there.

The *apostrophe* (') is used to indicate:
1 short forms, to show that some letters have been omitted (▶ 6.3);

2 the **s**-genitive (▶ 10.7).

Capital letters

Capital letters are used in the following cases:

F14

1 This is my new car. **I**t's a Ferrari.

1 at the beginning of a sentence;

2 My name's **J**ohn **B**urton.
Where's **M**iss **R**oberts?
She's with **D**octor **G**reen.
Do you like **D**uran **D**uran?
The **P**rime **M**inister will be here soon.

2 for names and titles of people;

3 The **T**hames is the longest river in **B**ritain.
I'm studying at the **L**ondon **S**chool of
Economics.
St **P**aul's **C**athedral is in the **C**ity of **L**ondon.

Compare:
Are you going to **s**chool?
What's your capital **c**ity?

3 for proper nouns, names of things and places referring to a particular example;

4 She's **E**nglish, but her husband is **F**rench.

4 for adjectives of nationality;

5 My uncle is arriving on **T**uesday and will stay
until 12th **A**ugust.
Are you going somewhere at **C**hristmas?
The **M**odern **A**ge has seen many dramatic
changes.

5 for names of days, months, festivities and sometimes periods in history;

6 Have you read 'The **E**nd of the **A**ffair' by
Graham Greene?
I read 'The **N**ews of the **W**orld' every Sunday.
Michelangelo's **L**ast **J**udgment is in the
Sistine Chapel in the Vatican.

6 for titles of newspapers, magazines, books, films, plays, works of art, etc. (but usually only the main words such as nouns, adjectives and verbs);

7 Please send a **SAE** (stamped addressed
envelope).
She works in an **EDP** (electronic data
processing) firm.

7 for many abbreviations.

8 You know **I** like fast cars.

8 Notice that the pronoun **I** is always written with a capital letter.

Appendix G
List of common phrasal and prepositional verbs

In many cases, with phrasal and prepositional verbs, the preposition or adverb can help us to understand the meaning of the verb.

Away

G1 often refers to the idea of separation or distance.

A left-wing group **broke away** from the main political party.
(= separated themselves)
It was eight o'clock before I could **get away** from the office.
(= leave)
The police warned the public to **keep away** from the disaster area.
(= stay at a distance)
I try to **put away** £50 a month in my deposit account.
(= save)
The porter **turned** us **away** at the entrance to the building.
(= refused admittance)

Back

G2 often refers to the idea of (2) repression, (3) rejection.

I **got back** very late last night.
(= returned home)
A series of disasters has **set back** the space programme.
(= delayed)
The journalist admitted he was wrong and **took back** his allegation.
(= withdrew)
The expedition was forced to **turn back** because of the weather.
(= return)

Down

G3 often refers to the idea of (1) descent or decline, (2) repression, (3) rejection.

The doctor advised him to **cut down** his consumption of alcohol.
(= reduce)
The rebellion was **put down** with great cruelty.
(= repressed)
You should stop **running down** your country and be more patriotic.
(= criticising negatively)
The company offered him a job but he **turned** it **down**.
(= refused)

For

G4 often refers to the idea of a goal or a target.

I'll **call for** you and we can go there together.
(= come and collect)
There are millions of people **looking for** work.
(= trying to find)

When storm clouds appeared the ship **made for** the nearest port.
(= travelled in the direction of)
She's **standing for** Parliament at the next election.
(= is a candidate for)

In

often refers to the idea of entering.

Some burglars **broke in** during the night.
(= entered the house violently)
If you're in the neighbourhood **call in** and see me.
(= come into my house)
Please stop **cutting in** and let me finish what I'm saying.
(= interrupting)
There was a broken window in the bedroom and a bird had **got in**.
(= entered)

Off

often refers to the idea of (1) detachment or isolation, (2) movement away.

The two countries **broke off** diplomatic relations.
(= terminated)
There were no other houses nearby. They felt completely **cut off**.
(= isolated)
The gardener asked us to **keep off** the grass.
(= not to walk on)
I wanted to make an early start so I **set off** at seven o'clock.
(= started the journey)
The plane **took off** and disappeared among the clouds.
(= went up in the air)

On

often refers to the idea of continuation.

How is Jimmy **getting on** at school?
(= progressing)
The speech **went on** for a long time.
(= continued)
Everybody asked him to be quiet but he **kept on** shouting.
(= continued)

Out

often refers to the idea of making an exit, which may result in an appearance or a disappearance.

A fire **broke out** in the engine room.
(= appeared, started)
It was cloudy in the morning but then the sun **came out**.
(= appeared)
The cat was trapped in the house and couldn't **get out**.
(= escape)
He blew on the candle and the flame **went out**.
(= was extinguished)

Over

G9

 often refers to the idea of (1) communication, (2) transfer.

The theory was very complicated and was difficult to **put over**.
(= explain)
Because of the fighting the army **took over** from the police.
(= replaced, assumed control)

Through

G10

 often refers to the idea of (1) emergence, (2) making contact.

Concorde was the first civilian plane to **break through** the sound barrier.
(= penetrate)
Most people **go through** a difficult period in adolescence.
(= experience and emerge from)
Is that the switchboard? Can you **put** me **through** to extension 56?
(= connect)
The line is engaged. I can't **get through**.
(= make contact)

Up

G11

↑ often refers to the idea of (1) rise or increase, (2) creation, (3) appearing.

I **got up** early because I wanted to have plenty of time.
(= rose from bed)
The price has **gone up** since last month.
(= risen)
I don't believe his story. He's just **making** it **up**.
(= inventing)
They **set up** a new office in Australia.
(= established)
Nobody was expecting him at the party. He just **turned up**.
(= appeared unexpectedly)
I always buy lottery tickets but my number never seems to **come up**.
(= appear)

G12 In many other cases the meaning of the phrasal or prepositional verb seems to have little or no logical connection with the normal meaning of the adverb or preposition. The following list contains some of the more common examples.

If the engine **breaks down** I can't repair it.
(= stops functioning properly)

After 1918 the Austro-Hungarian Empire **broke up** into a number of small states.
(= disintegrated)

The meeting was **called off** because of the bad weather.
(= abandoned)

I **came across** her photograph in an old magazine.
(= found)

Cut up the potatoes into small cubes.
(= cut into small pieces)

We've **fallen out** with our neighbours over the noise.
(= stopped being friends)

We had hoped to go to Scotland but our plans **fell through**.
(= didn't happen)

Do you **get on with** the other people at work?
(= have a good relationship with)

She was very depressed but now she has **got over** it.
(= recovered)

He pretended to be French but his accent **gave** him **away**.
(= betrayed)

The bank robbers saw that the building was surrounded by police so they **gave** themselves **up**.
(= surrendered)

The bomb **went off** inside a crowded supermarket.
(= exploded)

The doctors and nurses **looked after** me very well in the hospital.
(= cared for)

All the children were **looking forward to** the start of the holiday.
(= awaiting with pleasure)

He was worried about the noise and asked the mechanic to **look over** the engine.
(= examine)

Look up the word in the dictionary if you can't understand it.
(= consult)

The photo was so badly focussed that we couldn't even **make out** who was in it.
(= distinguish)

I don't want to **put** you **off** taking the job but there are problems.
(= discourage from)

Have you got any friends in London who can **put** you **up** for a night?
(= give accommodation to)

We're moving because we can't **put up with** the noise any longer.
(= tolerate)

Everybody wanted to buy milk and the supermarkets soon **ran out**.
(= had no more left)

The cat was walking in the road and was **run over** by a lorry.
(= knocked down and crushed)

The sun went down and darkness **set in**.
(= became established)

He **takes after** his mother – she's very untidy too.
(= resembles in behaviour)

I'll dictate the message and you **take** it **down**.
(= write)

She's Spanish but most people **take** her **for** a Scandinavian because of her blonde hair.
(= identify mistakenly)

He seemed so honest and sincere – I was completely **taken in**.
(= deceived)

The doctor advised him to **take up** golf to get some exercise.
(= start practising)

I was a little sceptical about seeing the play but it **turned out** to be very interesting.
(= proved)

Appendix H
Prepositions after adjectives, verbs and nouns

accuse of
He was **accused of** murdering his wife.
accustomed to
She wasn't **accustomed to** driving in the city.
afraid of
Are you **afraid of** heights?
agree with; about; to
I **agree with** you.
We didn't **agree about** the best place to meet.
Everybody **agreed to** help.
angry with; about
She was **angry with** her husband.
She was **angry about** losing the money.
annoyed with; about
The secretary was **annoyed with** her boss.
She was **annoyed about** missing her lunch.
anxious about; for; to
Helen was **anxious about** her son's illness.
She was **anxious for** the doctor to arrive.
She was **anxious to** contact her husband.
apologise for
I must **apologise for** keeping you waiting.
approve of
The manager didn't **approve of** the staff wearing jeans.
argue with; about
Please don't **argue with** me.
Why do we always **argue about** money?
arrest for
The old man was **arrested for** shoplifting.
arrive at/in
Finally we **arrived at** the hotel/**in** London.
ashamed of
Aren't you **ashamed of** getting drunk every night?
astonished at/by
The audience were **astonished at/by** his appearance.
aware of
Nobody was **aware of** the reason for the delay.
bad at
I'm very **bad at** remembering names.
believe in
Do you **believe in** ghosts?
blame for
The government were **blamed for** the rise in inflation.
boast about
He was always **boasting about** his adventures in Africa.

borrow from
The money was **borrowed from** a bank.
choose between
You have to **choose between** your career and your family.
clever at
I'm not very **clever at** investing money.
comment on
The President didn't **comment on** the newspaper reports.
compare with
You can't **compare** your work **with** mine.
complain about
We certainly can't **complain about** the service here.
concentrate on
I'm going to **concentrate on** passing the driving test.
concerned about; with
We're all very **concerned about** his health.
The next lecture will be **concerned with** the Renaissance.
confused about; by
I'm a little **confused about** how the computer works.
The teacher **confused** me **by** speaking so fast.
congratulate on
I must **congratulate** you **on** the success of your film.
conscious of
He wasn't **conscious of** being followed.
consist of
The flat **consists of** four rooms.
crazy about
He's **crazy about** football.
curious about
I'm **curious about** how the problem started.
decide on
Have they **decided on** a date for the wedding?
delighted about; with
Jimmy's **delighted about** passing the exam.
Jimmy's **delighted with** his birthday present.
depend on
You need a car – you can't **depend on** public transport.
die of
Thousands of people **died of** starvation.
different from
The Canadian accent is **different from** the American.

difficulty in; with
Older people have **difficulty in** learning
languages.
I had some **difficulty with** the Physics exam.

disappointed at/about; with
I'm very **disappointed at/about** Martin's
behaviour.
I'm very **disappointed with** Martin.

discussion about
The council had a long **discussion about** the
new road.

disgusted at/about; with
We were **disgusted at/about** Peter's attitude.
We were **disgusted with** Peter.

divide into
The cake was **divided into** four equal pieces.

doubtful about
She was **doubtful about** whether to apply for
the job.

dressed in
All the children were **dressed in** uniform.

effect on
The incident had an **effect on** the girl's
development.

enthusiastic about
The critics were not **enthusiastic about** the
new novel.

envious of
Other women were **envious of** her sense of
style.

excited about
I was **excited about** making the trip.

excuse for
Please **excuse** me **for** arriving so late.

experienced in
She isn't **experienced in** working with
computers.

explanation for
There's no scientific **explanation for** this
phenomenon.

famous for
Sydney is **famous for** its opera house.

fed up with
I resigned because I was **fed up with** the job.

feel about
How do you **feel about** going out this evening?

fond of
She's very **fond of** her cat.

forget about
Don't **forget about** the appointment at four
o'clock.

forgive for
I'll never **forgive** her **for** the way she treated
me.

friendly with
Monica is very **friendly with** my wife.

frightened of; by
Are you **frightened of** the dark?
He was **frightened by** a sudden loud noise.

good at
Are you any **good at** repairing cars?

guilty of
I've sometimes been **guilty of** neglecting my
family.

hear about; of
Did you **hear about** what happened last night?
Where is Togo? I've never **heard of** it.

hopeful about
We're all very **hopeful about** the future of this
project.

ill with
He can't come because he's **ill with** measles.

impressed with/by
The crowd were **impressed with/by** the
player's speed.

independent of
Young people want to be **independent of** their
parents.

informed about/of
The government was **informed about/of** the
crisis.

insist on
I **insist on** helping to wash the dishes.

interested in
I'm very **interested in** astronomy.

interfere with
Please don't **interfere with** the controls of the
heater.

involved in
As a young man he became **involved in**
politics.

jealous of
She has always been **jealous of** her sister's
popularity.

joke about
This is a serious matter, not something to **joke
about**.

keen on
I'm not very **keen on** tomatoes.

kind to
All the nurses were very **kind to** me.

know about
Did you **know about** their divorce?

lacking in
She's very shy and **lacking in** self-confidence.

laugh at
I can't wear this – everyone will **laugh at** me.

listen to
Listen to me when I'm speaking to you.
long for
We're **longing for** the holiday to start.
look at
He waved but she refused to **look at** him.
married to
She was **married to** an Irishman.
matter with
What's the **matter with** Alec today?
mistake for
Nobody could **mistake** him **for** an expert.
name after
We **named** our son **after** his grandfather.
nice to
She's very nervous; so please be **nice to** her.
object to
Would you **object to** answering some personal questions?
opposed to
The union was **opposed to** any workers losing their jobs.
pay for
I broke the window so I'll **pay for** a new one.
pleased about; with
The doctors were **pleased about/with** his progress.
My father won't be very **pleased with** me.
popular with
The film is **popular with** teenagers.
praise for
His novels were **praised for** their realism.
prepare for
We'll have to **prepare for** the journey.
present with
I was the one who was **presented with** the bill.
prevent from
The hostile crowd **prevented** him **from** speaking.
protect from
We wore hats to **protect** ourselves **from** the sun.
protest about
The students **protested about** the additional exams.
proud of
Being rich is nothing to be **proud of.**
provide with
All the staff are **provided with** identity cards.
punish for
Nobody should be **punished for** what he hasn't done.

quarrel about
The committee **quarrelled about** who was to blame.
react to
I wasn't sure how to **react to** the warning.
refer to
The report **refers to** two factories.
related to
The robbery was **related to** a previous crime.
rely on
You can **rely on** me to help you.
remind of
His voice **reminds** me **of** someone I used to know.
respected for
She is widely **respected for** her work with refugees.
responsible for
Nobody knows who was **responsible for** the explosion.
result in
The earthquake **resulted in** hundreds of deaths.
same as
Your car looks exactly the **same as** mine.
satisfied with
Why can't they be **satisfied with** what they've got?
save from
The princess was **saved from** a fate worse than death.
sensitive to
Babies are very **sensitive to** their mother's voice.
serious about
You're not **serious about** solving the problem.
shocked at/by
We were all **shocked at/by** the news.
sick of
I'm **sick of** listening to your complaints.
similar to
In some ways Japanese writing is **similar to** Chinese.
skilful at
He's very **skilful at** any kind of carpentry.
smile at
The receptionist **smiled at** me.
sorry for
I felt **sorry for** the man who had been arrested.
succeed in
We didn't **succeed in** finishing the crossword.
suffer from
The old lady **suffered from** rheumatism.

surprised at/by

A lot of people were **surprised at/by** the team's success.

suspicious of

I was **suspicious of** his reason for visiting me.

sympathetic to

Foreign newspapers were **sympathetic to** the rebels.

take care of

The babysitter will **take care of** him.

take part in

Thousands of people **took part in** the demonstration.

thank for

I **thanked** him **for** being so kind.

think about; of

Think about it carefully – you could lose your money.

If I don't go I'll have to **think of** an excuse.

tired of

They got **tired of** waiting and went home.

typical of

It's **typical of** her to say something sarcastic.

upset about

He was very **upset about** damaging the car.

wait for

Wait for me – I'm coming.

warn about/of

The news reports **warned** us **about/of** the danger.

worry about

There's no need to **worry about** him – he's quite safe.

wrong with

What's **wrong with** the car? It won't start.

Index

Abbreviations used: *adj* = adjective; *adv* = adverb; *conj* = conjunction; *n* = noun; *prep* = preposition; *v* = verb